Mugsiv

Barrister & Princ

CW01481549

Editorial arrangements, Introduction and Conclusion © Barrister and
Principal
Chapter 1 © Sally Tomlinson
Chapter 2 © Gajendra Verma
Chapter 3 © Zdeněk Matějček
Chapter 4 © Vladimír Smékal
Chapters 5 © Petra Samková
Chapter 6 © Tony Cline
Chapter 7 © J. H. M. Hamers, M. Tcholakova
Chapter 8 © Věra Pokorná
Chapter 9 © Sarah Ford, Birmingham City Council
Chapter 10 © Mohammed Mehmet, LB Camden
Chapter 11 © Rehana Minhas, Denise Trickett, Education Leeds
Chapter 12 © Danara Meluzínová
Chapter 13 © Bradford MDC
Chapter 14 © Maggie Power, Eileen Sparks
Chapter 15 © John Rex
Chapter 16 © Elena Ivanova
Chapter 17 © Zipora Oshrat, Judith Lapidot-Berman
Chapter 18 © Krystyna Węgłowska-Rzepa, Jolanta Kowal
Chapter 19 © Clare Beckett, Maggie Pearse
Chapter 20 © Susana Gonçalves
Chapter 21 © Marie Macey

All rights reserved. No part of this publication may be reproduced, stored
in a retrieval system, transmitted or utilised in any form or by any means,
electronic, mechanical, photocopying, recording or otherwise without
permission in writing from the publishers.

Published by nakladatelství [publishing house]Barrister & Principal,
Martinkova 7, 602 00 Brno, Czech Republic, +42 0 545211015,
fax +42 0 545210607, www.barrister.cz, e-mail: barrister@barrister.cz

Collection coordinated by British and East European Psychology Group,
University College London.

UK Orders: www.beepg.co.uk, e-mail: beepg@btinternet.com
47 Yokecliffe Drive, Derby DE4 4EX, UK; tel: +44 (0)1629 822915

ISBN 80-86598-40-3

TOGETHER WE WILL LEARN:
ethnic minorities and education

Vladimír Smékal, Hilary Gray
and Christopher Alan Lewis (eds.)

Our title respectfully echoes: Šaj pes dovakeras / Můžeme se domluvit
(Together we can agree: University of Olomouc, 1993) by ethnologist, Dr
Milena Hübschmannová, and S Romy žít budeme (With Roma we will live:
Portál, 1998) by psychologist Dr Pavel Říčan

ACKNOWLEDGEMENTS:

We sincerely thank headteachers and staff of the special and mainstream schools in north east Brno, and all the children and parents who worked with us on the research project: *The encouragement of the optimal development of personality and intellect of socioculturally disadvantaged children as a way towards respecting human rights.*

Eva Polášková managed the conference: **Minority v pluralitní společnosti / Minorities in multicultural societies**, September 1 - 3, 2000.

Members of the research team in the **Faculty of Social Studies, Masaryk University, Brno, Czech Republic** are acknowedged as authors in the following papers.

Especially we thank **Marta Hudečková, Věra Khaouni-Ivicová, Eva Bánová** and **Kateřina Holubová,** our interviewers from the Brno Roma community.

The project, and the associated international conference, were funded by the **Human Rights Project Fund of the British Foreign and Commonwealth Office**, administered by the British Embassy, Prague.

Financial support was also given by **The Council of Europe, the Ministry of Schools, Youth and Sport of the Czech Republic,** and **Brno City Council**.

Dedication:
The authors and editors dedicate this collection to our friend and 'keystone', Miroslava Novotná, lecturer in the Faculty of Education, Masaryk University, Brno. She is greatly missed by Czech educational reformers and by her friends in Britain and across Europe.

CONTENTS:

AUTHORS AND CONTRIBUTORS

Clare Beckett is Lecturer in the University of Bradford, UK. She tutors on the Masters program in Gender and Women's Studies, and on the Criminal Justice Development course.

Tony Cline is Professor of Educational Psychology and Head of the Centre for Education Studies in the University of Luton, UK. He was previously Principal Educational Psychologist of the Inner London Education Authority. He coordinated the MA course for educational psychologists at University College London. His latest of many publications in special needs and intercultural education is the research report for the UK Department for Education and Science: *Minority Ethnic Pupils in Mainly White Schools*, (www.dfes.gov.uk/research).

Antonia Dvořáková is currently engaged in Native American Studies as International Fulbright Scholar at the Centre for the Study of Indigenous Nations, The University of Kansas, USA. She plans to conduct her doctoral studies in the Centre for Personality and Ethnicity Development, Masaryk University, Brno.

Sarah Ford is an experienced teacher of children under 8 years of age, including pre-school children. She is an experienced psychologist in the multicultural city of Birmingham, UK. She is now a Senior Psychologist and is involved in co-ordinating Birmingham's program for developing inclusive education for all pre-school pupils with special educational needs: *Success for Everyone under Five*.

Susana Gonçalves is Professor of Psychology at the College of Education of Coimbra, Portugal. Her current interests are moral and social development, multicultural education and the role of higher education as a context for value and attitude development. She coordinated the project that lead to the recent book: *Multicultural Education and Human Rights Education: materials for schools and teachers*.

Hilary Gray was for twenty years educational psychologist in the multicultural city of Derby, UK. Since 1992, she has been secretary of the British and East European Psychology Group. She contributed to Professor Smékal's monitoring of the first Czech educational reforms (Obecné and Občanské školy), and was joint consultant for the project: *The encouragement of the optimal development of personality and intellect of socioculturally disadvantaged children as a way towards respecting human rights*.

Johan H. M. Hamers teaches diagnostic and treatment procedures with respect to learning disabilities to doctoral students at the University of Utrecht, the Netherlands. Publications are in the fields of dyslexia, teaching thinking, and learning potential assessment.

Elena Ivanova is Professor of Psychology in the University of Kharkov, eastern Ukraine. She is interested in psychological aspects of human rights, namely people's knowledge and perception of human rights and their attitudes to them.

Stanislav Ježek, Research Centre for Personality in the Context of Ethnicity, Masaryk University, Brno, Faculty of Social Studies , was devoted statistician on the project: *The encouragement of the optimal development of personality and intellect of socioculturally disadvantaged children as a way to respecting human rights.*

Paul Johnson is Co-ordinator of the Bradford Education Service for Traveller Children. Paul has worked in the field of Traveller education for the past fifteen years. He has delivered Traveller Awareness sessions in many part of the UK and in Europe.

Jolanta Kowal is economist, statistician and specialist computer scientist. She lectures and manages the Laboratory of Computer Science, Psychology Department, University of Wrocław, Poland. Interests and publications focus on multicultural aspects of the psychology of C. G. Jung, the relation between economy and psychoanalysis, and methodology of human sciences, where she especially uses multivariate analyses, and small but representative qualitative research samples.

Judith Lapidot-Berman is Deputy Head, Head of the Science Department and Head of Advanced Studies for In-Service Educators at Gordon College of Education, Haifa, Israel. Research interests include interethnic relationships, minorities, and misperceptions of scientific terms among different ethnic groups. She teaches the course: *Genetics of the Multicultural Israeli Population.*

Christopher Alan Lewis is Lecturer in psychology at the University of Ulster at Magee College, Northern Ireland. He was joint consultant on the project: *The enouragement of the optimal development of personality and intellect of socioculturally disadvantaged children as a way towards respecting human rights.* He has published widely, including in the areas of the psychology of religion and social identity, and is co-editor of the journal *Mental Health, Religion and Culture* (Taylor and Francis).

Marie Macey is Senior Lecturer in Sociology in the Department of Social Sciences and Humanities, University of Bradford, UK. Her master's degree is in education and prior to moving to Social Sciences she worked in the School of Education. Her specialism is race and ethnicity, with a particular focus on gender and ethnicity, and she has researched and published extensively in these areas.

Jan Mareš is doctoral student in the Faculty of Social Studies, Masaryk University, Brno, and Research Fellow in the Centre for Personality and Ethnicity Development. Formerly he was research fellow and latterly coordinator of the project: *The encouragement of the optimal development of personality and intellect of socioculturally disadvantaged children as a way towards respecting human rights*. Prior to that he was research fellow in the Faculty of Social Studies Centre for Children, Youth and Family.

Zdeněk Matějček is child psychologist and senior researcher at the Prague Psychiatric Centre. He is also Lecturer in Psychology at Charles University, Prague. His interests include social psychology of childhood, psychological development, and family relations. His recent publications include *School of Parents* (Prague: Maxdorf, 2000, in Czech).

Mohammed Mehmet is former Assistant Director of Education in the London Borough of Camden, UK, where he coordinated the strategy for raising the attainment of ethnic minority pupils, which won national 'Beacon' status. He is currently Director of Regeneration and Education in the London Borough of Islington with a strategic role to ensure that the borough's Neighbourhood Renewal Strategy and Education Development Plan are integrated to optimum effect.

Danara Meluzinová is an experienced teacher who has trained special school teachers for fourteen years. She now works in the non-profit making organisation Společenství Romů na Moravě (The Society of Roma in Moravia), coordinating educational centres in six cities in Moravia, which is the eastern half of the Czech Republic. Her work now includes training Roma classroom assistants, a role that is relatively new in the Czech Republic.

Rehana Minhas was Divisional Co-ordinator for Multi-Ethnic Education in the Inner London Education Authority (Hackney), UK from 1984 to 1987, working across all schooling phases and with the entire curriculum. From 1990-2000 she was LEA and OfSTED (national) inspector in the London Borough of Harringey. She is now Strategic Manager for Equalities in Education Leeds (Leeds LEA).

Tereza Osecká was research and administrative assistant throughout the project: *The encouragement of the optimal development of personality and* *intellect of socioculturally disadvantaged children as a way towards respecting human rights.* She also helped arrange the Conference: *Minority v pluralitní společnosti / Minorities in multicultural societies.*

Ziporah Oshrat is Deputy Head and Academic Dean of Gordon College of Education, Haifa, Israel. She teaches Educational Psychology and is a member of the Multicultural Educational Resource Center. Research interests include educational psychology, burn-out, stress, ethnic groups, minorities. She edited the book *Israel – a Multicultural Society* (1998).

Michaela Pavelková was researcher in the project: *The encouragement of the optimal development of personality and intellect of socioculturally disadvantaged children as a way towards respecting human rights.* She is now practising graduate psychologist in the Pedagogical-Psychological Counselling Centre, Bruntál, North Moravia.

Maggie Pearse is Lead Tutor on the BA Honours course in Community Work at the University of Bradford, UK. She works extensively in the voluntary sector, including with asylum seekers from many countries, which brings her into frequent contact with east European Roma. She is joint author with Jerry Smith of *Community Groups Handbook* (1990, Home Office / HMSO).

Milan Pilát, Department of Psychology, Faculty of Arts, Masaryk University, Brno coordinated his colleagues' conventional and dynamic testing of Czech and Roma children on the project: *The encouragement of the optimal development of personality and intellect of socioculturally disadvantaged children as a way towards respecting human rights.*

Věra Pokorná is Associate Professor of educational psychology at the Charles University in Prague. She is the author of a monograph on theory, diagnosis and therapy of learning and behavioural disabilities of children. She is the mother of four children and has eleven grandchildren.

Maggie Power is a Senior Lecturer involved in initial teacher training at Bradford College, UK. Her interests are in preparing teachers to meet the needs of pupils from diverse language backgrounds, narrative studies and drama.

John Rex was the founder of Sociology Departments in the Universities of Warwick and Durham in the UK. He served on the UNESCO International Experts Committee on Race and Race Prejudice in 1967 and is now Professor Emeritus in the Centre for Research in Ethnic Relations, University of Warwick.

Petra Samková-Bučková was researcher on the project: *The encouragement of the optimal development of personality and intellect of socioculturally disadvantaged children as a way towards respecting human rights.* Since then, she cooperated in a Phare project: *Improvement of relations between the Roma and Czech communities.* She is now an educational psychologist in a centre for children with language disorders in Brno.

Michaela Šafářová was research assistant throughout the project: *The encouragement of the optimal development of personality and intellect of socioculturally disadvantaged children as a way towards respecting human rights.* She also helped arrange the conference: *Minority v pluralitní společnosti / Minorities in multicultural societies.*

Vladimír Smékal lectured in Psychology at the Faculty of Arts, Masaryk University, Brno, from 1958 and was elected head of department in 1989. He taught developmental and personality psychology, psychometrics and research methods. Since 1998 he lectures in the Department of Psychology at the School of Social Studies of Masaryk University, and since 2000 is head of the University Research Centre for Personality in the Context of Ethnicity. He was host of the project: *The encouragement of the optimal development of personality and intellect of socioculturally disadvantaged children* and of the Conference: *Minority v pluralitní společnosti, Minorities in multicultural societies.* His most recent book is *Pozvání do psychologie osobnosti (Invitation to Personality Psychology)* (Brno: Barrister and Principal, 2001, in Czech).

Eileen Sparks is Senior Lecturer in Education at Bradford College, UK, where she has worked for twelve years. For eighteen years before that, she worked with children in mainstream secondary schools who had learning or behavioural difficulties, then as an Advisory teacher. For the last three years she has been involved in a European Project to encourage teachers to undertake further training that promotes inclusive practice.

Maya Tcholokova was Assistant Professor in Special Education at Southwestern University until 1999. She was Co-ordinator of the Centre for European Research in Special Education at the Faculty of Primary and Pre-school Education, Sofia University St. Kl. Ohridski, Bulgaria until 2001, where she is now international projects officer. Her main research is funded by the Soros Foundation, and relates to Learning Potential Assessment.

Sally Tomlinson is Emeritus Professor in the University of London, UK, and Research Associate in the Department of Educational Studies, University of Oxford, UK. Recent publications include *Education in a Post-Welfare Society*

(2001, Open University Press); *Exclusion, the Middle Classes and the Common Good* in eds., Daniels, H. and Garner, P.: *Inclusive Education: world yearbook of education* (2000, Kogan Page); and *Ethnic Minorities and Education: new disadvantage* (2000, Falmer Press).

Denise Trickett has been involved in equalities issues in education for many years, both in Britain and internationally. She is currently working for Education Leeds as Ethnic Minority Achievement Adviser. She has been a headteacher, and is currently an OfSTED inspector.

Svatava Vaculová was researcher on the project: *The encouragement of the optimal development of personality and intellect of socioculturally disadvantaged children as a way towards respecting human rights.* She is practising graduate psychologist at the DROM Roma in Brno, where legal and other advice and support are available for Roma families and children.

Tomáš Urbánek is academic researcher in the Institute of Psychology, Czech Academy of Sciences, Brno, where he specialises in methodology and statistical analysis.

Gajendra Verma is Professor of Education in the University of Manchester, UK. He served on the UK Government's Committee of Enquiry, The Swann Committee, which led to the Report: *Education for All* (1985). He has published widely in multicultural education, identity, equal opportunities etc and conducted several European and international projects in the area.

Jarmila Volná was the first manager of the project: *The encouragement of the optimal development of personality and intellect of socioculturally disadvantaged children as a way towards respecting human rights,* in which she also cooperated with the family interviews and the courses for teachers. She is now clinical psychologist and also doctoral student of Social Psychology at the Faculty of Social Studies, Masaryk University, Brno, where she teaches principles of Adlerian psychology and researches adolescence. She is also the executive vice-chair of the Czech Society for Individual Psychology.

Krystyna Węglowska–Rzepa is psychologist, psychotherapist, and deputy director (teaching) of the Psychology Department, University of Wrocław, Poland. Interests and publications include education and social behaviour of children and youth, and life span psychology. Her research about archetypal symbols is based on C. G. Jung's psychology and on humanistic and existential psychology. Practice includes designing sociotherapeutic programs for young people.

INTRODUCTION: INCLUSIVE EDUCATION, EASTERN EUROPE, AND SEVERE MARGINALISATION

Hilary Gray, University of Nottingham, UK,
Vladimír Smékal, Masaryk University, Brno, Czech Republic,
and Christopher Alan Lewis, University of Ulster, UK

The papers in this volume were presented at the conference: *Minorities in a multicultural society*, which was the culminating event in the project: *The encouragement of the optimal development of personallity and intellect of socioculturally disadvantaged children as a way towards respecting human rights.* The project researchers were psychologists from the Faculty of Social Studies, Masaryk University, Brno, Czech Republic, supported by psychologists from the Universities of Ulster and Nottingham in the UK. The project was funded by the British Foreign Office Human Rights Project Fund, and the conference also by the Council of Europe, by the Czech Ministry of Schools, Youth and Sport, and by the City of Brno. Most of the contributions are from the Czech Republic, Poland and Bulgaria in former communist central Europe and from the UK, with papers also from Portugal, Israel and the Netherlands.

The original project and the conference were concerned with a twofold human rights challenge, firstly that which faces all states in respect of their ethnic minority communities, and secondly the particular problems that face post-totalitarian countries. Education systems are societies' crucibles, so the issue of fair education for ethnic minority children sharply focuses priorities relating to inclusion. This conference included papers from some of the most experienced minds in universities and local education authorities in east and west Europe. We include new central European research, as well as reports from British local education authorities of monitored strategies for the education of children from various ethnic groups.

Any imbalance in numbers of papers is due to the injustices of twentieth century international politics. However, for such international discussions to be valid, there must be a degree of similarity between circumstances. Roma and Traveller children come from probably the most marginalised ethnic groups in Europe, and their education represents significant challenge (European Commission, 1999a, p.14; UK OfSTED, 1996). Similar concern about children from marginalised and underachieving[1] ethnic groups is today the focus of educationists' attention in both east central and west Europe. In Britain this is because some other ethnic minority groups now make satisfactory progress (Gillborn & Mirza, 2000; Mehmet, p.108[2]; Minhas & Trickett, p.120). In east central Europe there are concerns about the social and economic pressures that arise when a large proportion of one marginalised ethnic group are without industrial or post-industrial skills. We assert at the outset that this attention to particular, marginalised ethnic groups does *not* imply a genetic theory of racial differences: Roma have experienced centuries of stigma, then the holocaust, then forced assimilation; African Caribbeans in Britain are descendants of slaves in the British Empire. We believe such circumstances are sufficient to explain differences at least for practical purposes such as educational policies.

Implications of the communist period for education

In east and central Europe, sixty years of first nazi then communist totalitarianism followed monarchies with weak constitutions without or almost without break. We need not document that human rights abuse was severe. Privileged access to society's many varieties of support also occurs in capitalism, with more or less powerful systems of prejudice regarding gender, disability, age and race. For example, regarding ethnic abuse, the Lawrence Report (Macpherson, 1999) registers the depth of institutional racism in British public life, especially in police and security systems which until the Race Relations Amendment Act (2000) were exempt from national laws against racial discrimination. But the single party communist states' direct ownership and control of all facilities and services gave them immediate power over every aspect of individuals' lives in a way that democracy reduces. The site of our project, the Czech Republic, was the western part of the first Czechoslovak Republic from 1918 until 1938, with the exception of some border changes in the North. It was then was the nazi Protectorate of Bohemia and Moravia, then until 1989 the western part of the Czechoslovak Socialist Republic (ČSSR). There were two widespread purges in communist Czechoslovakia, the first in the 1950s and early 1960s, the second during the

---

[1] For purposes of discussion, we refer to Roma as 'severely marginalised' echoing the opinion of the European Commission (1999a, p.4). We refer to some ethnic groups in Britain, eg Bangladeshi Muslims, as 'marginalised', and to larger British African Caribbean and Pakistani groups, whose children's needs have also been poorly met by the education system, as 'underachieving'. Just as attention to individual groups does *not* imply a genetic theory of difference, so the term 'underachievement' is *not* to suggest that the problem lies with the pupils, their families or their communities: we propose that such situations are at least two way, and that with appropriate policies, the needs of all can be met in mainstream education. See also Gilborn and Mirza (2000, p.7).

[2] In this introductory chapter, page numbers given alone or with Author's names refer to papers in this collection.

so-called 'normalisation' period after the 1968 Russian invasion ended the Prague Spring's 'Socialism with a Human Face'. This second wave was also widespread and severe if this time mainly bloodless (Šimečka, 1984; Swain & Swain, 1993, pp.170-173).

All governments use their education system for political objectives, including for some degree of equality (Verma, below pp.33-35). For Western states, it promotes internal social cohesion (eg European Commission, 1993); equality was communism's primary goal, with the assumption that uniform delivery of education would yield equality of outcome (Verma, below p.34; Smékal et al., below p.53). Until the middle of the twentieth century most education systems still regarded 'knowledge' as fixed and the teacher as its transmitter. Then English and American teaching diverged most widely into group and individual topic based discovery styles (Alexander, 2000; Cookson et al., 1992). In fact English child centred experiential learning, which was sometimes unwisely child determined, is often blamed for the disastrous standards of literacy and mathematics identified by the OECD (2000) and in the *Third International Mathematics and Science Study* (Keys et al., 1996). On the other hand, east European states tended to maintain whole class teaching, within which Alexander (2000) found an interactive, deliberate use and teaching of language that was strongest in Russian primary schools compared with schools in the other four countries[3] in his comparative study. The Czech Language Curriculum for Basic school seems to call for something similar (ČR MŠMT, 1996, p.6)[4].

The success of Czech teaching of literacy and mathematics shows in the OECD and TIMMS international comparisons, when Czechs were world leaders in quantitative reading, world sixth in mathematics and world average in prose reading. But in spite of this success, some reforms are based on the view that the knowledge oriented system of education was too much an instrument of the five year plans. These encouraged manual and industrial skills and failed to facilitate both critical thinking and information processing skills (Kotásek, 1996; Koucký, 1996; Koucký et al., 1999; Piťha & Helus, 1994; Vondráček et al., 1997).

---

[3] France, India, USA, UK

[4] Correct language. Most Slav languages are highly inflected, and so the debate about correct language and especially the teaching of grammar is more complex than regarding English. Since the establishment of the National Curriculum, British education has also moved to more teaching of grammar, (eg Carter, 1990; UK QCA, 2000). However, developmental linguistics (eg Cummins, 2001; Labov, 1969) suggests that it can be counter-productive to focus heavily on 'received' knowledge, including 'received' knowledge about language. Regarding inclusion of children from ethnic minorities, the discussion about teaching language often coalesces around the use of mother tongue teaching or support in preschools and schools, although of course the debate is very much wider (see Power & Sparks, p.134, and Conclusion, p.190).

Psychology in the Cold War

Psychologists are among the guardians of their countries' standards of equal opportunities within various public services. Within education, this role developed through trust in more or less scientific assessment packages, although these are certainly more valid for best targeting of scarce resources than for guaranteeing each individual pupil's human right to be educated to his or her potential (UNICEF 1989, Article 29). Within special education, psychologists' responsibility for equal opportunities rests in part on their 'gatekeeper' role *vis à vis* segregated schooling and / or additional help in mainstream school.

The communist states of east and central Europe used various tactics to weaken psychology and the other human sciences. There was direct repression through party management of research and teaching (Hoskovec & Hoskovcová, 2000). Also psychology departments were broken up and staff distributed around related departments. This happened in Russia in 1955 (Brushlinsky, 1995), in Czechoslovakia during the 'normalisation' period, and in Romania's early phase of repression. In Romania the ban on teaching and practice was progressively tightened from 1977, the strongest ban, (Ordin MEI 2906/1982), remaining in place until 1989. The east European history of the psychology of individual differences and of testing is complex. Testing or 'pedology' was banned by the Central Committee of the USSR Communist Party's 1935 Resolution concerning pedological perversions, and many practitioners were sent to the Gulag (Smékal, 1995). The psychology of individual differences only slowly reappeared after Kruschev's 1956 'Cult of the Personality' speech (Hoskovec & Hoskovcová, 2000).

The context of severe marginalisation: the Roma people

Consistent with the Amsterdam Treaty 1997 Article 13 (European Union, 1997) against discrimination including racial discrimination, various European Commission reports, (eg European Commission, 1999a, p.14, 1999b) state that the situation for Roma is more difficult than for most other ethnic minority groups, in respect of health, housing, education and employment[5] in seven central and southeast European countries all of which have Roma populations in excess of three per cent. All seven countries now have some legislation to protect minorities. In particular none of these countries registered Reservations that are relevant to minority affairs when ratifying the European Convention on Human Rights (Council of Europe, 2002a).

---

[5] For example, economically expensive unemployment is high in the majority workforces (Bulgaria (16%), Czech Republic (8%), Hungary (6%), Poland (18%), Romania (19%), Slovakia (19%); Slovenia (8%), but the EU Accession Reports for individual countries' progress towards admission criteria mention unemployment rates between fifty and ninety percent for Roma adults (European Commission, 1998 - 2001).

Regarding the Czech Republic, Smékal et al. (p.52) and Samková-Bučková et al. (p.59) give some information about the traditional Roma beliefs and practices which were held in place by a system of shaming. They included the elderly and male dominated hierarchical extended family which is probably of Hindu origin, (eg Frazer, 1995; Preinhaelterová, 1996) and the concept of mánuš or purity which regulated bodily and group integrity (Frazer, 1995; Johnson, p.129; Rao, 1975).

Roma were decimated in the holocaust in the nazi Protectorate of Bohemia and Moravia (Crowe, 1995; Frazer, 1995; Kenrick, 1995). Smékal also notes how the communist state then refused legitimacy to those surviving (mainly in Slovakia). First national minority status was withdrawn from Roma, then settling was enforced (ČSSR Decree 74/1958). Later there was migration west to industrial towns and cities where the holocaust had been most severe (ČSSR Decree 502/1965). There is substantial research evidence (eg Ogbu, 1993)[6] suggesting that such forced assimilation makes it more likely that the members of the ethnic group concerned will find themselves locked into intractable 'caste like' economic, social and educational positions that are more difficult to escape and that fuel interethnic conflict with their cycles of disparity.[7]

Educational implications for Roma today

Statistics are complex because forced assimilation reduces willingness to declare ethnicity, but estimates suggest that almost one half of all Czech Roma children are in segregated special education (European Roma Rights Centre, 1999; ČR MŠMT Ústav pro informace ve vzdělávání, 1999). Similar proportions are cited in the EU Access reports for the other six countries (European Commission, 1998 - 2001). Until 1999 in the Czech Republic (ČR, 1999) parents had no right to reassessment for their child. Many more substantial changes will follow with the major Education Bill, information towards which was laid before Parliament early in 2002 (ČR MŠMT, 2002).

Roma is an indoeuropean language with complex syntax but said to have some limitations regarding content words that are relevant to industrial society. The first Czech codification was published in central Europe in 1991 (Frazer, 1995; Hübšmannová, 1991). Five[8] of the seven EU Access countries with highest Roma populations have ratified the European Charter on Minority Languages, but only in Slovakia is the Roma population high

---

[6] The electronic lists: Forced-Migration-History@jiscmail.ac.uk and Forced-Migration@jiscmail.ac.uk which are accessed via jiscmail@jiscmail.ac.uk are sources of information and opinion about this issue.

[7] Although early soviet Russia recognised Roma as a national minority with certain rights, the postwar history is similar in most communist countries (Crowe, 1995; Huttenbach, 1991).

[8] Hungary, Slovakia and Slovenia have signed and ratified the Treaty; the Czech Republic and Romania have signed but not yet ratified it.

enough (possibly 10%) that their language is registered as relevant under the Charter (European Commission, 1999c; Council of Europe, 2002b). However, there are many projects directed at change, for example Roma classroom assistants and preschool 'Zero grade' classes, and it seems that mother tongue support is offered in schools, dependent on local factors such as the head teacher's opinions (eg below Kowal & Węgłowska-Rzepa, p.162).

The papers in this volume
The political history and differences in educational style are extremely complex. But our papers raise questions including the following:

I.   What principles, hypotheses and needs underlie the aim of inclusive education?
II. What are the minority and majority processes that prevent ethnic minority children, especially those from marginalised groups, using the education systems offered by host societies?
III. Has assessment of children's special educational needs a role in fostering inclusion?
IV. What are the processes which help ethnic minority children progress as successfully as those from majority groups. In particular, can children from marginalised communities succeed when they are included in local mainstream schools?
V.   How can education systems foster majority and minority will to reverse the minority cultures of hopelessness and successfully facilitate celebration of diversity by majority children?

Broadly, our five Sections offers some answers to these five questions.

Section I of the book consists of two papers about principles of inclusive education. Gajendra Verma sets out different concepts of equal opportunities, and the varying perspectives of the stakeholders involved, including the state, the migrant and settled minority groups, and the teachers. Sally Tomlinson describes the development of the concept of inclusive education, which began with passive acceptance that all children have the right to a place at their local school and now consists of demands for many kinds of need to be actively met in local schools. For both authors the role of the teacher is central to positively meeting diverse needs: there are unresolved dilemmas in teachers' traditional responsibility to educate every child to potential, and also in their newer responsibilities regarding high quality relationships extending outside the classroom to colleagues, parents and community leaders.

The three papers in Section II are from east Europe. Zdeněk Matějíček sets out the intergenerational transmission of tolerance or prejudice via the parents' assurance of trust or communication of fear. He establishes one theme of this book: since this transmission is barely conscious, we can assume that reversing the fear at the base of prejudice will be through emotional, not knowledge based, processes. Vladimír Smékal et al. draw on secondary sources to describe Roma history and traditions, and on primary sources including socioeconomic variables to consider the risks for Roma children's attitudes to education, and how to reverse those risks. Petra Samková-Bučková et al. describe unique comparative research about disadvantaged Roma and Czech children's upbringing and their mothers' attitude to education, which is consistent with the contrast between collective and individualistic styles of child rearing.

Tony Cline opens Section III by thoroughly considering fair assessment of ethnic minority pupils' educational needs. Firstly he details how British law and professional practice have developed, then he lists four principles for fair assessment. He shows how classical, norm based assessment fails to guarantee these principles, and how more recent UK legislation still meets them inadequately. Vygotsky's (1978) developmental psychology suggests that assessments are more valid if they are 'dynamic', that is, if they take into account the child's response to teaching that is appropriate to his or her particular needs, which may include the need for teaching in mother tongue. Two forms of dynamic assessment are discussed in this volume. Věra Pokorná explains Feurerstein's Vygotskian critique of the concept of intelligence and his Instrumental Enrichment programs for moderating cognitive functioning: this is assessment in the sense of the dynamic learning context provided for the children by their teachers. J. H. M. Hamers and Maya Tcholachova describe dynamic *tests* developed to help ethnic minority children in the Netherlands and which have also been used with Roma and Turkish minority children in Bulgaria.

Sections IV and V represent local authority strategies for reversing relatively unsuccessful excluding education, and inclusive methods for schools to use. Section IV consists of six reports of good practice. Sarah Ford reports the strategy of Britain's second largest multicultural city, Birmingham, for including all preschool special needs pupils in mainstream nursery schools (materská škola). Mehmet's evidence from the London Borough of Camden where more than a hundred mother tongues are represented by the children, and Minhas and Trickett's from the large multicultural city of Leeds, should both be read in the context of major national campaigns to monitor and improve all UK children's literacy and numeracy skills (Minnis & Higgs, 2001; the National Literacy and Numeracy Strategies, UK DfES, 2002a, 2002b). Many city education departments now break this pupil achievement data down for the various ethnic minority groups, including some marginalised groups such Bangladeshi Muslims, and significantly underachieving groups such as Pakistani and African Caribbean (Gillborn & Mirza, 2000)[9]. These papers from Mehmet and from Minhas and Trickett suggest that the gap is narrowing between the skills of pupils from some marginalised groups and those of the average British child. Both authors describe local government strategies and school based methods which are facilitating this improvement.

One powerful local government strategy is the appointment of same ethnicity classroom assistants who can act both as role models for minority pupils and as successful intermediaries between majority and minority. Danara Meluzínová of the Society of Roma in Moravia spells out the factors for them to work successfully. Bradford in the north of the UK has a high proportion of Muslim families, including members of several marginalised groups. Paul Johnson describes inclusive education for children from Bradford's marginalised Traveller families, then Maggie Power and Eileen Sparks describe experiential teaching methods that actively involve ethnic minority families and that are highly appropriate to children from marginalised groups, especially from groups like Roma who have an oral language tradition.

The seven papers in the final Section V take us to education designed to promote positive intercultural understanding among adults and among children. First, John Rex sets out the broad sociological context of ethnopolitical prejudice and of different forms of multiculturalism and equality of opportunity. Elena Ivanova is monitoring new human rights education in newly independent Ukraine, a state which demonstrates one of Rex's types of multicultural society, where members of the former ruling nation (Russia) are now a large minority. In probably the most highly charged interracial arena in the world, Ziporah Oshrat and Judith Lapidot-Berman discuss the effect of ethnically mixed study groups on Druze and Jewish trainee teachers' attitudes to each other, and return us to the problem of the emotional base for successful interethnic relationships.

The book finishes hopefully: Maggie Pearce and Clare Beckett describe exciting community and higher education projects in the city of Bradford which reduced stereotyping of one of Britain's most marginalised groups, the Bangladeshi Muslims, and also led them to a helping role vis a vis both their own and the wider community. Jolantha Kowal and Krystyna Węgłowska-Rzepa describe the use of ethnic symbols to enhance Polish children's intercultural tolerance, while Susana Gonçalvez describes work to facilitate Portuguese teachers' reflections on racism and to promote their majority pupils' tolerance. Both these papers describe multicultural work with an *emotional* component, rather than only knowledge. Finally Marie Macey describes changing attitudes in British education, from majority dominated assimilation to a degree of welcoming of diversity, with still far to go in establishing zero tolerance regarding racist harassment, and other

---

9 See Footnote pp.107-108 for description of the monitoring of pupils' achievements and disaggregation of data by ethnicity, gender and socioeconomic status.

features that promote intercultural education (see also Cline et al., 2002 for British shortcomings).

Central and local government can drive change, but schools need not wait. In our Conclusion, we trace four broad methods for schools to positively engage with the problem: multilevel work with families and communities, experiential learning and use of mother tongue, delivery of intercultural education via the whole curriculum, and the establishment of zero tolerance of racism (Conclusion, below p.192).

Where the editors and authors stand

This book is international mainly in its Czech and UK reference. However, the several papers specifically about Roma and Travellers clearly reveal the twofold human rights challenge facing the new east European democracies: to simultaneously activate their human and civic rights systems as well as responding to the human rights of their sometimes severely marginalised minorities. The postwar demand for cheap labour was western as well as eastern, so very substantial ethnic diversity developed soon after World War II in all the cities represented here, including Brno (see Daniel, 1994; European Roma Rights Centre, 1999; Kenrick et al., 1995; Smékal, below p.51ff). We have long known that the intergenerational cycle of disadvantage sucks ethnic minority groups into its field of material and emotional need (eg Rutter & Madge, 1976). To suffer holocaust then forced assimilation (above p.17; Smékal, below p.52) was extremely harsh, but British people should certainly ask themselves how far Commonwealth immigrants in the 1950s and 1960s were in effect forced, not by quotas, but by hunger and appalling public services in their countries of origin.

Specifically regarding special education, it seems that around the world the process of moving from segregated to inclusive education has often begun worthily with pupils with physical needs (eg UNESCO, 1994, 1996, 1999). The UNESCO (2000) Dakar declaration bids us

...take account of the needs of the poor and the most disadvantaged, including working children, remote rural dwellers and nomads, and ethnic and linguistic minorities, children, young people and adults affected by conflict, HIV / AIDS, hunger and poor health, and those with special learning needs... (UNESCO, 2000).

This clearly includes children from Roma and Traveller families, from other groups which have experienced the processes of forced migration and assimilation to which Ogbu (1993) refers, and from groups in Britain and the west such as Bangladeshi Muslims and some African Caribbean and Pakistani groups. The communist states' legislation met Dakar requirements, but this was effected by segregating about half of the Roma children. This book points to the probability that such pupils can be better educated by inclusive means. We hope these papers will assist education administrators and practitioners in post and in training. We also hope it will help generate interest in the new democracies' substantial challenges.

References

Alexander, R. (2000). Culture and Pedagogy. Oxford: Blackwell.

Brushlinsky, A. (1995). Psychology in Russia. Paper presented to the British Psychological Society, History of Psychology Section York.

Carter, R. (1990). Language in the National Curriculum: the LINC reader. London: Hodder & Stoughton.

Cline, T., D'Abreu, G., Fihosy, C., Gray, H., Lambert, N. & Neale J. (2002). Minority Ethnic Education in Mainly White Schools. London: UK Department of Education and Skills. Project 1872000.(http://www.dfes.gov.uk/research)

Cookson, P. W., Sadovnik, A. R. & Semel, S. F. (Eds.) (1992). International Handbook of Educational Reform. Westport, CT: Greenwood Press.

ČSSR (74/1958). Zákon o trvalém usídlení kočujících osob. (Law on permanent settling of caravan people).

ČSSR (502/1965). Usnesení vlády ČSSR o opatřeních k řešení otázek cikánského obyvatelstva. (Governmental decree of the Czechoslovak Socialist Republic on the method of resolving the question of the Gypsy population).

ČR MŠMT (Ministry of Schools, Youth and Sport) (1996). Český jazyk, učební osnovy rok 1-9. (Czech Language teaching syllabus Grades 1-9). Prague: Fortuna.

ČR MŠMT (Ministry of Schools, Youth and Sport) (393/2002). European Integration: Materials and documents related to EU problems: survey of legislative and non-legislative tasks; longterm objectives of education and development of the education system of the Czech Government. (http://www.vlada.cz/1250/vrk/eu.htm)

ČR MŠMT Ústav pro informace ve vzdělávání (Ministry of Schools, Youth and Sport, Office for information on education). Statistická ročenka školství 1999. Prague: MŠMT.

ČR (1999) čj.10 (433/99-24). Education Regulation. Prague: MŠMT

Crowe, D. (1995). A History of the Gypsies of Eastern Europe and Russia. Tauris: London.

Council of Europe (2002a). European Convention on Human Rights: reservations. Strasbourg: Council of Europe. (http://conventions.coe.int/treaty/en/WhatYouWant.asp?NT=005)

Council of Europe (2002b). European Charter on Minority Languages: declarations. (CoE Treaty 148).
(http://conventions.coe.int/treaty/EN/DeclareList.asp?NT=148&CM=8&DF=12/07/00)

Cummins, J. (2001). Language, Power and Pedagogy. Clevedon: Multilingual Matters.

Daniel, B. (1994). Dějiny Romů (History of Roma). Olomouc: Palackého Univerzita Press.

European Commission (1993). The European Discussion of Education (Green paper). Brussels: European Commission.

European Commission (1999a). Countering Racism, Xenophobia and Antisemitism in the Candidate Countries. (http://europa.eu.int/comm/external_relations/human_rights/doc/com99_256_en.pdf

European Commission (1999b). EU Support for Roma communities in central and eastern Europe. (http://europa.eu.int/comm/enlargement/docs/pdf/roma.pdf)

European Commission (1999c). Regular Report on Slovakia's Progress towards Accession. http://europa.eu.int/comm/enlargement/report_10_99/pdf/en/slovakia_en.pdf

European Commission (1998–2001). Enlargement Overview. (http://europa.eu.int/comm/enlargement/overview.htm)

European Roma Rights Centre (1999). A Special Remedy. ERRC Budapest. Country Series, 8.

European Union (1997). The Amsterdam Treaty 1997. (http://www.europa.eu.int/en/agenda/igc-home/intro/home_en.htm)

Frazer, A. (1995). The Gypsies of Europe. Blackwells: Oxford.

Gillborn, D. & Mirza, H. S. (2000). Educational Inequality: mapping race, class and gender. Office for Standards in Education. (http://www.ofsted.gov.uk/public/docs00/inequality.pdf)

Hoskovec, J. & Hoskovcová, S. (2000). Malé dějiny české a středoevropské psychologie (Short History of Czech and Central European Psychology). Praha: Portál.

Hübšmannová, M. (1991). Romsko-český slovník. (Roma-Czech Dictionary). Státní pedagogické nakladatelství: Prague

Huttenbach H. R. (1991), (ed.). The Gypsies in Eastern Europe. Nationalities Papers, 19, 3, (Special Issue)

Keys, W., Harris, S., & Fernandes, C. (1996). Third International Mathematics and Science Study. First National Report. Windsor, Berkshire: NFER

Kenrick, D. (1995), (ed.). The Gypsies During the Second World War (Vol. 2): in the shadow of the swastika. Hatfield: University of Hertfordshire Press.

Kotásek, J. (1996). Structure and Organisation of Secondary Education in Central and East Europe. In Educational Reforms in Central and East Europe: special issue, European Journal of Education, 31, 1.

Koucký, J. (1996). Educational Reforms in Changing Societies: Central Europe in a period of transition. In Educational Reforms in Central and East Europe: special issue, European Journal of Education, 31, 1.

Koucký, J., Čerych, L., Hausenblas, O., Jallade, J-P., Kotásek, J., Kovařovic, J. & Švecová, J. (1999). Czech Education and Europe: pre-accession strategy. Phare project CZ 9405 01 03 01 UIV Tauris.

Labov, W. (1969). The Logic of Non-standard English. Georgetown, USA. Georgetown University Press.

Minnis, M. & Higgs, S. (2001). Evaluation of the National Literacy and Numeracy Strategies. Windsor: National Foundation for Educational Research. (http://www.qca.org.uk/ca/5-14/eval_nlns.asp)

Macpherson, W. (1999). Report of the Committee of Enquiry into the Death of Stephen Lawrence. (http://www.cre.gov.uk/pdfs/slinqlea.pdf)

Ogbu, J. U. (1993). Differences in cultural frame of reference. International Journal of Behavioural Development, 16, 3, 483-506.

OECD Organisation for Economic Cooperation and Development (2000). Literacy in the Information Age. Final Report of the International Adult Literacy Survey. (http://www.oecd.org/publications)

Piťha, P. & Helus, Z. (1994). Návrh učebních osnov Obecné školy (Program for Common Schools). Prague: ČR MŠMT (Czech Ministry of Schools)

Preinhaelterová, H. (1996). Tradiční velkorodina v hinduistické Indii (Traditional big family in Hindu India). Romano džaniben roč. 3, 1-2. www.volny.cz/dzaniben

Rao, A. (1975). Some mánuš conceptions and attitudes. In F. Rehfisch (ed.), Gypsies, Tinkers and other Travellers. London: Academic Press.

Rutter, M. & Madge, N. (1976). Cycles of Disadvantage. London: Heinemann.

Šimečka, M. (1984). The Restoration of Order: the normalisation of Czechoslovakia. London and Bratislava: Verso.

Smékal, V. (1995). Psychology in East Europe. In H. Gray, N. Foreman & N. J. Hayes (eds.), Psychology in a Changing Europe. Proceedings of the British and East European Psychology Group. Banska Bystrica, Slovakia. (http://www.ulst.ac.uk/beepg/infm)

Swain, G. & Swain, N. (1993). Eastern Europe since 1945. London: Macmillan.

UK DfES (2002a). The National Literacy Strategy: Framework for teaching. Nottingham: DfES Publications. (http://www.standards.dfes.gov.uk/literacy/publications)

UK DfES (2002b). The National Numeracy Strategy: Framework for teaching. Nottingham: DfES Publications. (http://www.standards.dfes.gov.uk/numeracy/publications)

UK OfSTED, UK Office for Standards in Education (1996). Education of Travelling Children. London: The Stationery Office. HMR 12/96/NS. (http://www.ofsted.gov.uk/public)

UK QCA Curriculum and Qualification Authority (2000). National Curriculum: English. London: The Stationery Office. (http://www.nc.uk.net/servlets/NCFrame?subject=En)

UK Race Relations Amendment Act (2000). London: TSO The Stationery Office.

UNESCO (1994). The Salamanca Statement and Framework for Action on Special Needs Education. UNESCO Special Education Program, 7 Place de Fontenoy, 75352 Paris 07 – SP.

UNESCO (1996). Legislation Pertaining to Special Needs Education. Special Education program. Place de Fontenoy 7, 75352 Paris 07-SP.

UNESCO (1999). Bringing forward the Salamanca Statement. Regional workshop Central and Eastern Europe. Annex 5: Bulgaria, Czech Republic, Macedonia, Poland, Romania, Slovenia. http://www/unesco.org/education/educprog/sne/bucharest/annex5/slovenia.htm

UNESCO (2000) World Education Forum, (Dakar, Senegal) - Final Report UNESCO Special Education Program, 7 Place de Fontenoy, 75352 Paris 07–SP. http://www.unesco.org/education/educnews/20_10_16/report.htm

UNICEF (1989). Convention on the Rights of the Child. (http://www.unicef.org/crc/crc.htm)

Vondráček, J., Tomek, K., & Kitzberger, J. (1997). Národní škola. (National Schools). ČR MŠMT, SPN.

Vygotsky, L. S. (1978). Mind in Society: the development of higher mental processes. (ed. M. Cole). Boston, MA: Harvard UP .

SECTION I

PRINCIPLES OF
INCLUSIVE EDUCATION

1. SCHOOL MANAGEMENT TO MEET THE NEEDS OF ALL CHILDREN

Sally Tomlinson, University of Oxford, UK

In many countries with developed systems of special education, a major aim over the past twenty years has been the inclusion of as many children as possible in the mainstream education system. A major impetus for this has been a moral and egalitarian realisation that segregating children was not a humanitarian practice. In most cases it ensured that children received an inferior education and went on to lives of dependency and powerlessness. Governments also recognised that special education was very expensive!

The move away from long established systems of segregating children with disabilities and learning problems has been established with difficulty. Teachers in mainstream schools argued that they could not give attention to all the class if they had to deal with a few 'problem' children, that they were not trained to deal with children with learning difficulties, that the school organisation and curriculum was not suitable, and that they did not have enough help and resources. Other professionals, particularly from the medical and psychological professions, argued that the children needed specialised treatments. In Britain, educational reforms have put schools into competition with each other for pupils and for funding in an 'educational market', and examination results are published school by school. This has led some headteachers to search for pupils who will be high attaining and undemanding and reject pupils who are troublesome or difficult to teach. Children likely to be excluded from mainstream schools include those from low socioeconomic backgrounds, with parents with a minimum of education, pupils from ethnic minority backgrounds, particularly African Caribbean boys, and Gypsy and Traveller[10] children. There is considerable conflict between the principles of inclusion and the principles of marketisation

---

[10] In Britain children from European nomadic groups are variously known as Gypsy, Traveller, or Roma (see Liégeois, 1987).

and competition between schools and pupils. Further, policy makers have difficulty producing policies which will incorporate equity and human rights principles, despite the New Labour government's assertion that:

We support the United Nations Educational, Scientific, and Cultural Organisation 1994 Salamanca World Statement on special educational needs, which calls on governments to adopt the principle of inclusive education, enrolling all children in regular schools unless there are compelling reasons for doing otherwise. (UK DfEE, 1997 p.44).

The concept of inclusion has moved away from earlier notions simply meaning the integration of children with disabilities and special educational needs (Warnock Report, 1978), to refer to the enrolment and successful participation of all groups of children in mainstream education, and a corresponding change in the pedagogies, curriculum, organisational structures, policy making, and cultural understandings within education systems and the wider society. Inclusive education is now an international movement, and journals such as *The International Journal of Inclusive Education* provide a forum for researchers, practitioners and policy makers, to share ideas for promotion of educational practices which will prevent individuals being marginalised on the basis of their race, ethnicity, culture, gender or disability. There are numerous definitions of inclusion but most are along the lines of Armstrong's (1999) statement:

Inclusive education refers to a system of education which recognises the rights of all children and young people to share a common education environment in which all are valued equally regardless of difference in perceived ability, gender, class, ethnicity or learning styles.

Five organising principles for inclusive education were set out in the 1980s in the State of Victoria, Australia. These were as follows:

- every child has a right to be educated in a regular school;
- categorisation is personally and educationally unhelpful;
- mainstream school based services serve pupils better than segregated facilities and resources;
- collaborative decision making (between teachers, parents and other professionals) must be encouraged;
- all children can learn and be taught (Semmens, 1993).

However, in Australia as in other countries, putting inclusive principles into practice has proved difficult, especially as schools have continued to find that incorporation of all groups of children is a problem and that school management for inclusive education needed careful thinking and planning.

Whole School Approaches

The consensus emerged among practitioners and policy makers during the 1990s that for inclusive education to be successful, whole school approaches are needed (eg Smith & Tomlinson, 1989). The traditional orientation of special education has been to identify children who were failing or were troublesome, segregate them from other children and provide teaching and resources in a different setting. The whole school approach encourages every professional to help change mainstream classroom practices so that children will not need to be removed. This involves[11]:

- changing traditional assessment practices;
- evaluating current classroom practices, curriculum, organisation and pedogogies;
- planning to change practice;
- planning for support in the mainstream;
- recording and evaluating new practice;
- involving parents;
- providing initial and in service training;
- improving relations between professionals.

Assessment

The instrument most commonly associated with assessment has been the intelligence test. Psychologists have usually been regarded as crucial figures in the assessment process because they work within a scientific model of mental testing. However, in England by the 1970s psychologists themselves were becoming anxious that IQ tests were being used in a political context, or as Tomlinson wrote:

IQ has never existed as a pure scientific concept. Most interpretations of IQ data have demonstrated political overtones. (Tomlinson, 1981 p.65).

In Tomlinson's study of children being assessed and referred to special schools for children with learning difficulties it was apparent that beliefs held at that time about the possible lower IQ of working class and Black children was leading to their over placement in special education (Tomlinson, 1982). In both the USA and Britain there has continued to be much anxiety about the way tests are interpreted, particularly since the publication in the USA of *The Bell Curve* (Herrnstein & Murray, 1994), a book which appeared to argue

---

[11] Core Standards include strategic direction of SEN provision, identification, assessment and planning, effective teaching, ensuring maximum curriculum access, evaluation skills, promotion of social and emotional development and positive behaviour, and ability to develop communication skills.

that all the US social and employment problems are caused by women with low cognitive ability having children! Mirza argued forcefully in a recent article that tests could become part of:

...racist pseudoscience, measuring culturally–specific vocabulary, social class judgements and socially acceptable behaviour. (Mirza, 1998 p.114).

Because of the doubts about testing and because some intelligence tests were not good at predicting a pupil's future educational progress, teachers in Britain came to prefer diagnostic tests. Becker pointed out over twenty years ago, that the most effective way to help children learn new skills is to teach directly what we want them to learn (Becker, 1978)[12]. Traditional testing has reinforced the idea that problems and deficits lie within the children. Assessment instruments that are more directly related to curriculum aims, result in improvements in teaching strategies and in learning, and can be readily evaluated have become a feature of whole school approaches.

Evaluating Practice

Classroom teachers are usually subject to much advice from experts. Those schools that have adopted whole school approaches have put the classroom teacher at the centre to observe and evaluate current classroom practices, the suitability of the curriculum, classroom and school organisation, and the teaching methods used. This leads to what Thomas and Feiler (1988) called the ecological perspective. Teachers are able to locate a failure to match the teaching and learning environment to the individual child. Rather than asking for children to be taken out of the classroom, strategies and methods were developed which allowed the child to stay in mainstream classes (Clark et al., 1995).

Support

Schools which adopted whole school approaches quickly realised that this does mean extra staff in the classroom. In Britain peripatetic teachers, welfare assistants, parents and student teachers have all been deployed to assist in classrooms. This needs careful planning and organisation, using extra staff as individual helpers, whole group teachers, and activity managers. It also means that the headteacher and senior staff must be committed to supporting all their teachers in inclusive education. In 1993, legislation in England introduced the Special Educational Needs Coordinator (SENCO), that is, a named teacher for every school to be responsible for all children with special needs, and central government policy demonstrated support for

---

[12] An early example of this was the Early Learning Skills Analysis (ELSA) developed by Ainscow and Tweddle (1979).

the principles of inclusion and whole school approaches. A Code of Practice for all schools was introduced from 1994, and schools are expected to try to retain all children before calling in outside professionals. A Government paper: *Excellence for All Children* (UK DfEE, 1997) asserted that... *we are determined to show that all children with SEN are capable of excellence.*

Evaluating New Practice
All schools are expected to record individual progress, whether or not children take the nationally standardised Standard Assessment Tasks (SATs) at 7, 11 and 14, and General Certificate of Education examinations (GCSE's) at 16. Teachers are also expected to evaluate the success of their new practices.

Involving Parents
Traditionally, parents have been ignored or uninvolved in decisions made on and treatment of children regarded as having special educational needs. Often professionals have assumed superior attitudes to parents, many of whom are from lower socioeconomic groups and not knowledgeable about education. Whole school approaches require that parents are regarded as part of a team, and close partnerships developed if possible. In Britain, parents now have more rights of access to information, and are more closely involved in schools and classrooms.

Training
It is now well accepted that all teachers need initial and in service training, and those that have special responsibilities need to have particular skills. In England, the Teacher Training Agency (TTA) has developed national standards for young beginning teachers, SENC0s, Headteachers and subject leaders in secondary school. The national standards set out the professional knowledge, skills, and understanding expected when dealing with children with learning difficulties.

Professional Relations
As assessment processes for children with learning difficulties became more bureaucratised, interprofessional conflicts and tensions became more evident. In England, Tomlinson (1996) counted thirtyfour different professionals available to deal with each child. Although professionals work within a *service ideal* dedicated to doing their best for children, harmonious collaboration continues to be difficult. There is a *fragmented professionalism* which encourages a division of responsibility for individual children. Professionals around the world are becoming more conscious of the need to understand each other and work together.

Case Studies

The inclusion of all children via whole school approaches is not easy. The following two case studies illustrate some of the problems.

1. Four Secondary Schools

A study carried out by Clark et al. (1999) in four secondary comprehensive schools found that the schools all experienced difficulties in incorporating all children and had to face a series of dilemmas. At one school pupils with learning difficulties were offered Instrumental Enrichment programs managed by the school's SENCO (the teacher who coordinates special education in the school). The other teachers assumed that this intervention would transform attainments and the capacity of pupils to learn, and the SENCO felt these were unfair expectations. In all the schools teachers were concerned that there was more pupil misbehaviour and some pupils were excluded from school on disciplinary grounds. All the schools had adopted policies of in class support, but the SENCO supporter was often resented by teachers, and effective planning for support partnership was absent. The authors concluded that these four schools' model of inclusive education was based on outdated organisational theories which assumed that if the 'right' practices were adopted all problems would be solved!

2. Exclusion of Gypsy Traveller children from schools in Scotland

Lloyd and Norris (1998) used data from a government funded Scottish education project, in which interviews had been conducted with mainstream teachers, Travellers' teachers, Traveller parents and children. Scottish Gypsy Travellers have a distinct cultural identity and there is Scottish legislation which allows children reduced school attendance due to their parents' seasonal work. This research found that there were strong cultural clashes between teachers' values and expectations of the children, and the children's views of school. Teachers regarded older children as disruptives who did not value education. The children resented school where they were called names by other children, were not given enough teacher time and were regarded as potentially dishonest.

There are no easy answers to the problems inherent in managing schools to meet the needs of all children. This paper has described some of the whole school approaches and the principles involved in inclusive education, by which schools and all the professionals dealing with the children start out with the assumption that mainstream schools will do more to keep all children, whatever their background, ethnicity, and ability level, and not exclude them or refer them to segregated special education.

In 1994 The Salamanca *Statement* and *Framework for Action on Special Needs Education* was adopted by ninetytwo governments and twentyfive international organisations. The statement supported inclusive schools within broader societal goals and noted:

The trend in social policy during the past two decades has been to promote integration and participation and to combat exclusion. Inclusion and participation are essential to human dignity and the exercise of human rights. (p 11).

References

Ainscow, M. & Tweddle, D. (1979). Preventing Classroom Failure. Chester: John Riley.

Armstrong, F. (1999). Inclusion, the curriculum and the struggle for space in schools. Inclusive Education, 3, 1, 75–88.

Becker, W.C. (1978). National evaluation follow through: Behavior–Theory–based programs come out on top. Education and Urban Society, 10, 4, 431–458.

Clark, C., Dyson, A. & Millward, A. (eds.) (1995). Towards Inclusive Schools. London: David Fulton.

Clark, C., Dyson, A., Millward, A. & Robson, S. (1999). Theories of inclusion, theories of schools: deconstructing and reconstructing the inclusive school. British Journal of Educational Research, 25, 2, 157–178.

Herrnstein, R. J. & Murray, C. (1994). The Bell Curve. New York: Free Press.

Liégeois, J. P. (1987). School Provision for Gypsy and Traveller Children. Strasbourg: Council of Europe.

Lloyd, G. & Norris, C. (1998). From difference to deviance: the exclusion of Gypsy–Traveller children. Inclusive Education, 2, 4, 359–370.

Mirza, H. (1998). Race, gender and IQ: the social consequences of a pseudo–scientific discourse. Race, Ethnicity and Education, 1, 1, 111–128.

Smith, D. J. & Tomlinson, S. (1989). The School Effect: a study of multiracial comprehensives. London: Policy Studies Institute.

Semmens, R. (1993). Implementing policy: some struggles and triumphs. In Slee, R. (ed.), Is There a Desk with My Name on it? London: Falmer Press.

Thomas, G. & Feiler, A. (1988). Planning for Special Needs: a whole school approach. London: Blackwell.

Tomlinson, S. (1981). Educational Sub–Normality: a study in decision making. London: Routledge.

Tomlinson, S. (1982). A Sociology of Special Education. London: Routledge.

Tomlinson, S. (1996). Conflicts and dilemmas for professionals in special education. In (eds.), Christensen, C. & Rizvi, F. Disability and the Dilemmas of Education and Justice. Buckingham: Open University Press.

UK DfEE Department for Education and Employment (1997) (Green paper). Excellence for All Children. London. (http://www.dfes.gov.uk/consultations/docs/45_1.pdf)

UK DES Department of Education and Science (1978). Special Educational Needs. (The Warnock Report). London: HMSO

2. EQUALITY AND EDUCATION: A MULTICULTURAL PERSPECTIVE FROM THE UK

Gajendra K. Verma, University of Manchester, UK

Equality and Equality of Opportunity

One of the most widely debated topics in the context of education has surrounded the concept of equality and the related one of equality of opportunity. Yet, the reality within education and related services in most western societies has been the persistence of inequality and of inequality of opportunity. The issue of inequality in education is not a new one. There is a considerable body of literature both in Europe and other parts of the world that bears testimony to this. Much of the writing reflects concern that sections of the population or society are denied access to any meaningful schooling or only accorded access to schooling in which inequality operates against their chances of success (Verma, 1989, 1993a, 1993b).

Most European countries claim, and probably believe, that they espouse equality and that it is a central pillar of their law and administration. Unfortunately, however, arguments can readily be advanced to show that this is not the case. British society, for example, has long been characterised by well established and largely taken for granted inequalities of gender and social class, to which, more recently, should be added 'race', or ethnicity. British national history is full of examples of exploitation both of minority groups and of the working classes. The principles of stratification present in today's society are grounded in Britain's history of colonialism, imperialism, urbanisation and the industrial revolution. It is only in the last fifty or so years that there have been the beginnings of an ideological shift towards equalitarian issues arising from the labour movement, civil rights campaigners and women's rights, signaled in the United Nations' Declaration of Human Rights in 1948. More recently, social and educational reformers have begun to assert that States by their legislation, and perhaps more significantly by their administrative processes, are concerned to ensure the perpetuation of inequality, so that those who have retain their privileges, and those who have not, continue to be deprived of them. Such an arrangement is seen to serve the stability of the state well.

Particularly when it is analysed within the educational context, inequality is both a relativistic and generic term. Nevertheless, the term has an important part to play in any discussion relating to the effectiveness, and the effects, of the educational process. Inequality has been debated in the context of other forms of social stratification – those of gender, ethnicity, race, socioeconomic status and urban/rural differences. Such issues are very much at the heart of the 'equal opportunities' debate, particularly in western countries. There is no shortage of evidence to demonstrate that certain sections of society are not being given a fair chance to make progress in the fields of education, employment and other aspects of their lives. There is also a relativist element in the context of equality. For example, in many developing countries, female education beyond a very basic level is regarded as less important than male education. Even in some apparently sophisticated societies, inequality in educational access and opportunity between the sexes is not uncommon.

The paradox inherent in the definition of equality
Saunders (1989) teased out three core meanings of the word equality. These he identified as *formal equality, equality of opportunity, and equality of outcome*. He defined formal equality as equality under the law. Equality of opportunity meant that all individuals had an equal opportunity to reach their potential by developing their particular talents. He compared a society based on the notion of equality of outcome to a handicap race in which the runners' weights were so perfectly judged that they all arrived at the finishing tape together. He concluded, however, that *formal equality* was incompatible with the other two meanings. It was impossible to have equality of opportunity without compromising on the principle that everyone is equal and entitled to equal treatment under the law. For either of the alternative meanings of equality to be achieved, the law had to require, or at the very least to encourage, positive discrimination in favour of those who were, for whatever reason or in whatever way, disadvantaged.

For the majority of educationists, the idea of positive discrimination presents little in the way of problems. Few would argue against the proposition that every person is unique. The process of education is devoted to ensuring that, within the constraints imposed by genetic inheritance and upbringing, students achieve their potential. For those who, for whatever reason, need more help, it is a matter of professional duty to provide that help.

Equality of opportunity and equality of outcome are incompatible. It is not possible to ensure that everyone achieves to the maximum of his or her potential whilst also ensuring that everyone ends up the same. Equality of outcome is similarly incompatible with formal or legal equality. For everyone to end up equal it would be necessary to apply different principles to the way individuals are treated. Moreover, there is the problem of reconciling formal equality with equality of opportunity – a problem faced by teachers every day. What is to be done with a class of children or adolescents, all at different levels of achievement and commitment to learning? Formal equality would demand that the teacher should treat them all the same. Any attempt to concentrate on the less able or conversely on the most able, would be to deny the principle of equal treatment. If, on the other hand, formal equality was the basis of action, how could this be reconciled with equality of opportunity?

Edwards (1990, p.25) suggested that a realistic measure might be one adopted as the basis of equality in the Affirmative Action plans required of federal contractors in the USA. The composition of the workforce of a business ought to reasonably reflect the ethnic makeup of the local population, both in the numbers employed and their positions within the business' hierarchy. However, Edwards observes that there is a fatal drawback:

...the proportion of minorities that contractors must strive by good faith efforts to replicate in their workforce, is a measure of the current situation, which is itself the result of past discrimination.

There is a real difference between the concept of equality of opportunity as applied to individuals and to groups of people identifiable by their colour, culture or ethnicity. Marx saw no problem in a socialist society in which people were differently rewarded for different kinds of work. However, a great deal of intellectual effort was fruitlessly expended in trying to decide appropriate rewards for, say, a street cleaner as against a brain surgeon. The essential difference lies in the fact that equality of opportunity applied to groups reduces itself to a power struggle. Edwards (1990, p.32) argued that:

...the practice of equalising opportunities is an exercise in promoting fairness ... The moral strength with which we endow it, however, may be responsive to the reasons for inequalities of opportunity. When these stem from factors of race, sex and religion, the pursuit of equality of opportunity becomes a matter of justice.

The purposes of education
A distinction needs to be made between what governments see as the purposes of an education system and how educationists and teachers see them. For governments, schools are seen primarily as institutions, which will provide the state with appropriately educated citizens in sufficient numbers to meet the various needs of society. For educationists and teachers, schools

are places where children will be encouraged and enabled to reach their full potential as individuals.

The two sets of ambitions obviously have a good deal in common, even if they are not identical. Governments are concerned with outcomes: are there going to be enough scientists or engineers, or doctors, or mechanics or whatever, to meet the nation's needs? Educationists and teachers are concerned with process: what are the best methods to ensure that children reach their potential, become fully themselves?

Parekh (1986) set out the objectives of what he described as the *traditional and widely accepted view of education*. These were to:

- cultivate fundamental capacities such as critical reflection, imagination, self criticism, the ability to reason and to form independent judgements;
- foster such intellectual and moral qualities as the love of truth, objectivity, curiosity and humility;
- familiarise students with the great intellectual, moral, literary and other achievements of the human spirit.

Education acording to that view was concerned to introduce young people not merely to the cultural capital of their own community but also to that of mankind as a whole. They are to be taught the languages, cultures, religions, histories and geography of other communities so that their affections are enlarged and so that they learn to appreciate mankind's unity and diversity. However, Parekh observed that such a statement suffers from some serious defects. He argued that it is sociologically naïve and does not take account of the way in which its realisation in practice is constantly frustrated by the social context in which every educational system exists and functions.

For educationists and teachers, the priorities are much more along the lines suggested by Parekh. They are concerned with the processes which will result in citizens whose education has encouraged and enabled them to reach their full potential, to become, fully and completely, themselves. Moreover, teachers may well be constrained in various ways in what they teach. In Britain, teachers used to be allowed enormous freedom over what they taught. However, the introduction, through the 1988 Education Reform Act, of the National Curriculum and its associated testing regime has resulted in a situation in which teachers now have to deliver a centrally controlled curriculum, and pupils are expected to meet prescribed standards of performance. What is not constrained are the methods which teachers employ to attain their required ends.

The role of education in nurturing equality of all citizens, which is acknowledged in the government guidance to the National Curriculum in the UK, is also reflected in material from nongovernmental organisations, researchers and by local educational bodies. In addition it is referred to in a number of documents and materials at the European policy level. Issues of education and of citizenship are included under the heading of social justice and equality of opportunity in the green paper on European social policy (European Commission, 1993a). The green paper on the European Dimension of Education sketches out equal opportunities and citizenship as areas important to the development of quality education across Europe, where *Europe is not a dimension which replaces others, but one which enhances them* (European Commission, 1993b). Equality and citizenship underlie all aspects of education from the scholastic achievement of children to the research and development of appropriate teacher training (see also Verma, 1992).

Testing and equality of opportunity

Tests developed by psychologists have been extensively employed in many fields by managers, operating on behalf of government, none more so than in education. A classic example of this in Britain is the Education Act (1944), which introduced universal secondary education. No delivery structure was prescribed. Local Education Authorities (LEAs) were simply required to provide schools, which would educate pupils according to their 'age, ability and aptitude'. An earlier plan for selective secondary education formed the structural basis for the division of schools into three categories – Secondary Grammar, Secondary Modern and Secondary Technical. The Act determined the secondary education of all children beyond the age of 11 years within the State system for the following twenty years until 1965, when a Labour (socialist) government announced its intention to end selective education.

The device employed by LEAs to decide the type of secondary school that children were to attend was an intelligence test. Many criticisms have been levelled at IQ tests over the years but the one that should have revealed their limitation is this: the concept of general intelligence grew out of a measuring process. Normally, of course, concepts are developed then devices are developed to measure them. Psychologists arrived at the concept of general intelligence by the opposite process. The test to measure it was devised and its results were claimed to provide an accurate measurement of how much of it an individual had. No satisfactory answers have been found regarding what is being measured and whether intelligence has any existence outside the piece of paper giving the results of an IQ test.

As is generally known, most psychological tests are norm referenced. The test results are expressed in terms of a comparison between those obtained from the test subjects and those obtained from a large number of other people. If the reliability and the validity of the test has not been established and standardised on an appropriate population (for example age range, social class, gender, ethnicity or country of origin), any results are likely to be, at best, suspect and, probably, severely misleading. The consequences for *individuals* who are 'wrongly' assessed, with resultant restricted future educational and life–chance opportunities, can be considerable (Verma & Mallick, 1982). When that testing 'wrongly' assesses *particular sections of society*, those consequences are even more acutely felt.

Settlers, minorities and education

Most European societies are now demographically diverse, characterised by two and sometimes more distinct groups. The groups may be differentiated in terms of language or ethnicity or religion or cultural characteristics, or by a combination of some or all of these. Faced by such diversity, most countries have failed to recognise and respond to the challenges of the heterogeneous nature of their societies. This failure extends to many areas of state provision including the education services. A major obstacle to progress lies in the fact that education services function within the legal and social contexts of the states they serve.

Relationships between dominant and minority communities in society can take on complex patterns. The state of relationships between the two depends on how both the majority and minority groups respond to one another. Berry (1979) characterised four distinctive models:

- Integration: where a distinct identity and culture is linked with a general wish of society to maintain positive interethnic relations;
- Separatism: where the dominant group does not wish to maintain positive interethnic relations;
- Assimilation: where the dominant group adopts a positive attitude and a particular ethnic group does not seek to hold on to a separate cultural identity; and
- Marginality: where no separate identity is sought by a minority group but the majority group adopts a hostile attitude towards that group (Verma et al., 1994).

The main thrust of the educational response to the situation in the UK has been referred to as 'multicultural education', although it must be admitted that this is 'at best a very imprecise concept' (Verma et al., 1994) and that this response has been criticised on a number of grounds. What is interesting in the present context is the changing pattern of the broad school response. This is well illustrated in the Swann Report, commissioned by the Secretary of State for Education in the late 1970's:

The most obvious difference between the early days of assimilation and integration and the concepts of multicultural education is that, whereas the former focused primarily on seeking to 'remed'[13] the perceived cultural problems of ethnic minority children and to compensate for their perceived 'disabilities', multicultural education has usually

---

[13] 'remediate' – Eds.

tended to have two distinct themes – firstly, meeting the particular educational needs of ethnic minority children and secondly, the broader issue of preparing all pupils for life in a multiracial society. (UK DES, 1985, p.205).

Research evidence suggests that many of the conflicts that arise between the school and minority communities, and many of the cultural disparities that pupils experience, are caused by conflicting values, beliefs and behaviour (Pumfrey & Verma, 1990; Verma & Pumfrey, 1994). Some ethnic and religious groups are socialised in homes and communities in which the sacred is valued more than the secular, and in which traditional cultural beliefs and religious values are strongly held. The attitudes of the in–group towards the out–groups are formed on the basis of this socialisation process.

Newly arrived settlers in any country face enormous problems. They need, as well as more practical requirements, to come to terms with the culture (using 'culture' in its broadest sense) of the society in which they have just arrived. So too do their children. To a more limited extent, members of the 'host' society also need to adjust. For both groups, this presents challenges. Will this situation be seen as an opportunity to welcome and benefit from diversity? Further, can that diversity be treated as a resource from which can be generated vitality and creativeness or will it be seen as an excuse for retreating into prejudice and racism?

While newly arrived parents get on with the business side of living, bringing them into contact with other adults from the host community, they will also have opportunities to relax in the comfortable company of their own group, in ways that are denied their children. For much of their time, the latter will be in school, sitting beside other pupils from differing cultural, ethnic, language backgrounds, being taught by teachers who are also representatives of alien traditions. Much the same may be true also for children from minority groups that have long been considered, for a variety of reasons, as 'inferior' or 'different' in the eyes of mainstream society. Yet schools are the places where children learn to respond either positively or negatively to matters of equality, inequality and cultural diversity. This represents an awesome responsibility for teachers and schools.

The model where minorities are expected to fully emulate the culture and customs of the majority in order to achieve integration does not match the reality of a pluralist society. This is demonstrated in areas of the UK which have populations of many centuries standing such as the Black population of Liverpool or the continuing marginalisation of Travellers.

Tackling inequality
In many countries, there has been much debate and discussion during more than thirty years on how educational institutions and the curriculum

can be modified to meet the challenges of plurality in society. There is no consensus as yet as to how best to educate all children and young people in a culturally diverse environment. Educational reformers have been asking what contribution education should be making towards creating a society in which the life chances of all are enhanced and fairly distributed (UK DES, 1985). In most western societies, academics have developed various models in the last thirty years or so, and have used them to address the issues of inequality within the educational context. The most popular approaches to advocate and provide equality of opportunity have been multicultural and antiracist education. These have had some effect on the perceptions and practices of some teachers. This has, however, been mainly restricted to those who work in schools with substantial ethnic minority populations.

Teachers in schools where pupils from the mainstream culture are the norm have failed to see the significance of these approaches. A consequence has been that teachers have failed to change the ideological perceptions of society at large. There has been widespread failure to recognise inequality within the education system. Moreover, racial prejudice and discrimination in society at large remain at a high level in the UK. In Britain, and no doubt in other European countries too, there are those who accuse teachers and educationists seeking to address issues of equality and cultural diversity of meddling with social engineering. They argue that teachers should concern themselves solely with the teaching/learning process. A statement by the British Prime Minister, John Major, in 1992 at the Conservative Party Conference serves as an example of this thinking:

Primary teachers should learn how to teach children how to read, not waste their time on the politics of gender, race and class.

The answer to those critics is, or should be, that the pursuit of equality of opportunity is a moral issue and one which justice demands. If education is not, among other things, about inculcating a moral sense in children and young people, together with a respect for justice, what purpose does it serve, other than meeting the utilitarian demands of the state for an educated workforce?

The role of the teacher

Perhaps the most vital element in bringing about those desired changes is the person at the centre of all these endeavours: the teacher. Much has been written about what teachers ought to do, very frequently pointing out how they are failing to meet 'the challenge' (Verma, 1993b). A whole paper would not suffice to deal with this issue properly, let alone the last few minutes of this address. Instead of attempting the impossible, I intend to list just a few of the key attributes of teachers in the pluralist classroom. To promote equality and respond generously and sensitively to human diversity in the classroom, teachers need to be:

- conscious of the ethnically and culturally diverse nature of the society in which they are working;
- prepared to act as agents of change in the creation of a diverse, pluralistic and harmonious society;
- capable of recognising their own prejudices and overcoming them;
- able to identify discrimination in others and the institutions they work in;
- equipped to prepare children and young people for a life in pluralist societies;
- able to recognise the values of teaching which identifies and acknowledges the aspirations of all children and young people and seeks to enhance their chances of maximising their potential.

We live in an interdependent world, where we have to work and interact with nations of different races, cultures, ethnicities beyond our borders and with people of varying cultural, linguistic, religious and ethnic groups within our borders – the one affecting the other. In such a world of increasing interdependence – economically, socially and politically – multicultural education can play an important role in challenging stereotypes, prejudices and ethnocentric perspectives of both individuals and groups (Verma, 1993a, 1994).

It is of *critical* importance that this is recognised in our institutions by all concerned with the provision of educational and related services. We can no longer afford to look back to the past and take comfort in it. We must respond to the challenges of today and prepare ourselves and our young people to meet the challenges of tomorrow.

References

Berry, J. (1979). Research in multicultural societies: implications of cross–cultural methods. Journal of Cross Cultural Psychology, 10, 415–434.

Edwards, J. (1990). What purpose does equality of opportunity serve? New Community, 17, 1, 19–35.

European Commission (1993a). European Social Policy – Options for the Union. Brussels: European Commision.

European Commission (1993b). The European Dimension of Education. Brussels: European Commission.

Parekh, B. (1986). The concept of multicultural education. In S. Modgil, G. K. Verma, K. Mallick, & H. Modgil (eds.), Multicultural Education: the interminable debate. London: Falmer Press.

Pumfrey, P. D. & Verma, G. K. (1990), (eds.). Race Relations and Urban Education: promising practices. London: Falmer Press.

Saunders, P. (1989). The question of equality. Social Studies Review, 5, 2, 77–82.

UK DES Department of Education and Science (1985). Education For All: report of the Committee of Inquiry into the Education of Children from Ethnic Minority Groups, (The Swann Report). Cmnd 9453, London: HMSO.

UK Ministry of Education (1944). Education Act. London: HMSO.

Verma, G. K. (1989), (ed). Education For All: a landmark in pluralism. London: Falmer Press.

Verma, G. K. (1992). Cultural diversity in secondary schools: its nature, extent and curricular implications. In P. D. Pumfrey and G. K. Verma (eds.), Cultural Diversity and the National Curriculum (Vol. 1): the foundation subjects and RE in secondary schools. London: Falmer Press.

Verma, G. K. (1993a). Cultural Diversity in Secondary Schools: its nature, extent and cross–curricular implications. In G. K. Verma and P. Pumfrey (eds.), Cultural Diversity and the Curriculum (Vol. 2): cross–curricular contexts, themes and dimensions in secondary schools. London: Falmer Press.

Verma, G. K. (1993b), (ed.). Inequality and Teacher Education: an international perspective. London: Falmer Press.

Verma, G. K. (1994). Cultural Diversity in Primary Schools: its nature, extent and cross–curricular implications. In G. K. Verma & P. Pumfrey (eds.), Cultural Diversity and the Curriculum (Vol. 4): cross–curricular themes in primary schools. London: Falmer Press.

Verma, G. K. & Mallick, K. (1982). Tests and testing in a multi–ethnic society. In G. K. Verma & C. Bagley (eds.), Self Concept, Achievement and Multicultural Education. London: Macmillan.

Verma, G. K. & Pumfrey, P. (1994), (eds.). Cultural Diversity and the National Curriculum (Vol. 4): cross–curricular themes in primary schools. London: Falmer Press.

Verma, G. K., Zec, P. & Skinner, G. (1994). The Ethnic Crucible: harmony and hostility in multi–ethnic schools. London: Falmer Press.

SECTION II

DEVELOPMENT OF ATTITUDES

3. POSITIVE AND NEGATIVE FACTORS INVOLVED IN THE PROCESS OF CHILD SOCIALISATION

Zdeněk Matějček,
Charles University, Prague, Czech Republic[14]

The presumptions which may be considered as the common denominators of this paper are that we all take the cohabitation of the majority with the minorities as desirable if not vital and that this cohabitation be without detriment to anyone and as advantageous as possible to both majority and minority parties. If these presumptions are true then tolerance, acceptance, and integration mark the journey to our goal. Finally, some attitudes are so deeply rooted that it is particularly difficult to change or reform them. Later I will suggest just why all this is so slow and why in spite of good will, efforts and many investments we are not so successful in our striving.

1. Socialisation

Socialisation is the developmental process through which a child 'in–grows' into its society, starts feeling him or herself a member, connects his or her personal identity with the society, accepts its order, its norms, etc. This process starts at early childhood. However its first elements can be found as early as the prenatal period, and the process is predetermined by even earlier factors like parental attitudes of those who begot the child and then psychologically accepted him or her, that is, connected their fate with the child's fate, being substantively involved in the child's well being. The process of socialisation necessarily comprises the formation, progress and various transformations of attitudes towards other people (children or adults) and thus also to people who are somehow different, unusual, conspicuous or strange. To a child of the majority, these conspicuous and strange people are members of various minorities; to a child of a minority group, these are members of the majority.

[14]Professor Matějček's research of mental health of persons exposed in childhood to unfavourable psychosocial conditions was supported by grant IGA MZ ČR nr NF 5579–3 to Prague Psychiatric Centre.

2. Many forms of minority

At present the issue of ethnic minorities is widely debated in the Czech Republic, but minorities in our society are many and varied. Some have been here many years, some are forming just now, some are more sharply delimited, some less, some define themselves in one way, others in another. The fact is they are here and various comparisons among their specific mentalities are rich sources of information. There are religious minorities, socioeconomic minorities (it is as difficult to understand the world of the homeless as to understand the world of millionaires), social status minorities (for example aristocracy even in the contemporary Czech Republic). There are minorities defined by physical or mental characteristics (top sportsmen) or by a particular pathology (alcoholics, gamblers, substance abusers, etc). There are also minorities that I would describe as 'experiential'. I am talking about people who have experienced or are experiencing something affecting their lives which is unusual in a given society and the effect is long term or permanent, for example families with mentally retarded children or (even more typically) families in which a child has died. From them, in my opinion, we can learn much about the mentality of a minority.

Our great grandmothers had more children than we today, but it was quite common that one of them died. Thus the experience of losing a child could be shared with just about anybody in the neighbourhood, relatives etc. A family encountering this painful experience easily received sympathetic feedback and understanding support and had no reason to feel socially isolated. Nowadays a loss of a child by death is rare, so the affected families have none to share their experience and give understanding. Most of them repeatedly run into defensive attitudes on the part of the majority, that is 'unaffected' people, so they become socially isolated and accept the minority mentality with everything that is related to it.

3. The unconscious origins of interpersonal attitudes: resistance to rational change

Reason, judgement, logical thinking and everything that we call intelligence is a 'service' institution. The degree to which intelligence affects some of our attitudes is surprisingly low. Its main use here is to find 'logical justifications' for what has already been constituted, in order to find the strong, usually pseudo–rational arguments convincing ourselves that our views are correct, normal, in accordance with the will of God or any other higher authority.

Attitudes towards people around us and their differences and special features are formed in the depths of our personality, at the unconscious or nearly unconscious level, very early in development, when we are not yet capable of rational reasoning and when we copy the attitudes of the people in our closest social circle through the mechanisms of immediate imitation and immediate identification. Unfortunately this means that whenever we wish to change any aspect of these deeply formed attitudes, all rational approaches and procedures, logical argument, school teaching in the conventional style, lectures, explanations and so on are too weak as means of education. These are not effective investments. And they are usually deployed too late, at a time when our intelligence works in favour of what has been formed long ago without its assistance. These are the causes of poor results and failed hopes so far.

4. The intergenerational transmission of irrational attitudes

Attitudes founded on an irrational basis are necessarily and obviously passed from generation to generation. They are strong, or resistant to time and outside influences. The process of change is lengthy. And we are not patient enough in matters which span beyond a single lifetime. We are not psychologically equipped to persist in efforts the effects of which are out of sight. Thus the knowledge of our limited lifetime poses a barrier on the journey from tolerance to integration, which we mentioned at the beginning.

The passing of attitudes from generation to generation can easily be seen between parents and children in the child rearing process. What to tolerate and what not, what should be punished, what encouraged, what is the 'female' behaviour expected of girls and the 'male' behaviour expected of boys etc. Research studies (eg David et al., 1988; Langmeier & Matějček, 1975) evidence how lengthy is the process of changing these attitudes, even those that are unnatural, unhealthy, impractical or plain nonsensical. At the same time these studies show that the higher the respondents' education, the more they show facility towards modifications of their educational attitudes. Many nonsensical and unhealthy practices are maintained especially strongly in groups where the members are socially isolated due to low education, cultural deprivation, religious sect membership, wherever these features are found, in minority or majority groups.

Origin of basic trust in the specific attachment relationship

Evidence provided by ethological psychology and so called behavioural biology has shown that approximately during the seventh or eighth months of child's life, that is in the middle of the nursing period, a specific emotional relationship to the mother person starts to appear (eg Bowlby, 1968). The mother person does not necessarily need to be the biological mother (Schaffer & Emerson, 1964), only someone who provides the child with the feeling of life security and safety – whose simple presence removes the child's fear of the unknown and thus dangerous world. The great Erik Erikson attributes to this period the beginnings of the basic trust or mistrust in 'his or her people' and consequently in people in general (Erikson, 1963). In the child's intellectual development, he or she has just arrived at differentiating between the known and the unknown. If the unknown was not connected with the feeling of anxiety, the child would dart uninhibited into the unknown, and could find him or herself in great danger, could get lost, drown etc (Hassenstein, 1987). This mechanism tells him or her that the known is safe but the strange is dangerous. Unknown appearance, strange facial features, unusual behaviour all lawfully induce the primary insecurity and work against accepting this person as known and thus safe. This is another difficulty that must be overcome on our journey to tolerance and further on to integration.

The specific attachment relationship as the key to facilitating tolerance
However, here is the key to supportive tactics, strategies and measures, and to freeing the way to accepting, in spite of all the above, the other, conspicuous and dangerous. When and how do we build into the process of socialisation something new, something our conscience says is positive? When is the right time and opportunity to change the transmission of interpersonal attitudes between the generations?

At the end of the nursing period (and also later during the succeeding developmental stages) the child unconsciously perceives an unknown and strange person as potentially dangerous. However – and here is the key to a positive change – if something unknown and dangerous is perceived while experiencing the feeling of safety and security, the strange stops being dangerous, and is added to the sum of the child's experiences just as any other known fact. We can say that if a child learns to overcome the existential anxiety of the unknown in his or her mother's arms, he or she also learns not to be afraid of people who are different. This is the basis of tolerance. If this is really to happen, it means that those who are the donors of security of life to the child are ready to let their child acquaint him or herself safely with the unknown world. This kind of readiness is a positive factor in the desirable socialisation of a child.

Psychological deprivation is a negative factor. Its symptoms, uncertainty of life and distrust of people, are found for example in children raised in children's homes. When they reach adolescence or adulthood, they often show nonsensical, unmotivated, aggressive intolerance towards 'strange' or 'different' people. I have labelled this for myself as the 'one bag mentality of both cowards and slaveholders' (Langmeier & Matějček, 1975).

Approximately around the age of two years the children start to form the so called family identity that is the sense of membership of a wider group of people who belong together and for whom the child has a very specific value. This is an important step towards security of life. We think it is positive if this family group is open to the unusual during this developmental period. The family should give positive, reinforcing feedback wherever the child encounters any strangeness. On the other hand it is negative when the family is not capable of this. In such a case the child's basic distrust in the human world is maintained and even reinforced (Stern, 1977).

Then comes another very significant if not crucial period – the preschool period (Matějček, 1999). This is a period of preparations for life, including life that lies far ahead, not only for school. The child now developmentally crosses the boundaries of his or her family and enters the community of peers. In our country this is characteristically documented by the child's entering the kindergarten. Only in contact and relationships with other children can the foundations be laid of the so called prosocial traits such as cooperative play and work, shared fun, compassion and commiseration. This period is most probably the one in which foundations are laid for a particularly important relationship, a specifically peer relationship – friendship. Unfortunately it has not attracted much attention from our developmental psychologists. On the other hand, this is also a period during which the child internalises impressions of his or her environment that are most formative, when he or she is suggestible and accepts what is presented with an appropriate dose of authority.

This is the crucial time when it is possible to instate something new, something prosocial, to the intergenerational transmission of attitudes. Children in kindergarten are evidence of this. They accept various human peculiarities without any problems or aversion, only with their natural childhood curiosity. Integration of handicapped children into kindergarten is much more successful than attempts for integration at school age. This age is relatively the easiest for inducing helpful attitudes to those in need. Here again the positive factor is the knowledge and readiness of the educators, this time professionals as well as the family members, to induce and reinforce children's prosocial attitudes. The negative factors are their ignorance, unpreparedness or unwillingness to do this.

Now the child is in school. Middle school age, from eight or nine to twelve or thirteen years of age, is a period of maximum extraversion and social orientation. At this stage the child suffers most from his or her 'inferiority' if he or she deviates in any way from the social average or lacks (even if fictitiously) any abilities, knowledge, skills which are prized by children's community. Only exceptionally, our children value school achievement, which our adults value most. Our children most value physical appearance and even more physical abilities and dexterity, but also devotion to friendship, fidelity, openness, etc. This is also the time of the final gender differentiation and of accepting an identity in accordance with one's own sex. Boy and girl groups are now most apart, and they feel most ashamed in front of the other group. Also the burning feeling of difference has now a distinct boy and girl version and in the same way the values on which the acceptance of a 'different' classmate are based are differentiated according to gender. In middle childhood, peer norms are often preferred over family norms.

Thus not only the authoritative parent or teacher decides how acceptable is any different voice. Now there is also the rather powerful 'people's voice', the voice of peers, the voice of the community which the child entered in the previous period and which has now matured to a certain degree of independence. The opinions of child community are not just the sum of the attitudes of all of its members. Children are more influenced by the opinions of 'leaders'. This means that if these leaders have been exposed only to negative factors in the previous developmental stages there is a danger that now they will negatively influence the whole community. If however those who preponderate in the community trod the road of tolerance and acceptance of minority differences in the previous stages, negative attitudes of those 'unprepared', 'uneducated', 'ill–bred' will not have any broader influence.

Thus if we want to influence the attitudes towards any minority, be there only one of its members in the class, on the playground, in a club, we must understand the given group of children and work from the inside. Outside pressure now starts to cause aversion and counter–pressure, as was well illustrated in a Czech movie *Obecná škola* (Community school, director Jan Svěrák) where the teacher explicitly refers to the identity of the only Roma member.

This middle school process continues into older school age and adolescence, except the evidence may be a little different. Gender differentiation is now even more distinct than before and the opposition against authoritatively expressed opinions is also stronger. More than earlier, we must also take the child's intellectual maturity into account, which by itself, as mentioned above, does not form any attitudes but rather serves them by reinforcing them by logical justification. The child's intelligence thus becomes an auxiliary tool that is often very helpful wherever the person has successfully begun the path from tolerance through acceptance to integration. And on the other hand it may serve to support and justify the negative attitudes if the negative factors prevailed in the previous developmental stages.

Realistic hopefulness

Generally we may say that whatever was put into the child's personality in the previous developmental stages and is now maturing, will now be harvested as good or less good fruits. The fruits here may mean outside behaviour, actions, activity, work. It may mean loud, aggressive demonstrations on town squares for the purity of the race. But it may also mean a friendly handshake, help without asking for thanks, and authentic, unassuming, barrier–overcoming implementation of the principle of integration into the everyday life of our society.

The latter option, acceptance and integration of minorities as a highly important principle, was mentioned as the first presumption of all further thoughts in this paper. Now, at the end, I return to it. The goal is distant and the journey to achieving it is not easy. I only want to add that distant goals and difficult journeys are challenges which we should take on together, not letting anyone weary us, confuse us, or prevent us.

References

Bowlby, J. (1968). Attachment and Loss, Vol 1: attachment. London: Hogarth Press.

David, H. P., Dytrych, Z. & Schüller, V. (1988). Born Unwanted. Prague: Avicenum / New York: Springer.

Erikson, E., (1963). Childhood and Society. New York: Norton.

Hassenstein, B. (1987). Verhaltensbiologie des Kindes. Munich: Piper.

Langmeier, J. & Matějček, Z. (1975). Psychological Deprivation in Childhood. New York: Halstead.

Matějček, Z. (1999). Sozialentwicklung unter den Bedingungen der psychischen Deprivation und Subdeprivation. In T. Hellbrügge (ed.), Kindliche Sozialisation und Sozialentwicklung. Lübeck: Hansisches Verlagskontor.

Schaffer, H. R. & Emerson, P. E. (1964). The development of social attachment in infancy. Monographs of the Society for Research in Child Development, 29, 3, 1–77.

Stern D. F. (1977). The First Relationship: infant and mother. Fontana: Glasgow.

4. RISK AND PROTECTIVE FACTORS IN DEVELOPMENT OF ETHNIC MINORITY CHILDREN

Vladimír Smékal, with Antonia Dvořáková and Jan Mareš,
Masaryk University, Brno, Czech Republic

If a stranger sojourn in your land, ye shall not vex him. But the stranger that dwelleth with you shall be unto you as one born among you, and thou shalt love him as thyself: for ye were strangers in the land of Egypt. (Leviticus 20, 33–34).

The Czech Republic is host to many national minorities, settled and migrant, from developing and developed countries, both through our former soviet and our new western connections (ČR Council for National Minorities, 2002). For satisfactory coexistence, the majority must develop and maintain tolerance for differences. The minority, while maintaining their ethnic identity, must respect our legal system, which, as in Roman Law, is based on seven principles of good behaviour. Further, in post–totalitarian days, all our citizens, majority and minorities, are newly learning to use statutory human rights protection.

The Czech Government's Council for National Minorities believes there to be two hundred thousand Roma in our country, making them our largest minority after Slovaks. International media have recorded how they are also the focus of considerable concern and of hostility. This paper explains some of the difficulties, and records two projects which have investigated the facilitation of positive characteristics in Roma children.

Orientations and background
Theoretical orientations
Although personality and characteristic behaviours can change throughout childhood, especially in adolescence, yet some are due to the social environment provided for the individual child through family child rearing patterns, as well as to ethnic or other cultural traditions, also to pregnancy and childbirth conditions (eg Dragonas et al., 1996). The sociobiological perspective certainly overestimates the genetic effect. Memes (Dawkins, 1990) probably influence the personality as

much as genes (Csikszentmihalyi, 1993; Hillman, 1996). Many complex longitudinal behavioural genetic investigations employing both twin–sibling and also adopted–away designs converge at present on the probability that genetic factors explain only about half the human difference in what we refer to as 'personality', and also about half of what we call intelligence (Plomin, 1994; Plomin & Defries, 1998; Plomin et al., 2001).

Thus behavioural genetic studies support the position that vulnerabilities to many problems can be overcome, and positive characteristics facilitated, if only societies have the will to provide facilitating environments. What is more, children are more open to change than are adults, so we must look to education systems as the motor of change. Both intentional and also unintentional practices of individual teachers and of the cultures of schools (eg Anderson, 1982) have effects, in some cases longterm effects. Even children's behaviour out of school (eg the delinquency of its pupils) has been found to correlate significantly with the school culture that the head and teachers maintain (eg Rutter et al., 1979).

Roma in the Czech Republic

Roma originated in India and entered what is now the Czech Republic in medieval times (Frazer, 1995; Nečas, 1995). By the 16th century, many were settled with specialist crafts, eg metal working and music. The nazi holocaust decimated the Roma population in what is now the Czech Republic, only one thousand surviving (Frazer, 1995; Kenrick, 1995; Nečas, 1995). The communist regime banned travelling, Edict 74/1958 (ČSSR, 1958), and rehoused most Roma in flats, often on huge urban estates. More survived the holocaust in semi–independent Slovakia, especially in the rural east, and many east Slovak Roma were forcibly resettled by Edict 502/1965 (ČSSR, 1965) which operated a quota system for proportions of minorities in each township. These Slovak Roma became labour for industrial expansion in Czech towns and cities, where they were often housed in poor nineteenth century accommodation which many still occupy. Approximately seventy per cent of today's Czech Roma are therefore of east Slovak origin, ten per cent west Slovak, and ten per cent Hungarian. Ten per cent are Olach (Vlach) Roma, a subethnic group found throughout Europe, still travelling in some countries. Olach Roma more strongly venerate the ancient traditions of close extended families, family and social hierarchy, gender role differentiation, the important purification codes or mánuš which regulate sexual contact, food, and interactions with non–Roma or gadžo, and the courts to adjudicate on marriage rights, property ownership etc (Frazer, 1995; Hübšmannová, 1991; Johnson, below p.129; Rao, 1975; Romano Džaniben, 1996)[15].

---

[15] There is more information about Roma in the Czech Republic on the websites:
(http://www.romove.cz/)
(http://www.czech.cz/index.php?section=3&menu=0&action=text&id=30)

The Czech Education system

From 1948, Czechoslovak education took the Soviet model of 'uniform' or 'Basic' schools, which served all the local children from age six to age fifteen or more, except those deemed to need special education (ČSSR 29, 1984). The same lessons were delivered to all children. Internationally, many countries admire our prioritisation of mathematics and literacy, which operates from the beginning of grade one. However, a weakness in our education is the prioritisation of memory for rules and facts over investigation and problem solving. This largely continues today (Koucký et al., 1999), though newly legal Obecné (Common) schools (Piťha & Helus, 1994) and Národní (National) schools (Vondráček & Tomek, 1997) emphasise problem solving and more individualised teaching (Novotná et al., 1998).

This early Basic school emphasis on rules of literacy and mathematics assumes that children will have been prepared for such disciplines by families or by nursery school (mateřská škola). In fact most Czech children do attend nursery school from age three (Koucký, 1996). Children can begin the nine grades of Basic school at age six, although twenty per cent wait until age seven (ČR MŠMT, 1999a). Teachers grade children annually: those who fail the grade must repeat the year.

Most young Czechs continue at age fifteen or sixteen from Basic school to 'secondary school', (UK 'further education'). There are three core forms: academically oriented gymnasia, professional schools for nursing, administration etc, and thirdly a vast network of small and large apprenticeship schools. Formerly each was based on a state owned factory or farm: some are now privatised, many have amalgamated, many closed (Kotásek, 1996).

Concerning Roma, the communist system transferred a rising proportion (thirtythree per cent in 1975 to fortyfive percent in 1989) from Basic school to segregated 'remedial special' school (zvláštní škola), (European Roma Rights Centre, 1999), often using conventional IQ tests in the process. Although parents had some informal right to oppose the placement, until 1999 (ČR, MŠMT, 1999), there was no legal route by which they could have their children return to mainstream school.

Roma tend not to use nursery school, because child care is available at home via close extended families, older siblings, our three year maternity leave, and, since capitalism, unemployed parents. Also, few Roma have continued to any form of secondary education (UK further education). Again, until 2000 (Czech Regulation 19/2000) this was legally impossible unless the pupil had formally graduated from Basic school. Since 1996, the Czech Government has established special 'zero grade' classes, some in mainstream schools and some in special schools, to help accelerate the progress of children who have missed preschool. The government also funds Roma classroom assistants in mainstream and in special schools (Meluzínová, below p.125).

Risk and protective factors

Informal observations led us to hypothesise that Roma children are more impetuous, change the focus of their behaviour more frequently, and show greater lability of energy than do Czech children. Such characteristics represent vulnerabilities, especially if managed confrontationally by formal teachers with strict expectations of discipline. On the other hand, many Roma children appear to have good adaptability, to be inquisitive, and less apprehensive, characteristics which good teachers can develop into intellectual curiosity and sociability.

The absence of positive role models, either historic or present, is also a risk factor. On the other hand, a positive factor is represented by strong intragroup solidarity and family bonds. Although there are risks in strong maternal attachments where there is maternal depression, alcoholism and interpersonal conflict, Roma mothers display a strong need to protect their children and many unemployed Roma mothers consider awakening their children's interest for education to be their mission. Thus risks can be overcome within families. (See Samková–Bučková, p.59–67, for more about Roma families).

Empirical studies

1. Effectiveness of preschool classes

Nursery school can be a powerful protective factor (Schweinhart & Weikhart, 1993), but few Roma children attend. In 1996, the Czech government allowed education authorities to open free 'zero grade' classes to prepare children for Basic or special school. Sixty were operating by 2000 (ČR MŠMT, 2000). Dvořáková studied children in three zero grade classes in inner city Brno early in the school year 1999, with follow up six months later. Using a playlike atmosphere, she administered various items of verbal comprehension and reasoning, visuomotor, early literacy, and also self help skills. Children were age between five and seven years. All had major deficits for their ages, and all made substantial improvements in all items tested over the six months from pre– to post–test. We concluded that by helping reverse educational disadvantage, preschool helps improve reciprocal respect between the minority and the majority.

2. Testing, skills deficits, demographic factors and remediation

Using a mixed Czech and Roma sample, we investigated and confirmed Antonak's finding that basic skills were equally good predictors of children's progress as conventional intelligence tests (Antonak et al., 1982). We also confirmed that a substantial proportion of children change their developmental position relative to their peers (Hindley & Owen, 1980; Sameroff et al., 1993). Further, we replicated US findings (Mercer & Lewis, 1979; Reynolds, 1980) that the predictive validity of conventional intelligence tests is lower for minority than for majority children. During this psychometric investigation, we collected basic demographic data for the parents of Czech and Roma pupils age eight or nine, who were in mainstream and special schools in NE Brno where most Roma families live. Nine per cent of Czech and thirtyfive per cent of Roma pupils were in special school.[16]

Our basic demographic data reflects typical Roma deprivation. The education of seventynine per cent Roma fathers and ninetytwo per cent Roma mothers stopped at or before the end of Basic school (see above), compared with only twenty per cent Czech fathers and twentyfour per cent mothers. Regarding jobs, only seven per cent of Roma fathers and six per cent of Roma mothers were in semiskilled employment. The jobs of other employed Roma parents were unskilled. This contrasted with the Czech parents where eightytwo per cent of fathers' and sixty per cent of mothers'[17] jobs were semiskilled or better. Sixty per cent Roma mothers were on maternity leave, twice as many as Czech.

A specially devised, picturebased test of comprehension of prepositions and high frequency adjectives which was independent of reading skills was orally administered, in Roma as well as in Czech. We also devised written tests of Mathematics (Bartoňová, 1999; Vaňurová, 2000) and of Reading Comprehension (Novotná, 1999, 2000), which were in Czech as Roma has only been codified since 1991 (Hübšmannová, 1991). We also administered Raven's *Coloured Projective Matrices* (Raven, 1990), a test of nonverbal (spatial) reasoning. All tests were administered in 1999 with post–tests fifteen months later.

The deprivation would predict that Roma children's scores would be on average poorer than Czech children's, but for oral language comprehension as well as Raven's, we found this to be also the case even when statistically controlling for the effects of parent education and of family social class. Low oral language levels in particular clearly present a developmental risk (Luria, 1976). However, we also compared the progress over fifteen months of subgroups of children in mainstream and in special schools who had identical Raven's and oral language scores at first testing. The mainstream and special school groups improved equally in language comprehension, suggesting that the mainstream teachers were facilitating language development equally as well as the special school teachers. The mainstream Raven's scores improved insignificantly more than those of the special school children, (p = .23). However, the Reading comprehension (in Czech) and

---

[16] This predictive validity study is recorded in our Project Report to the Czech Ministry of Schools, Youth and Sport and to the British Embassy: Smékal et al.: *The encouragement of the optimal development of personality and intellect of socioculturally disadvantaged children as a way to respecting human rights*, April 2001.

[17] Levels of employment by Erickson, Goldthorpe and Portocarero's class schema (Ericksen & Goldthorpe, 1993) already in use in east Europe, including in the Czech Republic (eg Matějů, 1993).

the Mathematics scores of these mainstream children improved substantially more than those of the children in special school, (Reading, p = .01; Maths, p = .001). It must be emphasised that mainstream teachers in this part of the inner city had long experience with Roma children. However, we offer these comparisons as part of our theme that, with the right support, risk factors can be overcome, in this case in inclusive educational settings. The progress of these children in Reading and Maths is particularly encouraging given the key role of these skills in most countries' schooling, certainly in ours.

Discussion

In Czech Basic schools (p.27), the formal teaching of abstract rules of reading occupies a large part of each day for children at the very beginning of Grade 1, thus our system assumes that comprehension has developed in nursery schools or at home. However, it appears that especially Roma children still need considerable help in understanding simple spoken material before they can reasonably be expected to concentrate on abstract rules for reading it.

We showed that preschool education can be effective in preparing the children for various aspects of school, including improving concentration and oral language development (Empirical Study 1). What is more, Empirical Study 2 shows that Czech Basic schools are not so uniform as suggested by old totalitarian laws. Some schools are successful not only in helping relatively weak children to successfully engage with early reading and mathematics, but also in helping them to accelerate their more fundamental language comprehension problems.

Conclusion

These researches confirm that Roma children can be helped to break out of their long cycle of educational and employment disadvantage. We confirm that some mainstream schools are successful in this task, as is also one of the first new moves by the Czech democracy aiming to overcome young Roma children's vulnerabilities, that is, the establishment of zero grade classes.

We believe that the internationally well known words of Dreikurs (1973) best sum up the spirit of hopeful facilitation of those of us who are trying to contribute to this process: the atmosphere in which a child lives becomes the style of his own behaviour. In particular, if a child lives with criticism or tolerance he or she learns to be critical or tolerant, and if in an atmosphere of friendship and love, to show love in the world.

References

Anderson, C. S. (1982). The search for school climate. Review of Educational Research 53, 3, 368–420.

Antonak, R. F., King, S. & Lowry, J. J. (1982). Otis Lennon Mental Ability Test,

Stanford Achievement Test, and three demographic variables as predictors of Achievement in Grades 2 and 4. Journal of Educational Research 5, 6, 366–373

Bartoňová, M. (1999). Test of Mathematics. (In Czech) Unpublished. Brno: Faculty of Social Studies, Masaryk University.

ČSSR (74/1958). Zákon o trvalém usídlení kočujících osob. (Law on permanent settling of caravan people).

ČSSR (502/1965). Usnesení vlády ČSSR o opatřeních k řešení otázek cikánského obyvatelstva. (Governmental decree of the Czechoslovak Socialist Republic on the method of resolving the question of the Gypsy population).

ČR Council for National Minorities, Czech Government (2002). Ethnic Makeup of the Czech Republic. (http://www.vlada.cz/1250/eng/vrk/vybory/vybory.htm)

ČR MŠMT (1999a). Ústav pro informace ve vzdělávání. Statistická ročenka školství 1999. (Ministry of Schools, Youth and Sport, Office for Information on Education. Statistics for School Year 1999). Prague: MŠMT.

ČR MŠMT (1999b). Regulation 10, 433/29–24. Prague: MŠMT.

ČR MŠMT (2000). Ústav pro informace ve vzdělávání. Statistická ročenka školství 2000. (Ministry of Schools, Youth and Sport, Office for Information on Education. Statistics for School Year 2000). Prague: MŠMT.

Csikszentmihalyi, M. (1993). The Evolving Self. New York: Harper.

Dawkins, R (1990). The Selfish Gene. Oxford: Oxford University Press.

Dreikurs, R. (1976). Children the Challenge. New York: Harper & Row.

Dragonas, T, Golding, J., Ignatyeva, R. & Prokhorskas, R. (1996). Pregnancy in the 90s. (ELSPAC: European Longitudinal Study of Pregnancy and Child Rearing). Bristol, UK: Sansom and Company.

Erikson, R. & Goldthorpe, J. H. (1993). The Constant Flux: a study of class mobility in industrial societies. Oxford University Press

European Roma Rights Centre (1999). A Special Remedy: Roma and schools for mentally handicapped. Budapest: ERRC Country Report 8.

Frazer, A. (1995). The Gypsies. Oxford: Blackwell, Oxford.

Hindley, C. B. & Owen, C. F. (1980). The extent of individual change in IQ for ages between six months and 17 years, in a British longitudinal sample. Journal of Child Psychology and Psychiatry, 19, 329–350.

Hillman, J. (1996). The Soul's Code. New York: Random House.

Hübšmannová, M (1991). Kapesní Slovník: předmluva (Roma – Czech dictionary: Introduction). Státní pedagogické nakladatelství. Praha.

Kenrick, D. (1995) (ed). The Gypsies During the Second World War. Vol 2: in the shadow of the Swastika. Hatfield: University of Hertfordshire Press.

Kotásek, J. (1996). Structure and Organisation of Secondary Education in Central and East Europe. In Educational Reforms in Central and East Europe: special issue, European Journal of Education, 31, 1, 25–42.

Koucký, J. (1996). Educational Reforms in Changing Societies: Central Europe in a period of transition. In Educational Reforms in C and East Europe: special issue, European Journal of Education, 31, 1, 7–24.

Koucký, J. et al. (1999). Czech Education and Europe: pre–accession strategy. Phare project CZ 9405 01 03 01. Prague: UIV Tauris .

Luria, A. R. (1976). On Historical Development of Cognitive Processes. Praha: Academia (Czech Translation)

Matěju, P. (1993). Revolution for whom? Czech Sociological Review 1, 1, 73–90.

Mercer, J. & Lewis, J. (1979). System of Multicultural and Pluralistic Assessment: technical manual. New York: Psychological Corporation.

Nečas, C. (1995). Romové v Česku včera a dnes. (Roma in Czechlands yesterday and today). Olomouc: Vydavatelství University Palackého.

Novotná, M., (1999). Test of Reading Comprehension (in Czech). Unpublished. Brno: Faculty of Social Studies, Masaryk University.

Novotná, M., (2000). Test of Reading Comprehension (in Czech). Unpublished. Brno: Faculty of Social Studies, Masaryk University.

Novotná, M., Smékal, V., Klimusová, H., Beran, J., & Gray, H. (1998). Educational Reforms: Czech Republic. Paper at ERISEE/Civic Society Conference, London University School of E European and Slavonic Studies. (http://www.mtu-net.ru/sgerisee/papers/gray.doc)

Piťha, P. & Helus, Z. (1994). Občanské školy (Citizens' Schools). Praha: Portál.

Plomin, R. (1994). Genetic research and environmental influences. Journal of Child Psychology and Psychiatry, 35, 5, 817–834.

Plomin, R. & Defries, J. C. (1998). Genetics of cognitive abilities and disabilities. Scientific American, 278, 5, 62–69.

Plomin, R., Defries, J. C., McClearn, G. E. & McGuffin, P. (2001). Behavioural Genetics. 4th edition. New York: Worth.

Rao, A. (1975). Some mánuš conceptions and attitudes. In F. Rehfisch (ed.), Gypsies, Tinkers and Other Travellers. London: Academic Press.

Raven, J. C. (1990). Coloured Progressive Matrices. Oxford: Oxford Psychology Publishers / Pychodiagnostika sro Brno.

Reynolds, C. R. (1980). Differential construct validity of a preschool battery for blacks, whites, males and females. Journal of School Psychology, 18, 112–125.

Romano Džaniben (1996). Romano džaniben, 3, 1–2. Special issue: collection of ethnography about the Roma family in east Slovakia. (http://www.volny.cz/dzaniben)

Rutter, M., Maughn, B., Mortimore, P. & Ouston, J. (1979). Fifteen Thousand Hours. London: Open Books.

Sameroff, A. J., Seifer, R., Baldwin, A. & Baldwin, C. (1993). Stability of intelligence from preschool to adolescence: the influence of social and family risk factors. Child Development, 64, 80–97.

Schweinhart, L. J. & Weikhart, D. P. (1993). Summary of the Significant Benefits of High Scope Perry Pre-school Study through age 27. Ypsilanti MI; High Scope UK

Vaňurová, M. (2000). Test of Mathematics (in Czech). Unpublished. Brno: Faculty of Social Studies, Masaryk University

Vondráček, J. & Tomek, K. (1997). Vzdělávací progam Národní škola. (Educational program National Schools). Praha: Státní pedagogické nakladatelstvi.

5. THE ENVIRONMENT OF CZECH AND ROMA CHILDREN FROM DISADVANTAGED BACKGROUNDS

Petra Samková–Bučková, Jarmila Volná–Petrovská, Michaela Pavelková, Svatava Vaculová, Masaryk University, Brno; Tomáš Urbánek, Academy of Sciences, Brno, Czech Republic

Historical and research background

Grandparents and parents of many of today's Czech Roma came from rural east Slovakia to the cities of what is now the Czech Republic in organised movements of the population in the the nineteen sixties, when labour was needed for postwar industrial expansion (see Smékal, above p.52). In the traditional society found in Slovakia, the elderly were significantly respected and men had more authority than women (Šebková et al., 1996). This is possibly related to origins in the Hindu 'big family' (Preinhaelterová, 1996). In the mid century, many east Slovak Roma were settled in satellite communities on the edge of villages and towns, dependent on menial farm and domestic employment. Tradition held mothers responsible for their children's health and wellbeing. They were often paid in kind with food for the family. Fathers' responsibility was passing skills, for example music or metal work, to their sons (Hübšmannová, 1996; Zlnayová et al., 1996). These traditions have to some extent been broken by urbanisation and resettling.

The above information is based on ethnographic work by Hübšmannová and her colleagues in Prague. Regarding quantitative work, Viková from Hübšmannová's faculty systematically studied the interests and family activities of fifty Roma children, based on a questionnaire and their drawings of their families. This showed residues of the 'big family' with grandparents much in evidence and older daughters performing household tasks (Viková, 1996). Bačová (1991) studied various economically and educationally related attitudes of Roma families on Lunek 9, the huge estate of apartment blocks in Košice, east Slovakia. She found the various indicators of disadvantage (educational, accommodation, employment) to be significantly intercorrelated.[18]

---

[18] There is more information about Roma in the Czech Republic on the websites:
(http://www.romove.cz/)
(http://www.czech.cz/index.php?section=3&menu=0&action=text&id=30)

Research aims and design

We wished to make systematic exploration of the psychological environment of Roma children, and that of children from disadvantaged Czech families, in order to raise hypotheses for further investigation. We wished data collection to coax the mothers, whether Czech or Roma, away from their understandable suspiciousness. Based on group interviews with mothers in the industrial cities Brno and Ostrava, we created a rapport interview schedule. This included the topics Education which included three subtopics: Progress and skills, Homework, Relationships and attitudes to school; and Child rearing which included two subtopics: Rearing strategies, and Care. Other topics included Family relationships and Employment. The interview also collected basic demographic data and data about basic amenities of the accommodation such as toilets and hot water.

All interviews were audiorecorded. Four Roma women, all employed in their community, interviewed the Roma mothers. Three Czech doctoral students of psychology interviewed our Czech mothers. Interviewer training prioritised listener skills, and practice interviews were discussed between interviewers. With these conditions, we believe we achieved 'ecologically valid' (Stratton et al., 1988) material which reasonably authentically reflects the attitudes of the interviewees.

Three schools and the social work department of Brno City helped us enlist nineteen Czech mothers and thirtynine Roma mothers who met our criteria of social disadvantage: no parents had education above Czech Basic school (re Czech school system see Smékal, above p.53), and all parents were either unemployed or in unskilled employment according to Erikson and Goldthorpe's (1993) Employment Classification. (Another Czech subsample of relatively advantaged mothers is not discussed here).

Analysis of interviews

We wished our analysis to facilitate investigation and comparison of patterns of interaction and of feelings of control in the disadvantaged Roma and Czech families. Causal Attributions are two part statements in which the first part gives a preliminary or (in a loose sense) a 'cause' of the other part, which is the 'outcome', for example: *The children were ill for a week and somebody informed the social workers.* An interviewee's causal attributions thus reflect his or her 'informal theories' (Heider, 1958) about the persons and topics to which he or she refers. Thus Causal Attribution Analysis (Stratton et al., 1988) identifies these two part statements within the stream of interviewee talk, and codes each for:

- Main topic and subtopic: as in the list above.
- The 'agent': that is the person who initiated the preliminary (the children in the attribution above).

- The 'target': the person most affected in the outcome (the family in the attribution above). For this report, agents and targets were the mother interviewees themselves, the father, a child under eleven, an adolescent son or daughter, and adult close family, (a grandparent or an adult son or daughter). School personel and other public servants are also agents and targets.
- Dimensions: we refer to two in this paper: Control, that is whether or not the speaker seems to perceive the outcome as under the control of the agent; and Modality, that is whether the speaker seems to perceive the outcome as good or bad for the Target, that is the person most affected (Stratton et al., 1988).

Identification of attributions from our speakers' stream of talk yielded two thousand three hundred and eighty, one thousand one hundred and eighty from our from our thirtynine disadvantaged Roma mothers, one thousand two hundred from our nineteen disadvantaged Czech mothers. In this paper we consider attributions within the topics Education with its three subtopics Progress and skills, Homework, and Relationships and attitudes to school, and within the topic Child rearing, with its two subtopics, Strategies and problems, and Care for the children. Education is obviously relevant to parents' and children's interactions with the wider society, while the topic of Child rearing is relevant to relationships within the home, but certainly with consequences for the wider society.

Results

1. Basic Demographic data

Consistent with the 1991 Czechoslovak Census, our thirtynine disadvantaged Roma families were larger than our nineteen disadvantaged Czech families. More Czech parents were legally separated, although Roma fathers did tend to be away from home on labour gangs. One quarter of Czech families had toilets outside the flat while Roma families tended to live in nineteenth century blocks with communal toilet blocks often accessed from open, outdoor landings. Six of our thirtynine Roma families against only two of our nineteen Czechs were without running hot water. We believe these differences are of little significance for our tentative conclusions.

2. Attribution Analysis: Topic and Subtopic preferences

Table 1 shows the different preferences of the two groups of mothers for these topics and subtopics. Within the topic Education, Czech mothers preferred the subtopic School progress and skills, Roma mothers the subtopic Attitudes and relationships to school ($\chi^2 = 10.8$, p <.001, df = 2). Within the topic Child rearing, Czech mothers preferred the subtopic Child rearing strategies, while Roma mothers preferred the subtopic Care of the children ($\chi^2 = 32.5$, p < .001, df = 1).

Table 1: Number and percents of attributions in topics and subtopics relating to Education and to Child Rearing and Care

	Number	% of all Czech attributions	Number	% of all Roma attributions
School skills	86	7.1%	63	5.3%
Homework	45	3.6%	30	2.4%
Attitude to school	45	3.5%	70	5.9%
Child rearing	149	12.3%	87	7%
Care for children	58	4.8	91	7.7%
Total attributions, each ethnic group	1208		1182	

Attributions about education: Agents, control and satisfactions with outcomes
Continuing the topic Education, Table 2 shows whom our Czech and Roma mothers perceived as the agents in this topic, and whether they seem to perceive that these agents have control, that is, whether the agents could have changed the outcomes of the attributions. Finally (not shown in Table) we discuss how far these outcomes are perceived by the interviewee mothers as satisfactory or unsatisfactory for the Target, who was almost always the mother herself or her child or children.

Czech mothers prefer the subtopic School progress and skills, but both Roma and Czech mothers talk more about their children as agents in these attributions about Progress and skills, rather than about the parents, grandparents, teachers or other adults. For example, one Czech mother typically says: *He is very clever and active, so his results at school are very good.* Especially *Czech* mothers' attitudes seem to show that they regard the children's skills as more dependent on the children themselves than on themselves as parents.

Also there is little difference between the groups so far as perception of agents' control regarding School progress and skills. Further, it is interesting to note that mothers from neither group speak much of the schools (or staff) as agents regarding their children's skills. In fact Roma mothers hardly talk at all about teachers' activities vis à vis the children's skills. It is as though teachers' activities have no place in Roma mothers' consciousness, which may be the case given that education outcomes were so unsatisfactory for themselves.

Czech mothers give relatively more prominence than do Roma mothers to the subtopic of children's Homework, which is very important part of the Czech educational system, and on the whole speak of themselves as responding to their children's needs, for example: *My son isn't very good at reading so I have to practise it with him.*

Table 2: Education Attributions: Agents and their control or lack of it in three subtopics, as perceived by Czech and Roma mothers

Subtopic	Agent	Attributions from Czech mothers			Attributions from Roma mothers		
			Agent perceived with control	Agent perceived without control		Agent perceived with control	Agent perceived without control
School skills	Child	51	31	20	42	25	17
	Parents & grandparents	22	11	11	16	9	9
	School staff	13	9	4	3	2	1
	ΣΣ(% of all Education attributions)	86 (49%)			61 (37%)		
Homework	Child	23	8	15	14	6	8
	Parents & grandparents	13	9	4	11	6	5
	School staff	19	13	6	3	2	1
	ΣΣ(% all education attributions)	45 (25%)			28 (16.4%)		
Attitudes and Relationships to school	Child	7	3	4	19	4	15
	Parents & grandparents	3	1	2	14	7	7
	School staff	35	25	9	37	26	11
	ΣΣ(% all education attributions)	45 (26%)			70 (41%)		
ΣΣΣ Sum all Education attributions		176 (100%)			171 (100%)		

As we have seen, Roma mothers pay significantly more attention to Attitudes and relationships at school, that is, to how their children are accepted by teachers and schoolmates. For example, a Roma mother complains: *My daughter came home crying, and bringing a note, but the teacher won't tell me what happened: I am not satisfied with the school.* Or another: *The teacher is good: I am satisfied.* It is important that both Czech and Roma mothers overwhelmingly speak of school staff as agents in regard to these attributions about Attitudes and relationships, and overwhelmingly as agents with control of the outcome. However, (not shown in Table 2) Czech and the Roma mothers' perceptions regarding the effect of this control differed significantly in that for the Czech mothers, the outcomes were perceived as satisfactory, (positive), while for the Roma mothers the outcomes were perceived (as above) as unsatisfactory. For example one Roma mother reported that she had had to accept her daughter's unhappiness at school saying: *I had the feeling that he (the headteacher) had such long fingers that she would have problems everywhere, so we stopped trying to transfer her to a different school.* By contrast, Czech mothers on the whole accept that teachers have control regarding the mothers' and their children's relationships and attitudes to school, often seeing discomfort as worthwhile for their children's future.

Attributions about Child rearing: Agents, control, and styles of interaction
For these Czech mothers, child rearing strategies are very important. For example, they tend to give attributions like the following: *When she is furious I try not to pay attention to her, and she stops.* Roma mothers also talk about child rearing strategies, but give relative prominence to care for their children, in statements about getting dressed, preparing food, maintaining hygiene etc. For example: *If she's hungry, or will be hungry, she tells me, and I give her another (bread roll). She needs something sweet, so I give it to her every day.*

Attribution analysis also allows us to look at interaction styles which the mother interviewers perceived to exist between agents and targets. This reveals a tendency for Czechs and Roma to employ different styles when family adults interact with children.

Table 3: Family Adult – Child, Child – Family Adult interactions in the subtopic: Rearing strategies

Agent – Target:	Czech Attributions		Roma Attributions	
	Agent control	Agent non–control	Agent control	Agent non–control
Family Adult – Child	39 (26%) †	19 (13%)	16 (20%) †	3 (3.6%)
Σ	58 (40% all Czech Ch Rearing attns)		19 (24% all Czech Ch Rearing attns)	
Child – Family Adult	14 (9%)	36 (34%) ††	8 (9.6%)	26 (31%) ††
Σ	50 (33.5% all Czech Ch rearing attns)		39 (41% all Roma Ch rearing attns)	
ΣΣ	149*		87*	

*Adult – Adult and Child – Child attributions are excluded, as they are unimportant for this argument.

In contrast to Czech mothers, Roma mothers give twice as many attributions where the children are agents (or their needs are the triggering situation) and the adults are targets, or their actions or feelings are the outcomes, $\chi^2 = 6.62$, p = .011, df = 1). That is, there is a significant tendency for Roma mothers to talk about adults responding to children's needs or actions. What is more, it is important that, as in the above examples, the content of these attributions about child rearing tend to show Czech mothers talking about adults, mainly themselves, influencing the children according to some predetermined aim or criterion which they deem to be desirable, for example future behaviour of the child, while Roma mothers talk more about reacting to their children's needs and wishes. However, in case this latter information is taken as suggesting that Roma parents allow complete power to their children, the similarity should be noted in distribution of agent control and non–control in these attributions. In both ethnic groups, there tend to be a higher proportion of attributions where adult agents are spoken of as having control (Table 3, †) and child agents non–control (Table 3, ††). Thus both Roma and Czech mothers see these interactions as conforming to the pattern one would expect in the affairs of adults and children: relative power goes to the adults.

Summary and discussion

When talking about school, Czech mothers give relative prominence to their children's skills, Roma mothers to their own and their children's feelings of being accepted or rejected, that is, to Attitudes to school and relationships at school. While all mothers tend to see the teachers or headteachers as having control regarding these attitudes and relationships, Czech mothers are satisfied with the outcomes of this control, while Roma mothers tend more often to be dissatisfied.

Similar comparisons hold regarding Child rearing and care. Roma mothers prioritise Care for the child, and when talking about Rearing strategies tend to talk about reacting to children's needs or behaviour: the children are agents and the adults are targets. Czech mothers talk less about Care for their children and tend to talk about clear strategies in which they conciously act to achieve some longterm change in their children's behaviour.

These differences may reflect the recent history of the two ethnic groups, one a majority group, the other a minority which was subject to forced assimilation and migration. However, especially in view of the history of the Roma family as a 'big family' of Hindu type, we believe that a different level of interpretation is useful, namely of differences between individualistic and collectivist cultures. In the former, parents teach their children that the most important thing is to assert themselves and actively fulfill their own wishes and needs. By contrast, in collectivist cultures such as the Roma, self assertion is evaluated negatively. In such a society it is necessary to inhibit personal interests and to focus on wishes and needs of others. The goal of parents in collectivist societies is not the autonomy of the individual but more to facilitate cooperation and dependence by compliance without discussion (Markus & Kitayama, 1991; Rudy & Grusec, 2001).

Many problems and misunderstandings at school and in society follow from these different expectations of children, teachers and parents. Teachers expect independent children who accommodate easily to the demands of the school, whereas Roma families lead their children to be dependent and to think in collectivist terms. For Roma children, it is unacceptable if their prestige is based only on achievement: to them an achievement oriented culture feels non–accepting, even rejecting, and in this way their poor social and economic conditions are exaggerated.

References

Bačová, V. (1991). Hladanie rómskej identity (Searching for Romany identity). Sociológia, 23, 1–2.

Erikson, R. & Goldthorpe, J. H. (1993). The Constant Flux: a study of class mobility in industrial societies. London: Oxford University Press.

Heider, F. (1958). The Psychology of Interpersonal Relations. New York: Wiley.

Hübšmannová, M. (1996). Postavení a role některých členů tradiční romské rodiny (Role and status of some members of the traditional Roma family). Romano džaniben 3, 1–2. (http://www.volny.cz/dzaniben/)[19] (Special issue on the traditional Roma family in Slovakia in early and mid twentieth century).

Markus, H. R. & Kitayama, S. (1991). Culture and the self: implications for cognition, emotion and motivation. Psychological Review, 98, 224–253.

Preinhaelterová, H. (1996). Tradiční velkorodina v hinduistické Indii (Traditional big family in Hindu India). Romano džaniben 3, 1–2. (http://www.volny.cz/dzaniben/)

Rudy, D. & Grusec, J. E. (2001). Correlates of authoritarian parenting in individualist and collectivist cultures and implications for understanding the transmission of values. Journal of Cross Cultural Psychology, 32, 2, 202–212.

Šebkova, H. et al. (1996). Úloha nejstaršího syna v tradiční romské rodině (Role of oldest son in traditional Roma family). Romano džaniben, 3, 1–2. (http://www.volny.cz/dzaniben/)

Stratton, P. M., Munton, A. G., Hanks, H. G. I., Heard, D. H., & Davidson, C. (1988). Leeds Attributional Coding System (LACS): manual. Leeds: Psychology Department, University of Leeds, UK.

Viková, L. (1996). Obraz současné romské rodiny z pohledu dětí. (A picture of the contemporary Roma family from the child's point of view) Souvislosti, 3, 128–138.

---

[19] The quarterly journal: Romano Dzaniben which is published in Czech and in Roma carries abstracts in English, French and/or German. The web address gives information for ordering articles.

Zlnayova, E. et al. (1996). Postavenie a uloha ženy–matky a muža–otca v romskej rodine (Position and role of mother and father in the Roma family). Romano džaniben. 3, 1–2. (http://www.volny.cz/dzaniben/)

SECTION III

FAIR EDUCATIONAL ASSESSMENT

6. PRINCIPLES AND PRACTICE OF FAIR ASSESSMENT

Tony Cline, University of Luton, UK

The nature of the challenge

There is discrimination against some minority groups across Europe, often expressed in the denial of educational opportunities. One form that this takes is to expedite the admission of minority children into special schools and units. Recent statistics from the Czech Republic are an exceptional example: it appears that around sixty per cent of Roma children were being educated in segregated schools on the basis that they had special educational needs. In the United Kingdom the public debate on fair assessment of special educational needs (SEN) has not focused on Roma children or Travellers. It has concentrated on the children of immigrants from Commonwealth nations in the developing world, that is, the areas of the old British Empire that were least well developed economically when they gained independence.

A large number of immigrants arrived in Britain from the nations of the old British West Indies during the nineteen fifties and nineteen sixties. By 1972, children of African Caribbean origin constituted just over one per cent of all children in maintained primary and secondary schools in England and Wales. Yet in that year in special schools for the mildly educationally subnormal (ESN(M)) nearly five per cent of all pupils came from that group – over four times what might have been expected (Tomlinson, 1984). Not surprisingly, parents and community leaders reacted angrily to such figures. For the influential book that first drew British public attention to the topic Bernard Coard (1971) chose the title *How the West Indian Child is made Educationally Subnormal in the British School System*. Suspicion in minority communities was not dispelled by subsequent developments. The assessment of special educational needs was described by a Black pressure group as *a serious threat to the education of black children* (HBPGE, 1984).

A London Muslim newspaper at the time referred to some of the professional workers involved in the assessment of special educational needs as *immigration officials of a monolingual system*. These problems were not unique to the United Kingdom or Europe. In the USA the language of some academic commentators was just as strong. DeBlassie and Franco (1983) described the transfer of bilingual pupils to SEN provision as *tantamount to a 'rape' of these children* (p.55). In Canada, Cummins (1984, p.1) used the term 'deportation', having in mind a 1917 report in which a physician celebrated the successful use of mental tests to secure the deportation from the USA of large numbers of aliens, described in the jargon of the day as 'feeble minded'.

In fact by the mid–eighties the statistical picture had changed in some important respects. In Inner London there was some satisfaction that the percentage of children from ethnic minority backgrounds who were the subject of an SEN Statement reflected much more closely the percentages of each group in the school system as a whole. But there was no room for complacency: an analysis of specific SEN groups showed some continuing discrepancies, for example in schools for children with emotional and behaviour difficulties (ILEA, 1985, Table 12). Meanwhile in the USA it appeared that Black over representation had merely moved from one type of special provision to another (Tucker, 1980). A recent English survey of head teachers of special schools for children with moderate learning difficulties has confirmed that many of them now see a different group as over represented in their establishments – children of South Asian origin (Male, 1996). The terms of the public debate have changed on both sides of the Atlantic, but the major challenge to educators has not disappeared. In eastern Europe, of course, the challenge is even more formidable, as illustrated by the statistics for Roma pupils in special schools.

Before we look at how British professionals have responded to that challenge, I would like very briefly to look at the situation from the perspective of the families from minority communities themselves. What challenges do their children face in relation to schools? It will be evident that minority children and their parents may differ from other pupils in:

- experience and understanding of the school system and the classroom;
- cultural knowledge relevant to the national curriculum;
- proficiency in the main language used in the school system;
- experience of prejudice, discrimination and racism.

It would be wrong to exaggerate, but it would be equally wrong to ignore these differences. Each factor could contribute to the underachievement of an individual child from a minority family in school, leading to a misleading impression that the child has special educational needs. Our strategies for the identification and assessment of SEN ought to make provision for that possibility.

The response to the challenge

The most important single element in our society's response to the challenge was a change in the law nearly twenty years ago that affected all children and young people with special educational needs. Before describing the legal position, however, I will briefly consider the response of individual professionals, their associations and their employers.

The initial response from educationists

In the United Kingdom the debate on the over representation of Black pupils in some types of special school had a considerable effect on some of the educators most closely associated with the Black community. Many such staff (for example teachers of English as a second language) developed a hands-off attitude to special education by the early nineteen eighties. There was a healthy scepticism about traditional IQ tests and other norm based tests used in SEN assessment. There was a tendency to emphasise the stigmatising effects of SEN provision above its possible educational value. Inevitably, therefore, many such teachers were reluctant to refer bilingual children for SEN assessment, but at the same time were often among the first to become aware of a bilingual pupil who was having exceptional difficulties in school.

Meanwhile teachers in the SEN field appeared to do little to bridge this gap. The journals and textbooks on SEN failed to reflect the changing composition of UK society, and methodological innovations in SEN teaching rarely related to issues of bilingualism or ethnic and cultural pluralism. Only very gradually over the last decade has the gulf of misunderstanding between these two networks of teachers begun to be bridged (Cline & Frederickson, 1991). It is a long, slow process that now, happily, seems to be gathering momentum.

The response of professional associations and employers

In the UK, the Codes of Conduct of the Association of Educational Psychologists and the British Psychological Society set out general principles of non-discrimination, but do not specify practical implications. Even as late as 1995 joint guidance from these associations on preparing statutory advice on SEN was rather vague in its single reference to the assessment of bilingual pupils (AEP/BPS, 1995). This is regrettable: a clear code of conduct from a professional association can protect professional staff from the insidious pressures to cut corners that often occur in public services. The Stephen Lawrence Report (Macpherson, 1999) into an unsolved racist murder triggered considerable debate on institutional racism, which is leading many professional bodies, including the British Psychological Society, to review their guidance to members.

In general, local authority employers of educational psychologists in the UK ignored the issues covered here. But during the nineteen eighties a number of local education authorities in urban areas began to try to address racism across the whole range of their activities. Some of these, including Manchester and Leeds, developed formal statements of service policy for their educational psychologists that covered fair treatment of Black children and parents (Joyce, 1988; Manchester SPCGS, 1983). In the Inner London Education Authority (ILEA) we developed a formal Code of Practice covering all the activities of the Service, which included a number of measures designed to minimise bias in the assessment of SEN. In addition, we committed ourselves to gather evidence of relevant knowledge and skills that children and young people showed outside school, including competence in languages other then English (ILEA, 1986). Individual members of the Service have described the fundamental changes in attitude and practice that were stimulated by the review process leading up to the writing of this document (Booker et al., 1989).

The response of central government

The legal framework for SEN provision was reformed in 1981. So for nearly twenty years education law has provided some essential safeguards in this field for children and parents. For example:

- Local authorities must obtain parents' permission before a child is assessed (or go through a formal appeal procedure if they believe parents are unreasonably withholding permission).
- Parents have the right to have a friend or advocate support them in all SEN interviews.
- There are regulations specifying the number, format and scope of the professional reports on which a statement of SEN in based, that make clear that certain key professional perspectives must be included.
- Parents must receive copies of all these reports as well as the formal statement itself.
- Children must remain in mainstream schools unless a strong case is made for them to be educated elsewhere. (The criteria will be further strengthened in new legislation).
- All such decisions must be based on an analysis of the child's educational needs. The criterion is not whether or not a child has a disability or impairment but whether or not they can be educated successfully with the provision available for all children in their area.

In relation to children from ethnic minorities and SEN, government departments in the UK have an uneven record. For example, there was resistance for a long time to the idea that we should collect adequate official statistics on ethnic minority pupils in schools. But since 1981 the law has at least clarified one important issue in relation to children for whom English is an additional or second language (ESL). The Education Act passed in that year stated that a lack of competence in English (or Welsh in Wales) is not to be equated with SEN as defined in the Act:

A child is not to be taken as having a learning difficulty solely because the language (or form of the language) in which he is, or will be, taught is different from a language (or form of a language) which has at any time been spoken in his home. (UK DES, 1981, Section 1,4).

A subsequent Act of Parliament in 1994 required the Department for Education to issue a Code of Practice on SEN which was to be an authoritative point of reference for all who work in that field (UK DfEE, 1994). Unfortunately the Department failed to rise to the opportunity that this task offered. Like its predecessors, this new document paid relatively little attention to children from linguistic minorities. It did, though, represent an advance in official guidance in that there was at least an explicit attempt to offer general advice on the subject. The Code advised that particular care should be taken when the identification or assessment of SEN concerns children from minority ethnic groups, including children whose first language is not English. There were four recommendations in the relevant paragraph:

- Take care to consider the child within the context of his or her home, language, culture and community.
- Ensure, if necessary by the use of bilingual support staff, interpreters and translators, that the child and his or her parents fully understand the measures the school is taking.
- So far as possible, use assessment tools which are culturally neutral and useful for a range of ethnic groups.
- Make use of any local sources of advice relevant to the ethnic group concerned (UK DfEE, 1994, Section 2,18).

For the most part, the advice was helpful, but the notion of a 'culturally neutral' assessment tool was naïve and the recommendations were rather general. The National Association for the Development of Language in the Curriculum (NALDIC) published a more detailed guide. This highlighted points in the recommended procedures when additional specific actions might be needed if a child thought to have SEN had a first language other than English (Cline, 1995). The crucial procedural steps set out in the Guide, which are not made explicit in the 1994 Code of Practice, include:

- Involve ESL and bilingual support teachers actively at every stage.

- Record and review information on a child's knowledge and use of their home language and of English.
- Set and review specific educational aims covering language and cultural needs.
- Arrange appropriate language provision.
- Investigate social, cultural and language isolation and peer harassment as possible factors in the child's difficulties.
- Engage an interpreter/adviser from the parent's own community if needed.
- Where a child attends a religious or community school, include that school among the outside agencies to be consulted.

Such procedural steps are necessary. The UK Department for Education and Science is about to issue a revised Code of Practice (UK DfES, 2001), and I hope it will fill some of the gaps that were left in 1994. However, guidance on procedure is not sufficient in itself to meet the challenges described earlier. For that purpose sensitive and fair methods of assessment must be developed. Before I examine assessment methods in detail, I will consider what principles should underlie our approach to SEN assessment in any society, thinking particularly about the increasing number of societies that are pluralistic, multiethnic and multilingual in character – including both eastern and western.

Principles of fair assessment

This section will highlight four reasonable expectations of the process of assessment: theoretical integrity, practical efficacy, equity, and accountability (Cline, 1992). The first two of these have regularly featured in textbook accounts of SEN assessment, focussing, for example, on the concepts of validity and reliability. Here the last two will be given equal importance – equity and accountability. Drawing on my own earlier work and on principles adopted by Shah et al. (1997) I wish to suggest a more wide ranging series of questions that should be asked about any process of assessment:

Theoretical integrity

- Is the approach to assessment based on an acceptable model of SEN (or is the model on which it is based reliant on out–dated or misleading categories of handicap)?
- Is the approach to assessment based on an implicit model of human development that incorporates all aspects of development (or on a narrow view of what is important in development, for example focusing exclusively on intelligence)?
- Is it based on an acceptable model of the learning process that respects the autonomy and initiative of the learner (or does it appear to assume

a top–down, highly structured process for all aspects of classroom learning)?

- Does it explicitly focus on aspects of development that are important for successful learning (or does it emphasise only weakness, limitations, gaps in knowledge, and constituents of failure)?
- Do the process of assessment and the information it yields tend to foster inclusion, integration and the provision of support for children with SEN in ordinary schools (or is the process geared to classifying children's SEN in order to facilitate their transfer to segregated settings)?
- Is the assessment rooted firmly in a real life context and does it explore concerns in the context in which they occur?

Practical efficacy
- Does the assessment draw upon the richest sources of information available (or on thin evidence that comes from a restricted perspective on what the child is like)?
- Does it produce information that can lead directly to improvements in teaching and learning (or is the information it yields of limited value in planning how the child can best be taught)?
- Is the evidence on which the assessment is based replicable, and are opinions and interpretations that are reported clearly denoted as such?
- Does the way the assessment is conducted empower children, parents and teachers (or does it place them in a subordinate position so their observations as stakeholders in the situation are ignored)?

Equity
- Are the rights of children and parents (or carers) effectively protected?
- Does the process operate without bias with respect to gender, social class, ethnicity, language use and religion?

Accountability
- Do parents (or carers) give their permission before their children are assessed on the basis of a good understanding of how the process and possible outcomes?
- Is the process and the information it produces open and intelligible to children, parents, teachers, other professionals, and district administrators?
- Can a report of assessment be understood easily by all who have an interest in it?
- Is the process cost effective?

The assessment of special educational needs is carried out in different countries with children and young people at different stages of development who are reported to have a wide range of difficulties. The methods used will differ widely. However, these questions, which imply a set of robust general principles, should receive answers that are very similar across all these varying contexts and settings.

Fair methods of assessment

Much of the debate on fairness in assessment has focused on techniques and materials. In this discussion I wish to consider two methodological options – normative assessment and curriculum related assessment. Another option referred to as 'dynamic assessment' that has some potential for use with children from ethnic and linguistic minorities is dealt with in another paper in this volume by Johan Hamers and Maya Tcholokova (pp.83ff.).

Normative approaches to assessment

The conventional approach to the assessment of SEN and learning difficulties remains the normative approach. This approach involves comparing an individual's performance with that of a large sample of children of the same age. Its focus on the child with a difficulty has an implicit assumption that the source of any problems lies within the child: s/he suffers from disability or impairment of learning ability compared to most children of the same age. The educators' task is conceived on an analogy from diagnostic practice in medicine. The aim of assessment or analysis is to determine what category of disability the child suffers from. Underlying this approach are the following hypotheses:

- that individuals' traits and abilities are relatively permanent characteristics;
- that it is possible to identify the pattern of strengths and weaknesses in learning that are the result of these characteristics;
- that this pattern of strengths and weaknesses is the prime cause of the child's poor classroom performance with other factors having less importance;
- that a teaching program which remediates weaknesses and builds strengths can lead to improvement in performance.

This approach has been particularly associated with arranging segregated provision for children with SEN in separate schools or units. Over many years critics have argued that this approach cannot fairly be employed with children from cultural or linguistic minorities because their prior experience is likely to be significantly different from that of the population on which the norms are based (Cline & Shamsi, 2000). Some defenders of psychometric tests have responded by showing that some major normative tests such as IQ tests have good predictive validity with different populations, for example Reynolds and Kaiser (1990) in the US demonstrated that in large samples of children with a wide range of ability and achievement, normative IQ scores can sometimes predict achievement test scores as accurately for ethnic minority groups as for majority children. However, Valdes and Figueroa (1994) showed that these broad based, positive correlations may conceal important individual anomalies. These concerns have been expressed too in the UK and Europe, leading some professionals to reject the use of norm based instruments altogether. Others have argued that some of the problems could be overcome if local community norms were developed through the use of computerised approaches to assessment (Beech & Singleton, 1997). The concept of pluralistic norms has a substantial and chequered history (Baker 1988; Figueroa & Sassenrath, 1989; Mercer, 1979). There are serious problems in trying to implement the strategy in any setting where behaviour and performance norms are changing rapidly – such as within many minority communities in the UK and worldwide.

Even if stable norms could be established, there are other problems. The demands of a special separate assessment have to be reviewed very carefully if a fair assessment is to be achieved:

- What language is demanded by the assessment task?
- Is there a possibility that the materials that are used are culturally biased?
- What social demands are made by the assessment task?

The first two of these questions have received most attention in the literature. The social demands will also be crucial for many children from ethnic and linguistic minorities. For example, a 'quiz' or 'interrogation' style in an adult's language may intimidate children who do not encounter such questioning in their home milieu, or the notion of 'doing your best' or 'putting on a show' in a test situation may be alien to the cultural style a child has assimilated at home. An effective strategy for assuring fair assessment needs to address all these issues – language, bias and social context. However those challenges are tackled, one thing is clear: a short single interview with an unfamiliar adult using materials that have been standardised in an alien cultural context is not a fair or efficient way of assessing the special educational needs of a child from a minority community. In fact, when combined with a strategy of persuading parents not to press their legal rights, it is an abuse of professional power and status.

Curriculum Related Assessment
The second approach to consider is Curriculum Related Assessment (CRA). Here the focus of attention is not so much on the child as on the teaching program offered. The hypothesis is made that the current curriculum is not well suited to the learning needs of the child. The aim

is to match work on the curriculum very closely to the child's existing skills and knowledge. The psychologist or teacher analyses the learning tasks within the curriculum into component skill elements that can be approached in incremental steps. Then it is necessary to determine which elements the child has mastered and which require further work. In the school setting the approach is based on a series of assumptions:

1. The school curriculum for developing children's knowledge, understanding, skills and attitudes can be analysed into tasks that can be expressed in the form of behavioural objectives.
2. These tasks can be arranged into pedagogically viable sequences.
3. By checking frequently on a child's attainments within one of these sequences, teaching can be matched closely to the learning stage the child has reached.
4. Through a method of instruction that is very firmly under the teacher's control children can be led to:

   • *acquire new skills;*
   • *perform them with fluency;*
   • *maintain them after teacher support is withdrawn;*
   • *use them in new context;*
   • *adapt them to different challenges (Cline, 1992).*

There are a number of disadvantages. Firstly, many important aspects of the curriculum cannot in fact be analysed easily into a series of specific objectives. Secondly, the pupil is often placed in a passive and unchallenging role, thus this approach could have an adverse effect on pupils' motivation and on their engagement in other opportunities for more active learning, because they would learn to be passive and to rely on others to select and structure their experience for them (Cummins, 1984; Frederickson, 1992).

However, there are valuable positive features too. A CRA approach encourages a rigorous experimental strategy in work with children who are experiencing difficulties; it incorporates frequent brief checks on performance; it insists on painstaking efforts by the teacher to foster generalisation and adaptation of learning; and, in particular, it ensures that assessment will serve directly to improve methods of teaching. The focus is on improving the education that is offered to children in their mainstream classrooms rather than on classifying them with a view to separating out different groups.

Many educators, for example Lowden (1984), have argued that CRA methods are generally to be preferred to a norm referenced approach for work with bilingual children, because at least they involve no application of norms to individuals whose language and cultural experiences differ significantly from those of the population from whom the norms were collected. At the same time, however, the assumptions underlying these methods do not always hold for bilingual children. For example, because of their different prior experiences they may learn some tasks in a different order, which will invalidate the teacher–devised learning hierarchy on which the approach is based. Most seriously, if the whole curriculum is ethnocentric a CRA strategy will not compensate for the gap between what bilingual pupils need from their school and what they are offered. In addition, some CRA methods present pedagogical problems that are specific to bilingual pupils. For example, Cummins (1984) highlighted the fact that behavioural objectives are normally defined in a very prescriptive way. Yet

... if we focus in on one, possibly ethnocentric, way of demonstrating understanding, we may disqualify (or at least lose sensitivity to), different ways in which understanding may be expressed by children from different cultural backgrounds. (Cline & Frederickson , 1996 p.7).

Conclusion

What I have said about different methods of SEN assessment might be taken to imply that, if we choose an appropriate technique and materials, all will be well. That is not the case. It is also essential that the setting of the assessment empower the pupil's achievement. The ultimate question is not: Is the test fair? but: What is the context for this assessment? For many children, the context is a difficult one which undermines any confidence they have and dissipates their ability to show what they are capable of. It is the responsibility of psychologists and teachers to refuse to allow their technical and professional expertise to be abused in order to lend authority to an invalid process. Adopting an inappropriate normative approach simply allows problems (or advantages) of the setting to be interpreted as attributes of the child.

We should not underestimate the challenges and the costs of managing these processes more fairly and effectively. In the past a favourite metaphor for the process of educational assessment involved the notions of sorting and categorising. That is quick and simple, but it does not lead to effective educational provision. Later the metaphor of a template became fashionable: assessment was about achieving an exact match between the profile of a learner and the shape of a teaching program. As my account of CRA illustrated, this takes a little longer and requires more sophisticated expertise, needing careful management if used as a basis for successful inclusive education.

An alternative way of thinking about assessment and teaching is to describe the whole cyclical process as dialogue or conversation. Some forms of dynamic assessment justify that description (though not those which depend on a single test that produces a score looking very like an IQ score). The metaphor of assessment as dialogue should be welcomed by those who work with children from ethnic and linguistic minorities. If there is to be a conversation, it will take time to reach a conclusion, success will require a particular effort towards mutual understanding, and it will be possible for non–standard responding to be accommodated by flexible practitioners. As I have pointed out previously, the notion of assessment as conversation also reminds us that you cannot make sense of what the other person is trying to say, cannot even hear it, unless you have the context right. *A finely tuned hearing aid in a noisy environment picks up nothing but noise* (Cline, 1993 p.67). And in Europe at present – east or west – there is, of course, a great deal of noise surrounding the educational assessment of any child from minority communities.

References

AEP/BPS (1995). Statutory Advice to the LEA: guidance for educational psychologists. Durham: Association of Educational Psychologists and Leicester: British Psychological Society.

Baker, C. (1988). Normative testing and bilingual populations. Journal of Multilingual and Multicultural Development, 9, 5, 399–409.

Beech, J. R. & Singleton, C. (1997), (eds.). The Psychological Assessment of Reading. London: Routledge.

Booker, R., Hart, M., Moreland, D. & Powell, J. (1989). Struggling towards better practice: a psychological service team and anti–racism. Educational Psychology in Practice, 5, 123–129.

Cline, T. (1992). Assessment of special educational needs: meeting reasonable expectations? In T. Cline (ed.), The Assessment of Special Educational Needs: international perspectives. (121–134). London: Routledge.

Cline, T. (1993). Educational assessment of bilingual children: getting the context right. Educational and Child Psychology, 10, 4, 59–68.

Cline, T. (1995). The Code of Practice on Special Educational Needs: a short guide for those working with bilingual pupils. Watford, Hertfordshire: National Association for the Development of Language in the Curriculum.

Cline, T. & Frederickson, N. (1991). Bilingual Pupils and the National Curriculum: overcoming difficulties in teaching and learning. London: University College London.

Cline, T. & Frederickson, N. (1996), (eds.). Progress in Curriculum Related Assessment with Bilingual Pupils. Clevedon, Avon: Multilingual Matters.

Cline, T. & Shamsi, T. (2000). Language Needs or Special Needs? The assessment of learning difficulties in literacy among children learning English as an additional language: a literature review. London: DfEE. (http://www.dfes.gov.uk/research)

Coard, B. (1971). How the West Indian Child is Made Educationally Subnormal in the British School System. London: New Beacon Books.

Cummins, J. (1984). Bilingualism and Special Education: issues in assessment and pedagogy. Clevedon, Avon: Multilingual Matters.

DeBlassie, R. R. & Franco, J.N. (1983). Psychological and educational assessment of bilingual children. In D. R. Omark & J. G. Erickson (eds.), The Bilingual Exceptional Child, 55–68. San Diego, California: College–Hill Press.

Figueroa, R. A. & Sassenrath, J. M. (1989). A longitudinal study of the predictive validity of the System of Multicultural Pluralistic Assessment (SOMPA). Psychology in the Schools, 26, 5–19.

Frederickson, N. (1992). Curriculum–based assessment: broadening the base. In T. Cline (ed.), The Assessment of Special Educational Needs: international perspectives. 147–169. London: Routledge.

HBPGE (1984). Black Critics of 81 Act. London: Haringey Black Pressure Group on Education.

ILEA (1985). Educational Opportunities for All? research studies. (Fish Report Vol.2) London: Inner London Education Authority.

ILEA (1986). Anti–racist Developments in the Work of the Schools Psychological Service. Report to Subcommittees. London: Inner London Education Authority.

Joyce, J. (1988). The development of an anti–racist policy in Leeds. Educational and Child Psychology, 5, 2, 44–50.

Lowden, G. (1984). Assessing children with learning difficulties. In P. Williams (ed.), Special Education in Minority Communities, 95–108. Milton Keynes: Open University Press.

Manchester SPCGS (1983). Promoting Racial Equality: a statement of service policy. Manchester: City of Manchester Education Department School Psychological and Child Guidance Service.

Macpherson, W. (1999). The Stephen Lawrence Enquiry: report. (http://www.cre.gov.uk/pdfs/slinqlea.pdf)

Male, D. (1996). Who goes to MLD schools? British Journal of Special Education, 23, 1, 35 – 41.

Mercer, J. R. (1979). The System of Multicultural Pluralistic Assessment (SOMPA): technical manual. New York: Psychological Corporation.

Reynolds, C. R. & Kaiser, S. M. (1990). Test bias in psychological assessment. In T. B. Gutkin & C. R. Reynolds (eds.), The Handbook of School Psychology (Edn 2, 487–525). New York: Wiley.

Shah, T.A., Hall, W., Nelms, S., Parkes, J. & Richards, A. (1997). Whither professionalism in assessment? Newsletter of the British Psychological Society Division of Educational and Child Psychology, 79, 28–33.

Tomlinson, S. (1984). Minority groups in English conurbations. In P. Williams (ed.), Special Education in Minority Communities, 18–32. Milton Keynes: Open University Press.

Tucker, J. A. (1980). Ethnic proportions in classes for the learning disabled: issues in non–biased assessment. Journal of Special Education, 14, 93–105.

UK DES Dept for Education and Science (1981). Education Act 1981 (Special Educational Needs). London: Her Majesty's Stationary Office.

UK DfEE Dept for Education and Employment (1994). Code of Practice on the

<u>Identification and Assessment of Special Educational Needs</u>. London: Department for Education.

UK DfES Dept for Education and Science (2001). <u>Revised Code of Practice for the Identification of Special Needs</u>. (http://www.dfes.gov.uk/sen/documents/SENCodeOfPractice.pdf)

Valdes, G. & Figueroa, R. A. (1994). <u>Bilingualism and Testing: a special case of bias</u>. Norwood, New Jersey: Ablex Publishing Company.

7. LEARNING POTENTIAL TESTS FOR ETHNIC MINORITIES: A VYGOTSKIAN PERSPECTIVE

J. H. M. Hamers, Utrecht University, Netherlands and
M. Tcholakova, Sofia University, Bulgaria

Introduction

Intelligence tests are mostly applied in educational practice for purposes of selection and remediation. The empirical research regarding selection focuses mainly on issues such as reliability, validity and bias. Bias can be caused by cultural and language differences, examiner bias and 'test wiseness'. With respect to the remedial function, attempts to link intelligence test results to educational practice have never been very successful, problems being that there is no clear relation between the content of intelligence tests and school achievement tasks, and also that they lack a sound theory about the learning processes underlying the test scores. It is claimed that the procedure of Learning Potential Assessment (LPA) could meet these criticisms.

In this chapter we summarise several projects with children of minority groups, in which LPA procedures are applied. In one project, the reduction of test bias and item bias was the object of study. In addition, a Dutch learning potential test for ethnic minorities is presented and some experiences with the test in Bulgaria. In another project, curriculum related test items were used. The main intention was to bridge the gap between assessment and intervention. In a recent project, the emphasis was directed to the integration of testing and training by extending the training phase to a period of some months, so called diagnostic programs, one of which we describe. We first describe what is meant by LPA.

Learning Potential Assessment

LPA represents a conglomerate of testing procedures (Grigorenko & Sternberg, 1998; Guthke, 1977; Hamers, Sijtsma & Ruijssenaars, 1993; Lidz & Elliott, 2000), thus the foundations and practical issues presented in this chapter should not be considered as representative for the field.

In theoretical terms, LPA starts from the principle that a test should not only measure previously acquired knowledge but also the ability to learn

(Dearborn, 1921). In the context of this principle, two theoretical roots of LPA can be distinguished: Vygotky's Zone of Proximal Development (ZPD), and the cognitive theory of human intelligence. Vygotsky (1978) is regarded as the creator of the learning potential concept and his ZPD has become the key concept in LPA. He described ZPD as:

... the distance between the actual developmental level as determined by independent problem solving and the level of potential development as determined through problem solving under adult guidance or in collaboration with more capable peers (pp.85–86).

Luria (1961) transformed Vygotsky's concept into a training phase as part of test procedures. By comparing pretest and posttest scores, Luria intended to differentiate between a child's actual and potential performance level. With this procedure, he was able to establish a rediagnosis of mental retardation for children whose initial intelligence test scores were low. The cognitive theory of human intelligence (Sternberg, 1981, 1982) has redefined the concept of intelligence by asking questions like: How can individual differences in test scores be explained? The answer is based on research about cognitive processes which are fundamental for solving test items. This approach, in particular, is relevant for LPA because it offers a framework for the construction of training phases in learning potential tests.

In methodological terms, a learning potential test has the psychometric properties of a regular test. However, LPA differs from regular assessment procedures in respect of administration, because a training phase is incorporated into the test. In classical test theory, changes in test scores based on training during the test procedure are often considered to threaten the psychometric properties of the test. In LPA, however, it is assumed that changes induced by training may increase test validity. In Embretson's (1987) terms a main aim in LPA is to provide a better estimate of the ability construct, i.e. intelligence. This is particularly needed when the test does not measure the intended ability for all examinees, as may be the case as a consequence of the use of irrelevant processes or lack of prior knowledge on the part of the student. These differences between examinees can be reduced in several ways:

- by training examinees to obtain a relatively high level of performance;
- by optimizing the examinees' use of prior knowledge;
- by reducing the number of alternative processing strategies to solve items by training examinees to use one efficient strategy.

Research projects
1. Learning Potential Test for Ethnic Minorities
The main aim of this project was to develop a test, the *Learning Potential Test for Ethnic Minorities* (LEM: Hamers, Hessels & van Luit, 1991) which

could be used to determine the learning potential of Turkish and Moroccan children living in the Netherlands. The LEM is suitable for pupils age five to eight years. The concept of learning potential was operationalised in a train–within–test paradigm. This means that the training is an integral part of the test and consists of increasing help depending on the needs of the child. The child is taught each task by means of demonstration and practice, until the task is completely understood. The test instruction is nonverbal, an important requirement when testing children with little or no majority language. Depending on the task, training in the test consists of three procedures: repeating items, feedback (nonverbal right/wrong information) and demonstration.

Children enjoy the LEM. It also appeared to be non-biased: comparing LEM scores from children of the same socioeconomic status but different ethnic groups showed the latter to be closer than their scores on a traditional IQ test (RAKIT: Bleichrodt et al., 1984) although they were still lower than the scores of Dutch children with comparable socioeconomic status. Also it successfully recategorised young ethnic minority pupils: seventythree per cent of them achieved scores equal to or below standard score eightyfive on RAKIT (see above) while only forty–eight per cent did on the LEM. This important finding may prevent children from being incorrectly labelled as mentally retarded or from being unjustly referred to schools for the mentally retarded. Finally, the test also strongly differentiated between those children who had low scores on the intelligence test. It was concluded (Hamers, Hessels & Pennings, 1996; Hessels, 1993) that the LEM is a promising test for tackling problems such as inappropriate test content and 'test wiseness' by using familiarisation and training, and language bias by using non-verbal instruction.

Bulgarian expertise with the LEM

The *Learning Potential Test for Ethnic Minorities* (LEM) was introduced in Bulgaria in the year 2000 as a part of a research project aimed at assessing the learning potential of minority children in special schools. We assessed the learning potential of eleven Roma and nine Turkish boys and girls between age six years and seven years five months who had been labelled as mildly mentally retarded according to a standard intelligence test (*Coloured Progressive Matrices*: Raven, 1990). Their families were of low socioeconomic status and from settled Roma and Turkish communities. The former communist regime conducted an assimilation program in the mid–nineteen eighties, which was accompanied by violence. It included changing the names of minority populations, including Roma and Turks. After this, particularly the Turkish community became more and more suspicious and isolated.

The children were enrolled in a program for children with special educational needs (mental retardation) at the special school in Shumen.

The aim of the trial was:

- introducing the test to a culturally different population and setting;
- commenting on test administration;
- drawing conclusions about the further advantages of the test in Bulgaria.

We wished to observe how the children followed the instructions, how much help they needed to overcome the difficulties and perform the tasks, the characteristics of their behaviour and performance with respect to the particular tasks and to their ethnicity, and the final LEM scores, compared to the Raven's CPM with Dutch norms for the same age groups. Only five out of the twenty children demonstrated low learning potential scores in comparison to their initial IQ scores which were below seventy. The other thirteen showed average learning potential scores, while two out of twenty obtained respectively high and very high scores.

The five low scoring children come from the Turkish group, while the highest scoring children are of Roma origin. The Roma children tended to be motivated to start solving the tasks, accepting the nonverbal instruction with curiosity and asking what exactly they should do. They also wanted verbal feedback. Moreover, they tended to verbalize their answers during the process of solving the tasks. This is because these children usually speak Bulgarian at home and are used to verbal instruction at school. Furthermore, Roma children were much more open and friendly to the examiner, while some of the Turkish children were shy and even avoided eye contact, consistent with the response particularly of their community, to the communists' forced assimilation program. Their lower results can be explained by understandable rejection of the examiner as unfamiliar person.

Thus according to our use of LEM, fifteen out of our twenty children had been misclassified as mentally handicapped, or as having special educational needs.

2. Learning Potential Test with Curriculum related Tasks

In a second project (Hamers, Pennings & Guthke, 1994; Tissink et al., 1993) a test was developed called *Phonemic Awareness Test* (PAT: Hamers, van Luit & Tissink, 1995). The authors first identified and described the prerequisites for reading and spelling, such as short term memory, auditory segmentation, objectification, and phonemic analysis. Children in Grade 1 Dutch schools who experience difficulties in this domain are often labelled as lacking reading readiness. In constructing the PAT, each of these prerequisites was operationalised in pretests and posttests. The training phase consists of four instructional modes, which are increasingly supportive in finding the correct answer on a practice item: repeated presentation of the item (Mode 1), disclosure of the item structure (Mode 2), presentation of a solution strategy (Mode 3) and modelling (Mode 4). Each time an examinee is not able to solve a particular practice item correctly, the item can be presented via Modes 1 to 4, in that order. In this study, the analysis of test profiles made it possible to generate information for intervention purposes.

3. Assessment by Diagnostic Programs

Guthke (1982) introduced the idea of diagnostic programs and several other learning potential assessment procedures. He distinguished so called short term and long term tests (see Table 1). Most of the learning potential tests which have been designed so far can be assigned to one of the two types.

Table 1: Learning potential test procedures (modified from Guthke, 1982)

Procedure	Kind of stimulation provided	Design	References
Long term test	Heuristic or algorithmic strategies for solving test items	Pretest–training–posttest Test time: hours, on one day or several days	PAT (Hamers et al., 1995)
Diagnostic program	Hierarchically arranged program eg for reasoning	Train–within–test or Pretest–training–posttest Test time: several weeks or months	Inductive Reasoning 1* (De Koning et al., 1995; De Koning, 2000)

* 20 Lessons and a teachers manual

Diagnostic programs form a third type of assessment tool, which can last several weeks, months or a year. A diagnostic program, applied as learning potential assessment, should differentiate between low ability levels that could not be discriminated by scores on a traditional IQ test or on a pretest. In order to achieve this goal, we applied a modified version of Klauer's (1989) *Program Inductive Reasoning* (De Koning & Hamers, 1995). The population of four hundred and fifty pupils was composed of Dutch schools with more than eightyfive per cent of their pupils from low SES families, most of them from minority groups, particularly from Turkey, Morocco and the Netherlands Antilles.

Assessment by diagnostic program: Inductive Reasoning

Inductive reasoning is defined by Klauer (1989) as systematic and analytic comparison to discover regularity in apparent chaos and irregularity in apparent order. Regularities and irregularities can be discovered by paying attention to the attributes of objects (colour, for example) or relations between objects (size, for example). Objects can be people, animals, things, and situations. For each of the two types, Klauer determined three classes of tasks with the accent on finding, respectively, similarities, dissimilarities or a combination of both. The three classes of tasks involving either attributes or relations cover the whole area of inductive reasoning (see Table 2).

Table 2: Classes of tasks for search and comparison of attributes and relations (Klauer 1989)

	Name of task groups	Types of items
Classifying on basis of attributes:		
similarity of attributes	1. generalisation	class formation class expansion finding common attributes
dissimilarity of attributes	2. discrimination	identifying irregularities
similarity/dissimilarity of attributes	3. cross classification	4,6,9 matrix figures
Seriating on basis of relations:		
similarity of relations	1. recognition of relation	order series series completion simple analogies
dissimilarity of relations	2. differentiation of relation	disrupted series
similarity/dissimilarity of relations	3. system construction	matrix figures with complex analogies

Table 2 shows the three classes of task for sorting objects based on attributes (generalisation, discrimination and cross classification), and the three classes of task for seriation of objects based on their relationships with each other (recognition of relationships, differentiation of relationships and system construction). All these six types of task require an ability to determine similarities and dissimilarities in attributes or relations. Cross classification and system construction are considered as final stages of inductive reasoning. Tasks from the class of cross classification can only be solved when generalisation and discrimination tasks have been mastered, tasks from the class of system construction can only be solved when recognition and differentiation of relations tasks have been mastered.

The adapted program (De Koning, 2000; De Koning & Hamers, 1995) for minority groups comprises a total of one hundred and twenty tasks (problem plates), twenty plates for each class of task. Each plate presents the pupil with a problem which can be solved by inductive reasoning. The tasks are divided over the twenty lessons, six tasks per lesson. The lessons are conducted in dialogue form with the whole group. The pupils sit in a semicircle so they have a good view of each other, the teacher and the problem plate which is hung up in front of the class. The heart of the dialogue is the teacher's ability to incite the pupils to reason. The pupils are enticed to do so by the teacher guiding them by posing questions (Vygotsky's ZPD).

It is essential that pupils be instructed in finding similarities and/or dissimilarities in attributes or relations, so they must learn how to seek and compare attributes of objects, or relations between objects. Analogous to the process of inductive reasoning, four instruction steps are differentiated (see Sternberg, 1981):

- Step 1: Searching: attributes or relations which may be of importance in solving the problem are identified.
- Step 2: Comparison: similarities/dissimilarities in attributes or relations of these objects must then be found by repeatedly comparing the objects.
- Based on Step 2, the problem is solved in Step 3: Answer.
- Finally, the solution is monitored in Step 4: Checking.

Assessment by diagnostic program Inductive Reasoning: Results
For the diagnostic purpose of this study, the questions were:

- Do the inductive reasoning skills of children who follow the program improve to a greater extent than the inductive reasoning skills of children who do not follow the program?
- How effective are the two instruction methods?
- What are the individual differences in learning inductive reasoning? This last question could be of importance for categorising children but also to prevent sending them to special schools.

We compared retarded children's scores before and after the above program. The main results of the within group comparison showed that they were able to increase their test scores substantially. These improvements were maintained (De Koning, 2000; Hamers, De Koning & Sijtsma, 1998). The training procedure provides children with a fair chance to show their potential intellectual capacity. Testing this research group with a traditional IQ test, would lead to the conclusion that most of them were scoring below average or are moderately mentally retarded.

Also comparing the four hundred and fifty children who received direct instruction in inductive reasoning within the program with children who only received conventional teaching showed that direct instruction leads to significantly better results. A possible explanation for this finding is that these children are in special need of a complete orientation basis, meaning a careful orientation on the task, the strategy for solution etc, at least in the initial phase of the learning process (for more details about this project, see De Koning, 2000; De Koning, Hamers & Sijtsma, 2002).

Concluding remarks

This chapter introduced the concept of learning ability as the leading concept in learning potential assessment. First we presented a reliable test that is without evidence of cultural bias, the Learning Potential test for Ethnic Minorities (LEM). Although mean learning potential scores of Turkish and Moroccan children differed significantly from those of Dutch children, this difference was smaller than with conventional IQ scores. We discussed the use of LEM with children from severely marginalised and repressed ethnic minority communities in Bulgaria.

Domain specific tasks may become a new tradition regarding instrument development. We introduced subject specific learning potential tests in reading and spelling. Our overall results indicate that these tests can substantially modify initial scores and assess the likely response to intervention. Short term or long term learning potential tests are likely to provide a more positive image for many children, and diagnostic programs (eg Klauer, 1989) can be an attractive extension. These programs give the teacher insight into the (hidden) individual intellectual capacity of children in more extended real life learning situations in which they are challenged to think. The findings showed also that the positive changes in the experimental groups are substantial and are maintained, especially if the material is delivered by direct instruction.

References

Bleichrodt, N., Drenth, P. J. D., Zaal, J. N. & Resing, W. C. M. (1984). Revisie Amsterdamse Kinder Intelligentietest (RAKIT) (Revised Amsterdam Child Intelligence Test). Lisse, Nederland: Swets and Zeitlinger.

Dearborn, W. F. (1921). Intelligence and its measurement. Journal of Educational Psychology, 12, 210–212.

De Koning, E. (2000). Inductive Reasoning in Primary Education: measurement, teaching and transfer. Zeist: Kerckebosch.

De Koning, E. & Hamers, J. H. M. (1995). Inductief Redeneren 1 (Experimentele versie) (Inductive Reasoning 1 (Experimental version)). Utrecht: Universiteit Utrecht ISOR.

De Koning, E., Hamers, J. H. M. & Sijtsma, K. (2002). Inductive reasoning in primary education. Psychological Review (accepted).

Embretson, S. (1987). Toward development of a psychometric approach. In C. S. Lidz (ed.), Dynamic Assessment: an interactional approach to evaluating learning potential. New York: Guilford Press.

Grigorenko, E. L. & Sternberg, R. J. (1998). Dynamic testing. Psychological Bulletin, 124, 1, 75–111.

Guthke, J. (1977). Zur Diagnostik der Intellektuellen Lernfähigkeit (Assessment of Learning Ability). Berlin: VEB Deutscher Verlag der Wissenschaften.

Guthke, J. (1982). The learning test concept: an alternative to the traditional static intelligence test. The German Journal of Psychology, 77, 5–22.

Hamers, J. H. M., De Koning, E. & Sijtsma, K. (1998). Inductive reasoning in the third grade: Intervention promises and constraints. Contemporary Educational Psychology, 23, 132–148.

Hamers, J. H. M., Hessels, M. G. P. & Pennings, A. H. (1996). Learning potential in ethnic minority children. European Journal of Psychological Assessment, 12, 3, 183–192.

Hamers, J. H. M., Hessels, M. G. P. & van Luit, J.E.H. (1991). Leertest voor Etnische Minderheden: Test en Handleiding (Learning Potential Test for Ethnic Minorities: test and manual). Lisse: Swets & Zeitlinger.

Hamers, J. H. M., Pennings, A. H. & Guthke, J. (1994). Training–based assessment of school achievement. Learning and Instruction, 4, 347–360.

Hamers, J. H. M., van Luit, J. E. H. & Tissink, J. (1995). Leertoetsen voor Oudste Kleuters (LOK) (Phonemic Awareness Test (PAT)). Hilversum: OBD.

Hamers, J. H. M., Sijtsma, K. & Ruijssenaars, A. J. J. M. (eds.), (1993). Learning Potential Assessment: theoretical, practical and methodological issues. Amsterdam: Swets & Zeitlinger.

Hessels. M. G. P. (1993). Leertest voor Etnische Minderheden: theoretische en empirische verantwoording. (Learning Potential Test for Ethnic Minorities: Theoretical and empirical foundation). Rotterdam: Erasmus Universiteit, RISBO.

Klauer, K. J. (1989). Denktraining für Kinder 1. Ein Program zur intellectuellen Förderung (Inductive reasoning. A program for the stimulation of inductive reasoning). Gottingen: Hogrefe Verlag.

Lidz, C. S. & Elliott, J. G. (2000). Dynamic Assessment: prevailing models and applications. Amsterdam: JAI – Press.

Luria, A. R. (1961). An objective approach to the study of the abnormal child. American Journal of Orthopsychiatry, 31, 1–16.

Raven, J. C., (1990). Coloured Progressive Matrices. Oxford: Oxford Psychology Publishers.

Sternberg, R. J. (1981). Testing and cognitive psychology. American Psychologist, 36, 1181–1189.

Sternberg, R. J. (ed.), (1982). Handbook of Human Intelligence. New York: Cambridge University Press.

Tissink, J. (1993). De Constructie van Leertests met Curriculum(on)Gebonden taken (The Construction of Learning Potential Tests with Domain Specific Tasks). Utrecht: Utrecht University ISOR.

Tissink, J., Hamers, J. H. M. & van Luit, J.E.H. (1993). Learning potential tests with domain–general and domain–specific tasks. In J. H. M. Hamers, K., Sijtsma & A. J. J. M. Ruijssenaars (eds.), Learning Potential Assessment: theoretical, methodological and practical issues. Amsterdam: Swets & Zeitlinger.

Vygotsky, L. S. (1978). Mind in Society: the development of higher psychological processes. (M. Cole, J. Steiner, S. Scribner & E. Souberman, eds. and translation). Cambridge, MA: Harvard University Press.

8. REUVEN FEUERSTEIN'S METHOD OF INSTRUMENTAL ENRICHMENT AND ITS FIRST APPLICATIONS IN A CZECH SETTING.

Věra Pokorná,
Charles University, Prague, Czech Republic

Reuven Feuerstein devised one of the most famous and sophisticated stimulation programs. Born in 1922 in Romania, he emigrated to Israel after the World War II, and studied with Piaget and Rey in Geneva. He founded and leads the Hadassah–WIZO–Canada research institute in Jerusalem. He was interested in the development of cognitive functions because he realised the discrepancy between some Jewish children's performance in concentration camp settings where they successfully adapted to the extreme conditions, and their poor adaptation to the new cultural and social conditions as emigrants. These resocialisation problems of children well adapted to extreme conditions raised his interest in the practical applications of academic findings to children raised under normal conditions.

Feuerstein noticed that some children fail in school because they cannot cope with the formal school situation, but out of school they use complex skills in play and work. Others learn new skills but lose them within a day or a few hours, sometimes so profoundly that it seems they never met the particular skill or piece of information. Yet others can learn something but cannot apply it: they have not learned to think contextually, nor to organise their knowledge, are impulsive in thinking and acting, accept only single pieces of information, and fail to learn from their errors. Feuerstein's method is based on the analysis of these findings.

Three theoretical premises of the method

1. The questionability of intelligence as a given characteristic and the critique of IQ based assessment.

In the 1950's Feuerstein was one of the first scientists to oppose the view that intelligence is constant for life. He denies that actual intellectual performance measured by a test battery predicts future achievements in school and life. He claims that intelligence changes, and that children with inferior IQ can be taught and their development facilitated in such a way that they will achieve higher IQ scores. Lower intellectual performance is related to lower socioeconomic status and membership in minority ethnic groups; school and home performance can be inconsistent.

Assessment of intellectual abilities by intelligence tests refers to a hypothetical construct. Tests are positivist, measuring only present performance in unnatural settings. They cannot assess the child's ability to learn. The whole, expressed by the IQ, is a sum of individual parts and fails to express the structure of intellectual functions. Also, it claims its validity without any relation to a particular place or time, or to the child's day to day contexts, for example differences between atmosphere or approach to achievement in different schools, different psychodynamics in different classes and families (Sharron & Coulter, 1994).

Later, more voices questioned the results of intellect assessment, and talked about 'unrealised intelligence' (eg Lory, 1966). They too warned against thinking that a child's performances solving individual items of IQ tests were objective, when his or her cognitive abilities are insufficiently developed (Müller, 1974). Sindelar (1994) considers that the information processing difficulties of children with some learning difficulties distort the intelligence profile, so that it fails to reflect the child's capacities.

The overall IQ, which is composed of the average values of individual subtests, then loses its meaning as a descriptor of the child's intellectual capacity (p.84)... Scientific research has shown that the intelligence quotient is not a good predictor of school success... behaviour and learning disorders correlate highly with the defects of partial functions, much less with IQ. (p.100).

2. Structural cognitive modification
Feuerstein asks three questions:

1. Why is cognition so important? Cognition is a mental capacity for success. It makes use of experience, including emotional experience, and is related to the person's adaptability.
2. If it is important is it modifiable? The development of cognition is not only a better way to learning: it is related to the human need to develop relationships, thus involves emotions. We live in particular conditions. When they change, new functions develop. For Feuerstein (1990) it is an issue of faith that if we were determined we would not be free: we were created in the image of God. That excludes invariance. We are responsible for our lives and deeds. Thus he refuses terms such as dyslexia and learning disabilities, which only characterise a certain state that has been produced by certain conditions.
3. The third premise involves Feuerstein's Instrumental Enrichment intervention program, via Mediated learning:

3. Mediated learning

The engaged teacher sorts information, selects stimuli, changes the situation, interprets. He or she participates in the development of pupils' answers. What is important is the evaluation of information in the process of learning: we are all continually bombarded by neutral, thus emotionally meaningless, stimuli. Only when we understand the meaning of stimuli that affect us can we evaluate them as pleasant, important, correct etc, then they affect us emotionally and thus raise our interest. Neutrally presented information is also neutrally received, felt to be unimportant, thus disinterested teachers with neutral attitudes to the information they present get poor responses from the children. To mediate evaluation means passing the values themselves, passing moral attitudes without moralising. That is also why the individual exercise books of Feuerstein's program are called 'instruments': they are not created for the child to fill, but to help the teacher to develop the child's cognitive abilities and teach the strategies necessary for processing information about themselves and the world.

Each interaction should be mediating, and mediating interaction has two conditions. First is the *intentionality* of interaction, that is, children must feel that the material has been prepared for them and not for the lesson. A typical non–mediating teacher comes to the class and says: 'Open your textbooks on page XY'. But children must know the objective and reason for their work, its value and relationship with other activities and facts.

The other condition is *reciprocity* in interaction. Children must be stimulated, encouraged to comment, and not only give correct answers. They should learn to ask questions, participate by giving examples, while being lead to further associations and their evaluation according to given rules.

Teaching that is mediating makes possible the application of knowledge or 'bridging' (Feuerstein, 1990). The child not only solves this present problem, but must know how to use his/her knowledge: the teacher must provide situations in which a particular piece of knowledge or skill is useful. Mediated teaching also means mediating meaning, and the child must know the reason for a particular activity, its method, and its structure and relationship with earlier and later topics.

In the process of learning, children are often in new situations which induce uncertainty, so they are justifiably unconfident. Whenever possible the *feeling of competence* is mediated. Even more important than the evaluation of the child him or herself is the positive evaluation, with reasons, of the results of his or her work: he or she should be told of any progress achieved.

The Instrumental Enrichment program (IE)

The Instrumental Enrichment program (Feuerstein et al., 1980) consists of over five hundred pages of paper and pencil exercises divided into twenty instruments, each focusing on a specific cognitive deficit but also contributing to the acquisition of many other learning prerequisites. Feuerstein recommends that fourteen of the twenty instruments be regularly used in classes in three to five hour long weekly lessons for two years.

IE exercises may be divided into two categories, according to the level of literacy. Dot Organisation, Analytical Perception and Illustrations can be used with more, less or functionally illiterate individuals. Space Orientation I, II, III, Comparisons, Family Relationships, Calculations, and Templates use some vocabulary and require the teacher's assistance in reading the instructions. Categorisation, Temporary Relationships and Syllogisms require a relatively good level of literacy and verbal understanding. Other instruments outside the two year training may be used at various levels of development. These include Absurdities, Analogies, Convergent and Divergent Thinking, Illusions, Linguistic and Symbolic Understanding, Maps, and Auditory and Haptic Discrimination.

Each exercise involves a gradual increase in difficulty and complexity. The objective of the exercises is the development of the child's learning potential, which is meant in a wide context. Firstly, it is the *correction of deficient cognitive functions* on Luria's three levels (Luria, 1966). The first level is *input* where problems of imperfect perception of information appear. Second is the *elaboration* level, where the child may have insufficiently internalised the ability to use strategies or to evaluate the importance of information. The third is the *output* level, where, among other problems, the child may be hyperactive and impulsive, have insufficient verbal ability, or over use trial and error.

When working with Feuerstein's method the emphasis is on the *development of language*. Language is a tool of any intellectual activity, so a child must be able to use it to express any thought process, any strategy s/he uses. By using language the child internalises both the information and the strategy.

Children's *internal motivation* to learn is supported by the motto of the whole program: 'Just a moment, let me think!' At every exercise they are thus encouraged, and gradually it becomes part of their strategy, also controlling and limiting their hyperactivity. The children also take some responsibility for learning: the teacher should act to diminish the pupils' passivity, and demonstrate their competence and ability. Children are not ranked, but are motivated by the style of work, by every child's chance for success. The emphasis is on cooperation, listening, and limiting hyperactivity. Questions, not competition, stimulate the children, within the respect afforded to everyone's personal pace: 'Let me think about it'.

Children should learn to reflect their thinking and insight, to evaluate their learning abilities, and generalise ways of thinking. They should become aware of and internalise the fact that a different child may see a problem in a different way: in turn this has a direct bearing on their orientation in political life. Further, the process of mediation is very demanding on the teacher and assumes an open attitude to life.

Feuerstein's work on the development and refining of the instrument started in 1950. His cognitive development program was created in 1960. By the late eighties the method had spread through Europe (England and France) and North and South America (USA, Guyana, Venezuela). In Canada it is also used successfully with prisoners (ICELP, 1998). Today, there are training centres in Switzerland, Malta and Hungary and during the last few years there is slow awareness in our country (Pokorná, 2000). Since 1979, many studies have been published confirming the effectiveness of the program (ICELP, 1998). Despite this, there are critics. It seems that the biggest problem is to meet the premises of mediated teaching.

First Czech applications of the Instrumental Enrichment program

From 1995 to 1997, staff at the department of school and educational psychology of the Faculty of Education, Charles University, made a preliminary evaluation of Instrumental Enrichment. They and ten teachers were trained in four modules (Dot Organisation, Space Orientation I, Comparisons and Analytical Perceptions) by Professor Alex Kozulin of The International Centre for the Enhancement of Learning Potential, Hadassah – WIZO – Canada – Research Institute.

Our evaluation sample consisted of sixtynine pupils, the selection depending in part on teachers' willingness to try the methods. Most of the pupils were in mainstream primary (Czech Stage 1) schools, a smaller number were in special school (zvláštní škola). All the latter were Roma. Most of the pupils were of primary school age, thirteen were a year older. Three quarters of the sample were boys.

Methods

Teachers worked one hour weekly with whole classes or selected children for one school year (1996/97). Over this period children mastered two programs: Dot Organisation and Space Orientation I.

Evaluation was via several instruments, which were applied at the beginning and the end of the school year: Similarities subtest of *Wechsler Intelligence Scale for Children*, B, C and D (Wechsler, 1991); subtests of Raven's *Coloured Progressive Matrices* (Raven, 1990); and the following battery of questionnaires, all by Vágnerová (1995): *School Success Self–evaluation, Evaluation of Family – School Relationship,* and *Class Atmosphere Questionnaire.* Also, some evaluation, including WISC Similarities, was by qualitative methods: children gave reasons for their solutions, or were asked for another acceptable solution, making it possible to evaluate their thinking strategy. Finally, teachers themselves completed questionnaires designed to assess each child's school work, family – school relationship and class atmosphere.

Our findings and their interpretation

Children regarded their own school success, and their class atmosphere, as average, both before and after the program (sixth sten). They tended to evaluate their own family – school relationships as above average (seventh sten): this opinion probably reflects the fact that most of the children had school–related problems so for them family – school contact tended to be more frequent.

The children who improved in Raven's Matrices were initially the lower scorers: presumably these children had some reserves and so could profit more from the program.

The improvements in WISC Similarities scores were statistically significant for the complete sample (t = 2.93 p<0.01), for boys (t = 2.02, p<0.05) and for girls (t = 2.83, p<0.05). We attribute the average improvement in logical thinking on WISC Similarities to the program, since it was better than the improvement that would normally be attributed to development alone.

Most teachers evaluated the school success of their pupils, and also the family – school relationships, as average. These opinions showed positive but statistically insignificant improvements from the beginning to the end of the year: we believe this was associated with the work and attention they had given to the children. Teachers saw the relationships between the children as above average at the beginning of the program (eighth sten), and remaining so at the end. Although they are unchanged, we believe that this view of their children by the teachers is important because it signifies their positive attitudes towards their classes, which in turn were evidenced in their willingness to do the extra work with their children.

Conclusions and looking forward

Our data evidences some positive effects of Instrumental Enrichment, but we suggest that it be applied more than one hour per week. We have verified that it is usable with boys and girls of any age. The program appears mostly to affect verbal reasoning (looking for similarities and relationships): children were taught to verbalise their strategies and thus to develop their verbal reasoning even though the stimulation materials were non–verbal.

It was also interesting when teachers discussed the changes in their work and attitudes, after working with the program for one year: all stated that they enjoyed eliciting reciprocal problem solving from their children. Most talked about using these strategies in parallel with encouraging children to think tasks through independently in their regular classes.

Our preliminary program will develop into a course on Feuerstein's method for the development of cognitive functioning, which has been prepared as part of the Lifelong Education program for students of Psychology and Special Education at the Faculty of Education, Charles University. This will certify participants for the use of the individual instruments of Feuerstein's program in their schools.

References

Feuerstein, R. (1990) Theory of structural cognitive modifiability. In B. Presseisen (eds.), Learning and Thinking Skills: classroom interaction, 68–134. Washington DC: National Education Association Research for Better Schools.

Feuerstein, R., Rand, Y., Hoffman, M. B. & Miller, R. (1980). Instrumental Enrichment: an intervention program for cognitive modifiability. Baltimore: University Park Press.

ICELP International Centre for Enrichment of Learning Potential (1998). Bibliography on the Theory of Structural Cognitive Modifiability and Mediated Learning Experience and its Applied Systems: instrumental enrichment the learning potential assessment device and the shaping of modifying environments. Jerusalem: ICELP.

Lory, P. (1966). Die Leseschwäche. Entstehung und Formen, ursächliche Zusammenhänge, Behandlung. Erziehung und Psychologie, 1, 44–56.

Luria, A. R. (1966). Higher Cortical Functions in Man. London: Tavistock Publications.

Müller, R. (1974). Leseschwäche, Leseversagen, Legasthenie. Bd. I und II. Basel: Wienheim.

Pokorná, V. (2000). Teorie, diagnostika a náprava specifických poruch učení. (The Theory, Diagnosis and Treatment of Specific Learning Difficulties). Praha: Portál II. vyd. 267–273.

Raven, J. C. (1990). Coloured Progressive Matrices. Oxford: Oxford Psychology Publishers / Pychodiagnostika sro Brno.

Sharron, H. & Coulter, M. (1994). Changing Children's Minds: Feuerstein's revolution in the teaching of intelligence. Birmingham: Sharron Publishing Co.

Sindelar, B. (1994). Teilleistungsschwächen. Wien: Eigenverlag Dr. B. Sindelar.

Vágnerová, M. (1995). Dotazník sebehodnocení školní úspěšnosti dítěte, hodnocení vztahu rodiny a školy, hodnocení atmosféry ve třídě (School Success Self-evaluation Questionnaire, Evaluation of Family–School Relationship, Class Atmosphere Questionnaire). Psychológia a patopsychológia diet'ata, 30, 34–41.

Wechsler, D. (1991) Wechsler Intelligence Scale for Children (WISC–III). N.Y.: Psychological Corporation / Pychodiagnostika sro Brno.

SECTION IV

INCLUSIVE EDUCATION: GOOD PRACTICE IN SCHOOLS AND AUTHORITIES

9. A SUPPORT STRATEGY FOR INCLUDING CHILDREN WITH SPECIAL NEEDS IN MAINSTREAM EARLY YEARS PROVISION IN A LARGE MULTICULTURAL CITY

Sarah Ford,
City of Birmingham Local Education Authority, UK

Birmingham is the second city in the United Kingdom after the capital, London. Birmingham has a population of one million people including one hundred and fiftyeight thousand children and young people who attend approximately four hundred and forty schools. Approximately forty per cent of school pupils are from Black and ethnic minority families and approximately thirty per cent speak a first language other than English. Thirtythree per cent of pupils are entitled to free school meals on the basis of the family's low income – this is compared with a national average of eighteen per cent. Approximately three per cent of pupils have Statements of Special Educational Needs which means that the Local Educational Authority (LEA) has decided that the child's needs meet specified criteria for additional support following a period of measured, multidisciplinary intervention. A Statement provides additional resources, therapy, facilities and equipment to support their learning. This may be in a special or a mainstream school. Children's needs are assessed in their natural setting over time and information about their response to teaching is used to decide the detail of their special needs and the necessary provision as required by the 1994 Education Act (revised 2001), with its *Code of Practice for the Identification of Special Educational Needs* (UK DfES, 2001). For children under five, assessments and observations take place at home and in other preschool settings, in the children's first language and through play based dynamic assessment.

Birmingham has unequivocally set equal opportunities at the top of its political agenda (Birmingham City Council, 2001). Social and educational inclusion are central pillars of the city's commitment to equality for all its citizens. The *Early Years Development and Childcare Plan* is charged with ensuring that inclusion becomes a reality and that parents or carers and children have access to appropriate child care and education within their communities. The aim is to reduce segregated, distant placements for children and to increase the skill, confidence and expertise in local settings to allow all children to learn together in their local neighbourhood. This needs a fundamental change in social thinking towards attitudes that value diversity, as well as changes in resourcing and training.

Twentynine of Birmingham's schools are currently special segregated schools for children with either physical disabilities, hearing impairment, visual impairment, autism and communication disorders, general learning difficulties or profound and multiple learning difficulties. Inclusion of such children as their basic human right to be equal social members of their communities is very high on the political agenda in the United Kingdom. Birmingham now has a strategic plan for inclusion of all its children in local settings. Currently three special schools are undertaking co-location projects with mainstream schools so that sites and resources are shared and children with wide ranging educational needs are taught in inclusive settings.

Birmingham City Council believes that every child and young person should have an equal opportunity and right to attend a local mainstream early years setting or school with appropriate resources and support networks, if that is the parents' or carers' preference. This means they will have access to a common range of experiences and that they will attend wherever possible a local early years setting with all the other children in the neighbourhood. In Birmingham every four year old is entitled to a free nursery place at least part time and this year the target is for all three year olds to have a part time place at a nursery / early years setting as long as they can access the provision.

In the United Kingdom, the philosophy in early education is generally based on a hands-on learning-through-play model with opportunities to talk about experiences, think creatively, solve problems and accept challenge with confidence and enjoyment. A Foundation Stage Curriculum has been established by the Government's Department for Education to describe the experiences children should cover from the age of three to five years. The planning of activities should include each area of learning and each child's developmental level.

The *Success for Everyone under Five* Standards were developed in Birmingham as a direct response to the 1998 *Early Years Development Plan*. This required the establishment of preschool targets for inclusion that could be used to evaluate early years settings and support the development of further inclusive practice against Standards in Leadership, Management and Organisation, Teaching and Learning, Environment, Parent / Community Involvement and Staff Development.

In May 2000 a multiagency team began working to launch *Success for Everyone under Five* in two pilot areas of Birmingham. The team is made up of an educational psychologist specialising in the early years and a former teacher; a parent of a child with a disability who herself is a training consultant to voluntary agencies; a health visitor working in a city centre community with high levels of poverty; a teacher from one of our segregated special schools for children with physical disabilities; and a nursery officer who speaks community Asian languages and who runs parent and toddler sessions and support groups for Asian women who are isolated within the community.

The brief was to support all early years settings providing childcare and education. In Britain childminders are inspected and registered to care in their own homes for children whose parents are at work. Playgroups for children to learn and play together in a local setting are run independently and privately in a variety of community buildings, like schools, churches and leisure centres. Nursery schools are education establishments where children are taught an early years curriculum by teachers and nursery nurses, and some primary schools also have nursery classes. All of these preschool settings are expected to offer experiences that fulfil the requirements of the Foundation Stage National Curriculum.

The *Success for Everyone under Five* team was set up to help any of these preschool settings to complete a Profile of Progress against the Standards for Inclusion. The areas in the document covered are as above and each section is divided into several parts for staff to agree whether their practice is Emerging (as it were Beginning the journey ...), Established (Well on the way ...), or Advanced (Doing well: What next?) Each stage is positive and developmental and it is our role to help settings decide their priorities for development and an action plan. The team provided the training and support to enable them to work towards their target for further inclusive practice.

Birmingham LEA invited schools to cooperate as inclusion networks to promote local work between mainstream and special schools. Generous financial support was made available to groups of ten or more schools who produced an inclusion strategy that would eventually lead to the reintegration of pupils from the special schools into mainstream education. Strategies such as additional training and multi-agency working came up often so the *Success for Everyone under Five* project selected its pilot areas from among these networks.

The first pilot area for the project was three miles from the city centre. It is multiethnic with a mixed population of families from varied economic and social backgrounds. The second pilot area was six miles from the city centre. It consisted of one district that was really proactive in inclusion, and two that were not so forward thinking.

The launch of the project coincided with the end of the summer term and academic year. It was therefore decided to organise informal taster sessions to which all education service early years providers were invited from the pilot area. Attendance was excellent with only one setting unable to commit time to the meetings. Staff were rewarded for giving their time with strawberries and cream and an informal, social atmosphere was achieved. The team introduced *Success for Everyone under Five* and its explicit links to the Foundation Stage Curriculum. Examples of the Standards for inclusive practice were given and teachers were helped to see how the document would support school development planning rather than be an additional task to be completed for the LEA.

Feedback was excellent with all participants feeling very positive and enthused. Opportunities were given for participants to request the particular type of support they would like and need in their setting, and these were formally recorded and responded to individually following the session. These requests formulated the team's program of work in the pilot area for the next few months.

Success for Everyone under Five was piloted in two areas of the city but all preschool settings had access to the project materials. The support team wanted to be able to offer a service to those settings who did not fall into the pilot areas but who wanted to engage with the project. Therefore a two tier mode of service delivery was developed with a proportion of the team's time being designated for one-off training sessions. Preschool settings were introduced to the Standards, encouraged to record their practice, and devise an inclusion action plan. These early years providers come from the LEA, playgroups, childminding services and the private sector. The sessions were very well attended and positively received by all sectors.

Examples of the project in action included a nursery school setting up a parents' group to support and challenge the attitudes of parents whose children did not have special needs. This arose from Standard 23: *Involving Parents*. The nursery staff were aware that parents of other children were concerned about children with special needs being in the nursery and disadvantaging their own child. Information from a questionnaire supported this assumption and so a decision was reached to tackle parents' understanding of inclusive thinking and its benefits, not disadvantages, to their children. Other visits from the community supported this group as did parents with children with special needs.

Another example came from a private nursery. The managers were aware that their success in including one little girl with cerebral palsy lay in the attitudes of the other children who had grown up alongside her. They were aware however that not all of the staff thought in the same way. So they selected the Standard: *Sharing the Vision*, and formulated an action plan to provide all staff with regular training and support in developing awareness and understanding of inclusion.

A community day nursery for children from six weeks of age to five years worked on their outdoor environment. The Foundation Curriculum states that children learn indoors and outdoors, so practitioners need to consider the outdoor environment when planning children's learning. The Standards: *Planning for Learning* and *Improving the Premises* were selected and an action plan was formulated which involved the children, parents and local groups in designing a multisensory garden in which all children could participate and learn.

A community volunteer organisation for families became involved. They offered good, free support, but knew they were not attracting families with children with special needs. They worked on the Standard: *Involving other Agencies* and made links with the local Child Development Centre and Community Day Nursery, who in turn referred families to the playgroups. The volunteers in the parent and toddler group felt that for them the *Success for Everyone under Five* project was a real springboard towards inclusive practice.

Success for Everyone under Five also looked at the ways parents of children with special needs could use project materials to support the development of inclusive practice in settings their children already attended, or the Standards to select an appropriate preschool setting for their child. The first task involved people from home support services helping parents to work on a Standard together with the staff in their child's nursery. The second task led to the development of a parents' booklet which asked the same questions as each of the Standards in appropriate words for parents to use when visiting settings.

The pilot phase of the project ended in May 2001. A celebratory event was held and all those involved shared many of the good ideas and positive developments. The team then moved on to evaluate the outcomes of the pilot through questionnaires and semi-structured interviews with people in the pilot areas and people who had attended training sessions.

Currently work is under way to develop the training strategy framework based on the lessons learnt in the pilot project and during the evaluation. It is hoped that this framework will enable more settings to use *Success for Everyone under Five* materials on an ongoing basis. The materials have been updated with good practice examples, completed action plans and success stories from the pilot project. The materials now function as a resource pack as well as an audit tool of inclusive practice. It was a moving accolade for the *Success for Everyone under Five* team to hear at the celebration:

As a parent of a disabled child it is your utmost hope that they will live in a fully inclusive society without prejudice, but in reality I know this will take a long time.

Hopefully the *Success for Everyone under Five* project will be a step in the right direction.

References

Birmingham City Council (2001). Inclusion Consultancy. (http://www.bgfl.org/services/inclus)

UK DfES Dept for Education and Science (2001). Revised Code of Practice for the Identification of Special Needs. (http://www.dfes.gov.uk/sen/documents/SENCodeOfPractice.pdf)

10. DELIVERING EDUCATION FOR CHILDREN WHOSE FIRST LANGUAGE IS NOT ENGLISH

Mohammed Mehmet,
London Borough of Camden Local Education Authority

Introduction

The population of Camden is one hundred and ninety thousand. There are around four and a half thousand residents aged three and four and thirtyone thousand residents aged five to nineteen. About eighteen per cent of residents are from non–white minority ethnic groups, the largest being Bangladeshi at three and a half per cent. However, there are major differences between the profile for under sixteens and the population as a whole. Thirtyone per cent of under sixteens are from non–white minority groups and more than ten per cent are Bangladeshi. A further ten per cent are refugees, the largest group being from Somalia. The Child Care Audit of 1998 shows that the Bangladeshi community will grow by twenty per cent and the Black African community by sixteen per cent by the year 2006. There are over one hundred mother tongues, and over thirty per cent of the children in Camden's schools speak English as an additional language. Eligibility for free school meals is twice the national average.

Camden is amongst the most deprived boroughs in England, but is probably unique in its extremes of wealth and poverty, with intense geographical concentration of poor families, ethnic minorities and refugees reflected in the schools. Overall test and examination results are very good, being the best in inner London and comparing well against national averages, but severe underachievement is masked by overall success. Table 1 shows the percentage of pupils achieving expected standards at the end of primary and secondary education[20].

---

[20] **Disaggregation of UK pupil achievement data for ethnic group, socioeconomic status and gender.** All this data should be read within the major National Literacy and Numeracy strategies (Minnis & Higgs, 2001; UK DfES, 2002a, 2002b) which are producing steady improvements in average reading and mathematics skills in UK children, see for example Mehmet p. 108, Figure 6, 'All Groups'.

Pupils Achievement Data: All UK pupils must take nationally standardised tests, Standard

Table 1: Pupil achievement data, 2000

	Key Stage 2, % pupils achieving Level 4 or above			Key Stage 4, % pupils with 5 good GCSE passes
	English	**Maths**	**Science**	**5+ A*–C grades**
Camden	72	70	83	51.3
Inner London	68	65	78	35.4
National	75	72	85	47.5

Level 4 is the expected (criterion) level of achievement in the Standard Assessment Tasks (tests) at the end of UK primary education (age 11). Five or more A*–C grades at GCSE (General Certificate of Secondary Education) is the expected level of achievement at the end of UK secondary education (age 16).

However, consistent with the extremes of wealth and poverty, these overall scores mask both very high achievement and very low achievement. In particular, many children from working class, Bangladeshi and refugee backgrounds are achieving below these averages in Camden's schools. Addressing this is very high priority, especially in view of the predicted numbers within these communities.

Because attainment is closely linked to socioeconomic disadvantage and racial inequalities, Camden is developing its strategy for inclusive education within corporate and multi–agency approaches to tackling poverty, unemployment and discrimination. This is based on careful analysis of the achievement of all pupils, the identification of groups that are

Assessment Tasks (SATs), in English, Mathematics and Science at ages 7 (referred to as Key Stage 1), 11 (KS2), and 14 (KS3). Level 4 is used as the national benchmark or criterion of pupils' success in these SATs. Pupils take examinations in a range of subjects, usually at age 16 (General Certificate of Education, GCSE). These GCSE examinations are nationally standardised by four university consortia. Five good GCSE passes (at levels A* – C out of 8 levels) is used as benchmark of pupils' success at this stage.

Socioeconomic Disadvantage: All Local Education Authorities (LEAs) and the Department for Education and Skills (UK DfES – the Ministry of Education) collect this data in two groups: children whose family income does and does not qualify them for a Free School Meal (FSM). Qualifying for FSM is used in Britain as the index of socioeconomic disadvantage for educational matters.

Ethnic Minority Groups: Most Local Education Authorities (LEAs) with significant ethnic minority populations collect this pupil achievement data for each of the main ethnic minority categories of the UK Census; (http://www.statistics.gov.uk/census2001/pdfs/H1.pdf). From 2002 all schools must make every effort to elicit this data from parents for the School Census, after which time individual IDs will track children through their education. While group data is useful vis a vis policies, this individual tracking represents significant but surreptitious extension of computerisation of citizens' lives. – HG.

causing concern and the development of strategies, through close working with schools, the relevant communities and agencies (Camden LEA, 1999). Camden expects to raise the attainment of underachieving groups to the current average of the borough by the year 2002. By the year 2006 it expects to eliminate the attainment gaps between underachieving groups and all pupils.

Analysis

We know from educational research that there is a very close relationship between class, ethnicity, gender and educational achievement. Gillborn and Mirza's (2000) research confirms that whilst the effect of class, ethnicity and gender can overlap, they are often mutually exclusive. This is consistent with Camden's local experience where our approach to analysing test and examination data takes account of the interaction between these factors.

Figure 2

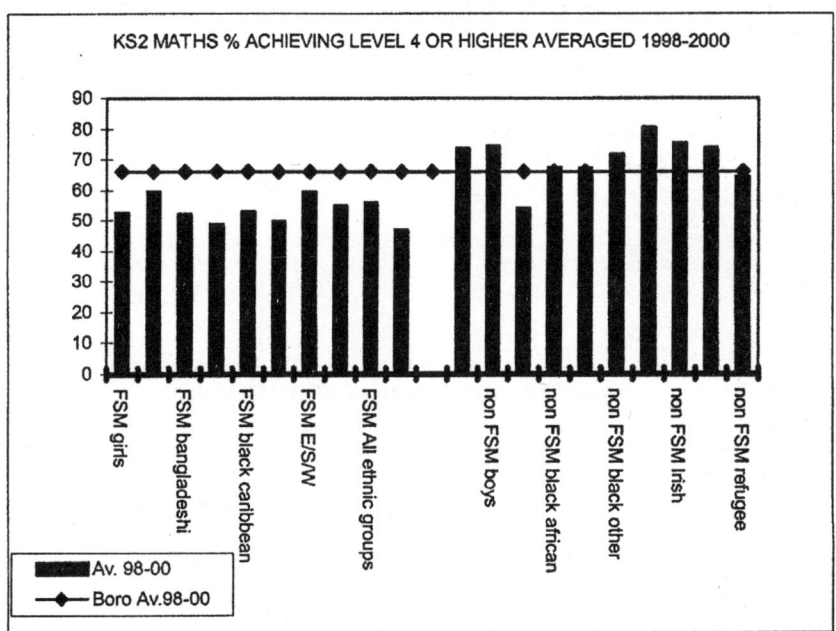

Figures 2 and 3 show (see the following page 116) the Key Stage 2 average scores, over three years, in English and Maths, for boys, girls, children on free school meals and the main ethnic groups in Camden. They show that all groups on free school meals (FSM) perform below the Camden average. They show that Bangladeshis, Black Africans and refugees are the lowest attainers. Bangladeshi and refugee students are achieving below the Camden average whether they are on FSM or not. It is important to note that at the end of Key Stage 2, Black Caribbean and Black Other groups are performing well.

Figure 3

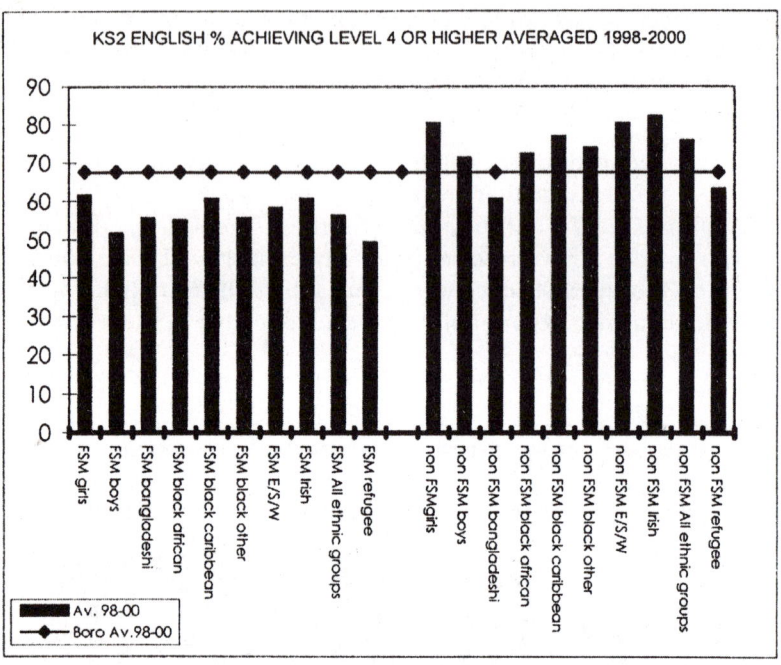

Figure 4

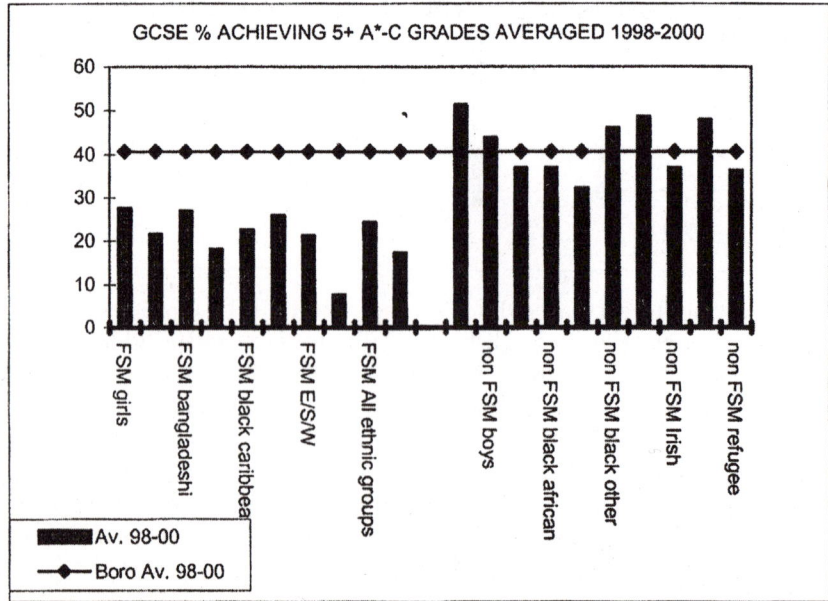

Figure 4 shows that the gap between students on free school meals and others has widened by the end of Key Stage 4 (age 16). The pattern of achievement of Bangladeshi and refugee students at this stage is consistent with end of Key Stage 2 (age 11), but the Black Caribbean and Black Other groups have fallen well behind white students. The achievement of refugee students is particularly worrying and this is demonstrated in Figure 5.

Figure 5

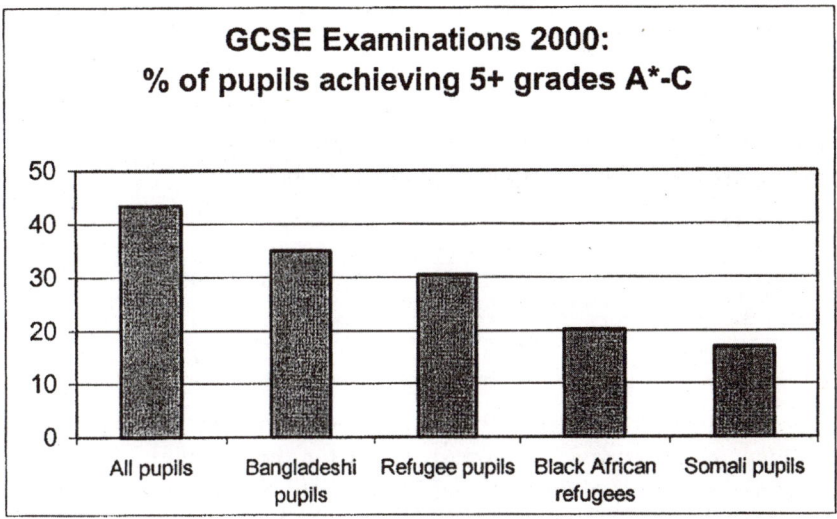

From this analysis, Camden has concluded that it needs to focus extra attention on raising the achievement of four distinct groups: working class children and boys in particular, Bangladeshi pupils, refugees and Black African in particular, and secondary aged Black Caribbean and Black Other groups.

We have closely tracked these groups' attainment over a five year period and the gap is monitored. For example, Table 6 (see p.118) shows the attainment of Bangladeshi pupils at Key Stage 2 English Tests compared with the average for all Camden pupils from 1996 to 2000.

Figure 6

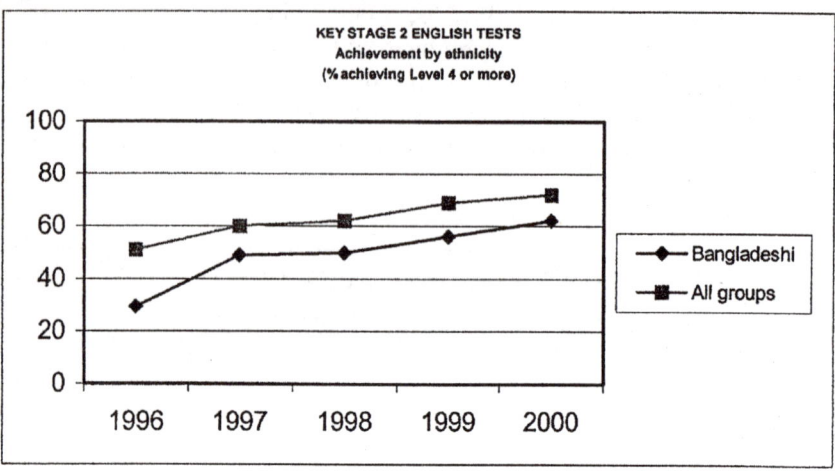

	1996	1997	1998	1999	2000
Bangladeshi	30	49	50	56	62
All Groups	51	60	62	69	72

The graph is encouraging in that the line representing Bangladeshi attainment is shadowing the upward trend for the borough as a whole, reflecting the success of the National Literacy and Numeracy strategies and other strategies (Minnis & Higgs, 2001; UK DfES, 2002a, 2002b). It also shows that in the last year the rate of improvement for Bangladeshi pupils is greater than that for all pupils, thus closing the gap. However, it is clear that as the gap narrows it becomes more stubborn.

Other Key Stage 2 and Key Stage 4 results for 2000 are also showing improvements for these groups, some of which are significantly greater than the average borough improvement. For example, Key Stage 2 Mathematics results for Bangladeshi pupils increased by twelve per cent whereas the attainment of all pupils remained the same as the previous year. Measured by the number of pupils with more than five GCSE passes at levels A*–C, Bangladeshi attainment increased by seven per cent, Black attainment by thirteen per cent and the overall attainment by three and a half per cent. If the LEA manages to repeat this pattern over the next two years then it will be able to eliminate many of the 'attainment gaps' by 2002.

Our approach to educational inclusion is a corporate rather than a departmental one and it attempts to take a broad view of inclusion which includes ethnic minorities, children with special educational needs, young people in public care, refugees, Travellers, pregnant school girls and able and talented pupils.

Strategies for Inclusive Education

1. Community involvement

For some time, Camden has worked closely with the relevant ethnic minority communities to research the reasons for this underachievement. In 1996–7 the LEA undertook a thematic inspection of Bangladeshi pupils' achievement. This found that teachers often lacked confidence in accurately assessing the learning needs of these pupils, thus placing a disproportionate number on a school's special needs register, instead of intensively teaching language and literacy.

In 1999, the LEA and Somali community representatives commissioned the Institute of Education to research the experiences of Somali pupils in schools, identifying their lack of knowledge of the British educational system as a key problem (Institute of Education, 2000). Also in 1999, the LEA and the Camden Black Parents and Teachers Association commissioned research on the Black Child in Camden (People Science Intelligence Unit, 2000) to learn more reasons for underachievement of secondary aged Black Caribbean students.

Research findings are disseminated to schools and educationalists through conferences and training sessions, and education advisers help schools integrate recommendations from these into their development plans, some times focussed on problems of particular groups, sometimes broader recommendations.

Camden is rich in community groups and voluntary organisations and the LEA is developing ways of brokering links and relationships between them and schools. The LEA will map all parent education programs across the borough and target community groups to relevant ones, as well as encouraging all schools to promote themselves as local community resources.

To ensure the ongoing involvement of local communities, Camden has established a Steering group on ethnic minority achievement comprising ethnic minority representatives from the Refugee Education Forum, the Bangladeshi Achievement Group, the Black Parents and Teachers Association, as well as education professionals and senior managers, as in Figure 7 (see over, p.120). These groups oversee the monitoring of agreed actions and where appropriate participate in the implementation process. Agendas are jointly agreed and the emphasis is on sharing knowledge, experience and learning. Recently the Steering Group has endorsed an action plan for raising the achievement of secondary aged children from African Caribbean backgrounds and produced leaflets and publicity materials for parents on how to report racial harassment in schools.

Figure 7

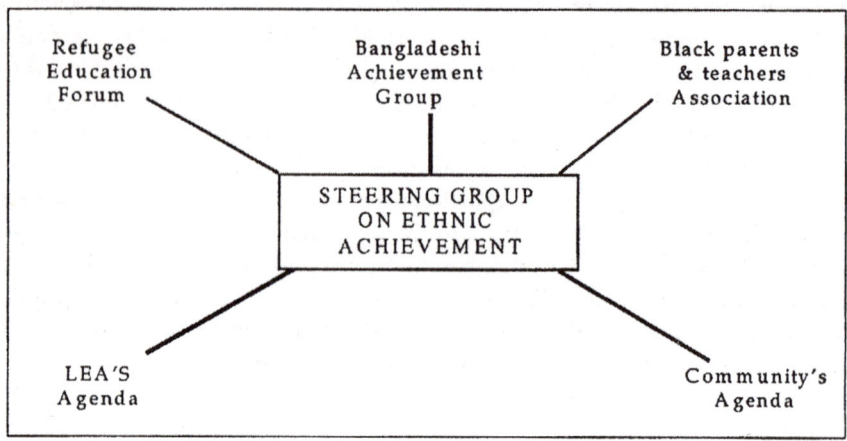

Camden has a large Roma community, including more than three hundred of school age, but our understanding of the needs and expectations of this group is at an early stage of development. LEA officers are currently meeting with Roma representatives to identify educational priorities and consider whether to include this group in the above consultative framework.

2. A corporate strategy

Camden's approach to educational inclusion is broad, including ethnic minorities, children with special needs, young people in care, refugees, Travellers, pregnant schoolgirls and able and talented pupils. We accept the recent joint UK Audit Commission / OfSTED report on *Local Education Authority Support for School Improvement* (2001) which concluded that Local Education Authorities (LEA's) influence for good was less significant than the influence of socioeconomic disadvantage for bad:

The success or otherwise of LEAs is...most likely to be judged by their effectiveness in raising expectations and overcoming the effects of socioeconomic disadvantage. (UK Audit Commission / OFSTED, 2001, p.6 para.21).

However, this implies a key role for the education service in developing corporate and multi–agency partnerships. As part of its inclusion strategy, Camden is investigating how to ensure effective, seamless coordination of all its programs, including government funded programs such as the Neighbourhood Renewal Fund, and programs for children and young people such as Sure Start and Connexions. The Council is also looking at how best to integrate the support that Education, Social Services, Health and the Voluntary groups offer to schools and families.

Critical is ensuring that race equality considerations are embedded in strategic objectives, planning, institutional behaviours. Our detailed action plan that responded to the public inquiry into the death of the Black teenager Stephen Lawrence (Macpherson, 1999) adopted the report's key definitions of a racist incident and institutionalised racism and a number of recommendations for examining Camden's institutional behaviours, for example, in employment policies and by improving the representation and participation of ethnic minorities in its decision making. We have targets for raising the number of education officers, school governors and teachers from ethnic minority communities, backed by appropriate, effective training. Key documents are translated into community languages. We have policies for minimising school exclusion, and all schools have procedures for monitoring and acting on racist incidents, with regular reports to parents, governors and the Local Education Authority (LEA).

3. Raising achievement and activities additional to the mainstream curriculum

Our central strategy for raising achievement is through the mainstream curriculum, National Literacy, National Numeracy, and Information and Communication Technology programs (Minnis & Higgs, 2001; UK DfES, 2002a, 2002b) and the target setting and school improvement strategies. The LEA has published a Curriculum Handbook for schools, with guidance on the multicultural dimension of all subject areas, and practical examples of how valuing of diversity can be demonstrated.

However, more needs to be done to tackle the above achievement gaps. The most significant supplementary program, the Ethnic Minorities and Travellers Grant, is largely devolved to schools, who must produce relevant policies and targets with advice from the LEA. A small team of specialist LEA staff work with classroom teachers to assess the language competency of non–English speakers and identify strategies for supporting the learning of children whose first language is not English. We discourage withdrawal, so this work is done within the mainstream curriculum and in partnership with the classroom teacher. We are developing specialist resources for schools with significant numbers of refugee pupils, with examples of texts, dual language books and tapes, and CD–ROMs, and also community developed material. The Somali research provided powerful evidence of the strong links between competency in mother tongue, self esteem and performance in mainstream education: the facility to show mother tongue skills in school can reverse apparently severe behaviour problems, via the pride given to the pupil.

All Camden pupils age eleven to fourteen have access to a mentor. Also government funded programs such as Excellence in Cities, the Social Inclusion Grant and Sure Start all provide support to disadvantaged groups in addition to that which schools are expected to offer through their mainstream curriculum. These include preschool visits and family literacy, numeracy and information technology programs to encourage the participation of 'hard to reach' groups, particularly in early years education. The LEA has developed various ways of involving parents in children's learning, for example weekly classes help bilingual parents to support children's learning, and a video in Sylheti encourages parents of Bangladeshi reception class (East European Grade 1) children to support regular attendance at school.

Conclusion

Camden recognises that its continued success depends on its ability to raise the attainment of all pupils and to accelerate that of underachieving groups. Camden believes that narrowing and eliminating 'gaps' is as important as raising general standards, as the only way of providing equality of opportunity (see also Mehmet, 2002).

It is encouraging that Camden's strategies that have run for several years of involving the ethnic minority communities in planning and monitoring are narrowing even the attainment gaps between the average and the poorest performing groups, such as the Bangladeshi children in Figure 6, stubborn though these gaps remain.

Camden recognises that inclusion in education cannot be achieved without considering social inclusion more generally. The Council has formulated its Corporate Strategy so that it links the LEA's work to the broader inclusion agenda, that is, poverty, unemployment, poor housing and health.

While we are convinced about the need for initiatives that are additional to the mainstream curriculum, the LEA is at an early stage of developing a rigorous method for measuring their actual impact on raising the educational attainment of the students who underachieve.

Camden's view is that national initiatives need to be adapted to local circumstances, and supplemented by a program of local action in consultation with schools, ethnic minorities, and other agencies. A key priority is to develop a broader approach to tackling socioeducational exclusion, and a more rigorous means of measuring the difference made by 'additional' activities. There is a long way to go but we have established a clear approach to meeting this challenge.

References

Camden LEA (1999). Raising Achievement Together: education development plan 1999–2002. (http://www.camden.gov.uk/learn/lea/pdf_files/Education%20Development%20Plan%20April%201999.pdf)

Gillborn, D. & Mirza, H. S, (2000). Educational Inequality: mapping race, class and gender. HMI 232. London: Office of Standards in Education. (http://www.ofsted.gov.uk/public/docs00/inequality.pdf)

Macpherson, W. (1999). Report of the Committee of Enquiry into the Death of Stephen Lawrence. London: Council for Racial Equality. (http://www.cre.gov.uk/pdfs/slinqlea.pdf)

Mehmet, M. (2002). Raising the Attainment of Minority Ethnic Groups. London: The Education Network (TEN).

Minnis, M. & Higgs, S. (2001). Evaluation of the National Literacy and Numeracy Strategies, 1999–2001. Windsor: National Foundation for Educational Research. (http://www.qca.org.uk/ca/5–14/eval_nlns.asp)

Institute of Education, London University (2000). Meeting the Educational Needs of Somali Pupils in Camden Schools. London: Institute of Education/London Borough of Camden (unpublished report).

People Science Intelligence Unit (2000). Camden Black Child Report. London: People Science Intelligence Unit/London Borough of Camden (unpublished report).

UK Audit Commission / OfSTED (2001). LEA Support for School Improvement. London: The Stationery Office. (http://www.archive.official–documents.co.uk/document/ofsted/lea/lea.pdf)

UK DfES (2002a). The National Literacy Strategy: Framework for teaching. Nottingham: DfES Publications. (http://www.standards.dfes.gov.uk/literacy/publications)

UK DfES (2002b). The National Numeracy Strategy: Framework for teaching. Nottingham: DfES Publications. (http://www.standards.dfes.gov.uk/numeracy/publications.)

11. COMBATING RACISM. TOWARDS MAINSTREAMING EQUALITIES IN EDUCATION: THE LEEDS EXPERIENCE

Rehana Minhas and Denise Trickett,
Education Leeds, UK

Leeds, in common with other Local Education Authorities over the last three decades, has developed specific policies to combat racism, in response to local and national struggles and to statutory obligations under Race Relations legislation. The concept of mainstreaming equalities has developed with a deeper understanding of institutionalised racism, and there has been an increased public awareness of institutionalised racism with the publication of the Macpherson Inquiry Report into the murder of Stephen Lawrence. The statutory obligations for public institutions to promote race equality and avoid unlawful discrimination have been strengthened in the Race Relations Amendment Act (2000). That institutionalised racism in education has contributed to the underachievement of ethnic minority pupils is well documented by official research. Key documents are the Swann Report (UK DES, 1985), recent OfSTED reports (Gillborn & Gipps, 1996; Gillborn & Mirza, 2000) and also in the work of practitioners and academic researchers such as Coard (1971) and Gilroy (1981).

The challenge of mainstreaming equalities in education is to ensure that race equality underpins all policy, resource allocation and practice with increased accountability. We believe that combating racism in education requires a holistic approach. A key drive is to establish an ethos of inclusive education with high expectations. This can only be achieved in partnership with schools' governing bodies and local communities. The window of opportunity created by the Race Relations Amendment Act (2000), the Council for Racial Equality Standards (UK CRE, 1999, 2000a, 2000b) and the national agenda for education inclusion needs to be maximised.

Education in Leeds and the Performance of Ethnic Minority Groups

Leeds has the second largest metropolitan Education Authority in England, which in April 2001 became Education Leeds. There are seventyfive nationalities residing in the city, but the main groups are of Pakistani, Indian, Bangladeshi, African Caribbean heritage. Leeds has two hundred and forty primary schools (east European Basic school first level), fortythree secondary schools (Basic school second level) and eleven special schools. The total student population is approximately one hundred and ten thousand of which thirteen thousand pupils are from ethnic minority groups, over ninety per cent of whom were born in England. The majority of the ethnic minority pupils attend schools in the poorest, inner city areas of Leeds (Form 7 Returns, Leeds LEA, 1999). The national OfSTED Report *Raising the Attainment of Minority Ethnic Pupils* (1999) notes that while the attainment of minority groups as a whole is improving, some groups continue to underachieve.

Gillborn and Mirza (2000)[21] in *Educational Inequality: mapping race, class and gender* take this further and comments on the performance of different ethnic groups across the UK over the past ten years:

- *Indian pupils have made the greatest gains in the last decade: enough to overtake their white peers as a group.*
- *Bangladeshi pupils have improved significantly but the gap between themselves and white youngsters is much the same.*
- *African Caribbean and Pakistani pupils have drawn least benefit from the rising levels of attainment: the gap between them and their white peers is bigger than a decade ago. (p.14).*

In other words, whilst on a national level the attainment of all groups is improving, the equality gap between some groups is getting wider.

Leeds Education Authority has monitored performance by ethnicity for four years, using the categories of the UK Census. Similar to the national picture, Pakistani and African Caribbean pupils are underachieving compared to their white peers, particularly at Key Stages 3 and 4 (fouteen and sixteen year olds). For example, Table 1 shows numbers and percentages of eleven year olds from a selection of the ethnic groups in Leeds who achieve at least the criterion Level 4 in national exams in English.

As Gillborn and Mirza (2000) report for sixteen year olds across the UK, Indian and Chinese pupils achieve better on average than Leeds pupils; Pakistani, African Caribbean, and Bangladeshi pupils achieve on average significantly lower Levels.

---

[21] See footnote pp.107–108 about disaggregation (break down) of UK pupil achievement data for ethnic group, socioeconomic status and gender

Table 1: English. Number and % of eleven year old pupils at or above Level 4: targets and actuals for four ethnic minority groups, for majority pupils, and for all Leeds pupils.

Ethnicity	1998			1999			2000		
	No of students	% at L4+		No of students	Target %	% at L4+	No of students	Target %	% at L4+
Chinese	41	66%		31	70%	74%	40	78%	88%
Indian & Sri Lankan	196	72%		180	76%	82%	177	80%	81%
Black Caribbean	179	48%		188	52%	64%	152	70%	70%
Pakistani	279	50%		319	54%	55%	358	64%	67%
White born UK	7091	67%		7494	71%	72%	7703	74%	74%
Average for all Leeds	8612	66%		8720	70%	71%	8884	74%	74%

(Data extracted from Leeds monitoring of, in all, eight ethnic groups.)

The Table shows a steady improvement in attainment over the three years for eleven year olds of all ethnic groups. Indian and now Chinese pupils succeed substantially better than Leeds average. Also it is very significant that among underachieving groups, Black Caribbean pupils showed a large improvement from 1998 – 2000, coming close to the Leeds average. Pakistani pupils still achieved lower results in relative terms, but from 1998–2000 also improved their performance compared to the Leeds average.

This compared with the situation among sixteen year olds in Leeds in 2000, where the different attainment of ethnic groups remained marked, using the indicator of number of pupils gaining five passes at levels A*–C in national examinations. Indian and Chinese students were above the Leeds average, Black Caribbean and Pakistani students still well below. (Data not shown.)

Strategies to raise the educational achievements of ethnic minority pupils and promote race equality

Education Leeds (2001) clearly states that the under performance of any group of pupils is unacceptable. Its strategy to improve the achievement of ethnic minority and promote race equality is one of the seven priorities in the Strategic Plan 2001–2006. Education Leeds works in close partnership with all of its schools in implementing the Education Development Plan, but it is important to point out that the key and direct responsibility for raising achievement lies with the schools and their governing bodies. The strategy is wide ranging, but some of the key areas are:

Target setting

As shown in Table 1, Education Leeds sets targets to reduce the differentials in performance of different ethnic groups, in line with the requirement from the UK Department for Education and Science relating to the Ethnic Minority Achievement Grant. School improvement advisers, as part of the statutory role of Education Leeds, advise schools on target setting on an annual basis, and encourage them to set targets by ethnic group. These advisers help schools to refine this target setting process and ensure that appropriately challenging targets are set.

Leadership and Management

There is a consensus (eg Blair & Bourne, 1998) that schools which were successful in raising the attainment of particular ethnic groups had a strong and determined lead on equal opportunities given by the headteachers (Gillborn & Gipps, 1996). Work with headteachers and senior school management is embedded into the strategy. All schools with high percentages of ethnic minority pupils develop their own Action Plan for raising the achievement of ethnic minority pupils. Progress against the Action Plans is monitored by a School Improvement Officer on a termly basis, through a visit to the schools. Additional support and training takes place in those schools that need more advice and help.

We regularly arrange focussed training and conferences for Headteachers and Senior Managers. Recent examples are *Raising the Achievement of African Caribbean Pupils; Issues for Bilingual Learners; Parental Involvement;* and *Discipline, Attendance, Exclusion and Racial Harassment.* We also arrange high profile regional conferences with national speakers, such as one entitled: *Challenging Inequalities,* and another entitled: *The Power to Change.*

School based projects

The UK Department for Education finances Local Authorities through the Ethnic Minority Achievement Grant (EMAG) to:

raise the achievement of ethnic minority pupils who have English as an additional language, ethnic minority groups at risk of underachievement and to meet the needs of refugees and asylum seekers. (UK DfES, 2000).

In Leeds the majority of schools use this funding to pay for Curriculum and Parental Support Assistants (CPSAs). All the CPSAs in schools are Black and/or bilingual, from the same ethnic and language backgrounds as the pupils in schools. The CPSAs give additional support to children in the classroom, mainly in literacy, numeracy and information technology. Much of their work is in mother tongue, especially with younger pupils. Their role is also to enhance cultural activities and understanding within the curriculum, and encourage greater involvement of parents in their children's education.

Education Leeds also funds a specific project to raise the achievement of African Caribbean pupils with three participating high schools. The focus is on raising awareness of teachers on race equality issues and on cultural issues relating to the needs of these pupils. Individual pupils are targeted for classroom support and pupils have a mentor to assist them in their learning.

Training

Underpinning the strategy is a high quality training program: *Teaching and Learning in Successful Multi–Ethnic Schools* for all teachers and support staff. Courses for senior management have already been mentioned. Six day courses are held for CPSAs on effective classroom practice. Staff meetings and training days take place for mainstream teachers on the National Literacy and Numeracy Strategies (Minnis & Higgs, 2001) and pupils who have English as an additional language. Training on equality issues takes place for school improvement advisers from Education Leeds, so that they understand the issues when they visit schools.

Commission for Race Equality: Learning for All, Standards for Race Equality in schools

Part of Leeds' strategy to promote race equality is implementation of the CRE Standards, which are a tool for schools to evaluate their performance in the area of race equality and ethnic minority achievement.

The Standards, each of which has specific criteria against which schools provide evidence, are:

- Policy, Leadership and Management
- Curriculum, Teaching and Assessment
- Admission, Attendance, Discipline and Exclusion
- Pupils – Personal Development, Attainment and Progress
- Attitudes and Environment
- Parents, Governors and Community Partnership
- Staffing – Recruitment, Training and Professional Development

Affirmative employment: increasing the number of teachers from ethnic minority groups

Campaign 300 was established in 1992 to increase the number of teachers from ethnic minority groups in Leeds, so that it reflects the ethnic proportions in the student population. Campaign 300 operates through training and recruitment, and by working in partnership with other institutions, such as further and higher education, and the careers service. Increased training opportunities are being sought through the Graduate Teacher Training Program.

Conclusion

Leeds has for many years been increasing its affirmative action on behalf of the Black and Asian presence in the city. A recent success is the improved achievements particularly of African Caribbean eleven year olds who have reached city averages, in comparison to the national picture which shows them among the groups who are still well below the national average (Gillborn & Mirza, 2000). Another key breakthough will be the point where proportions of ethnic minority teaching and non–teaching staff match those of the city's ethnic minority pupils, and we keenly anticipate this.

References

Coard, B. (1971). How West Indian Children are Made Educationally Sub–National in the British Educational System. London: New Beacon Books.

Blair, M. & Bourne, J. (1998). Making the Difference: teaching and learning strategies in successful multiethnic schools. London: HMSO.

Education Leeds (2001). Strategic Plan. Leeds: Leeds City Council

Gillborn, D. & Mirza, H.S. (2000). Educational Inequality: mapping race, class and gender. HMI 232. London: Office for Standards in Education. (http://www.ofsted.gov.uk/public/docs00/inequality.pdf)

Gillborn, D. & Gipps, C. (1996). Recent Research on the Achievements of Ethnic Minority Pupils. London: Office for Standards in Education.

Gilroy, P. (1981). The Empire Strikes Back: racism in Britain. London: Hutchinson

Minnis, M. & Higgs, S. (2001). Evaluation of the National Literacy and Numeracy Strategies, 1999–2001. Windsor: National Foundation for Educational Research. (http://www.qca.org.uk/ca/5–14/eval_nlns.asp)

UK DES Department of Education and Science (1985). Education for All: Report of the Committee of Inquiry into the Education of Children from Ethnic Minority Groups. (The Swann Report) Cmnd 9453, London: Her Majesty's Stationery Office.

UK CRE Commission for Racial Equality (1999). Equality Standard for Local Government. (http://www.cre.gov.uk/publs/cat_gov.html#remq)

UK CRE Commission for Racial Equality (2000a). Learning for All. (http://www.cre.gov.uk/gdpract/ed_lfa.html)

UK CRE Commission for Racial Equality (2000b). Achieving Racial Equality: a standard for sport. (http://www.cre.gov.uk/publs/cat_sport.html#sportstd)

UK DfES Department for Education and Science (2000). Ethnic Minorities Achievement Grant. (http://www.standards.dfes.gov.uk/ethnicminorities/raising_achievement/)

UK OfSTED (1999). <u>Raising the Attainment of Minority Ethnic Pupils</u>. HMI/170. London: OfSTED Publications. (http:// <u>www.ofsted.gov.uk/public</u>)

UK Race Relations Amendment Act (2002). London: TSO Stationery Office.

12. ROMA ASSISTANTS WORKING AT SCHOOLS AS A FIRST STEP TO HIGHER EDUCATION

Danara Meluzínová,
The Society of Roma in Moravia, Czech Republic

Classroom assistants are vital to support children from ethnic minorities, and so raise their educational levels. Since 1988, I have trained special school teachers. Now I work in a non–profit organisation: Společenství Romů na Moravě (The Society of Roma in Moravia). I coordinate educational centres in six cities in Moravia, which is the eastern half of the Czech Republic. Up to now, we have trained thirty Roma assistants. Their role and task are not yet properly understood: here are the most important goals and principles as they apply to the disadvantaged Roma children in the Czech Republic.

Goals
- The ultimate goal is to help the members of the ethnic minority achieve all professional levels in our society;
- to eliminate lack of education;
- to promote positive role models of the ethnic minority;
- to help the children from the ethnic minority know their own history;
- to help the ethnic minority children master the majority language;
- to help every child for whom we have responsibility find enjoyment and success in learning.

The cultural backgrounds
Czech education is mainly based on a tradition where teachers have unquestioned authority. On the other hand the Roma ethnic group comes from various cultures that have utterly different social and child development norms. Czech children understand better than Roma children that duties come before leisure. However, Czech culture places the individual above the group, while the collective Roma culture values the group, and decision making is shared. Also, Czech parents tend to punish their children's

failures while Roma parents tend to offer understanding and comfort (see also Samková - Bučková, above p.61–65).

The Roma assistant has to bridge this divide. His or her first responsibility is to the children and the families. He or she tries to change their attitudes to education, but the problem is two way, and we need good teachers who do not depend only on their authority, but can awaken children's individual abilities and enable the child's personality to assert itself.

To achieve change, classroom assistants must:
- understand the beliefs and practices of the ethnic communities whose children they are helping to educate. In the case of Roma children, this includes the subgroups such as the Olach communities and other groups (see Smékal, above, p.52);
- thoroughly know the history and language of the cultural groups and subgroups they serve;
- thoroughly know and be known by the local community of the ethnic minority they serve. In the case of the Roma community this includes being known by the various extended families in the local school area;
- be clear with the families that the role is preventative, guarding against complications and conflicts, not solving all present problems;
- refer families for help with housing and other services, not solve all welfare problems themselves;
- listen tolerantly to other ethnic groups;
- understand the language and literacy of the majority society, and other important school subjects;
- via regular visits to the families, contribute to gradual openness towards school, and mutual understanding between home and school;
- gain the trust of the families of the children in their care by careful explanations and encouraging interest in their children's education and in school events;
- introduce schools' staff to the exact nature of the assistant's role;
- observe when children are under stress, and watch to diagnose the source of that stress;
- manage small groups of children by positive methods;
- understand the problems of managing large groups of children.

He or she follows these tasks directly, by working with classes and even with mass media, and indirectly, through play, art, and by an adapted pedagogical environment.

Classroom assistants need:
- training in pedagogy and psychology;
- access to further education in skills and in management of children;

- ongoing support from education authority officials or school managers in developing their colleagues' understanding of the assistant's role;
- to be treated as experts regarding the children from the ethnic group they are serving;
- to be strong in resisting school's pressures to be a general assistant with tasks that are not directly connected with education;
- to be strong in rejecting pressures on children to complete demotivating tasks that do not assist his or her learning and lead to frustration;
- to work with teachers who are interested in the history and cultures of minorities - there is need for better teacher training in this respect;
- knowledge about local resources for meeting material needs, educational needs and emotional needs, in order to direct families to the appropriate help;
- the confidential facility to share frustrations with a sympathetic but realistic person who understands the constraints on teachers as well as the problems that ethnic minorities face.[22]

[22] See also UK DfES (2002): Teaching Assistants: a good practice guide. (http://www.teachernet.gov.uk/Professional_Development/managingmycpd/teachingassistants) This website contains much useful advice for classroom assistants and the teachers with whom they work. (Eds.)

13. EDUCATIONAL PROVISION FOR TRAVELLER CHILDREN IN BRADFORD

Paul Johnson,
City of Bradford Local Education Authority, UK

This paper briefly outlines the provision that Bradford Metropolitan Authority makes for Traveller children. The majority of local education authorities in England make similar provision. It describes practical measures taken to include Traveller children in the formal educational system, and some of the challenges to be overcome. There are major differences between the Czech Republic and England in both the educational systems and the characteristics of the Gypsy communities, however there are enough similarities to raise issues for discussion.

Context

The Bradford Metropolitan District, Yorkshire, incorporates a variety of communities: the City of Bradford and surrounding towns and villages including Haworth and Ilkley. The population of the area is approximately half a million. There are approaching three hundred Traveller children within the authority for some or all of the year. Throughout the area there are two council run sites, with places for about fortyfive families, also private sites, and also Travellers living in houses.

Terminology

In this paper I use the term Traveller and not Gypsy or Roma. The Traveller communities represented in Bradford include Romany, Irish, Fairground, Scottish and Circus. The word Traveller is used as an umbrella term to include these different communities and is the most common term of self–description. In English society in general the terms Gypsy and Gypo are used in a derogatory manner as terms of abuse. There are however Gypsies who dislike the use of the term Traveller and state that they are Gypsies and proud of it.

Romany Travellers retain the use of the Romany language to differing degrees, dependant on the value families place on it. The extended family is of great importance and generally there is a strong sense of belonging and cultural identity. There can be suspicion of Gaugo society seeking to undermine and devalue long held cultural values. Many families have strict hygiene rituals such as keeping separate washing vessels for different tasks. Strict codes of behaviour are applied to young people once they have undergone puberty.

The vast majority of society subjects the Traveller communities in Bradford, as in the rest of England, to dislike and racism.

Provision

The Bradford Education Service for Traveller Children was established on recommendation of, and mainly funded by, central government, in recognition of the fact that many Traveller children in the area were receiving no formal education. The education system in Bradford, as some other English local education authorities, was failing to meet the needs of children who the Plowden Report, *Children and Their Primary Schools* (UK DoE, 1967) described as ...*probably the most deprived in the country.*

Bradford local authority was not meeting its statutory responsibility. The Education Act 1944, as amended by the Education Act 1993 (UK DfEE, 1993) places LEAs under a duty to make education available for all school aged children in their area, appropriate to their age and aptitudes and any special need they may have. This duty extends to all children residing in their area, whether permanently or temporarily, and thus particularly embraces travelling children. In many Traveller communities there was no history and tradition of school attendance. Then and now: *Gypsy Traveller pupils are the group most at risk in the education system* (OfSTED, 1996 p.7).

Historically some Travellers who had attended school, although cognitively bright, had been placed in Special Schools. This experience was in the main negative for them. The Service was set up on the basis that Traveller children have the same rights as all other children, and their parents have the same responsibilities.

The government's commitment was restated by its minister Charles Clarke at a meeting of teachers of Travellers in November 1998:

The approach the Government takes is straightforward. It is that all children have a right to go to school and achieve their best. We are committed to improving the attendance and achievement levels of all Traveller children. Traveller children enrolled at school are of course funded in the same way as all other children. But in addition, as you know, my Department funds the specific grant program involving the expenditure of some eleven million pounds in this financial year to meet the additional needs of Travellers and of displaced persons. This money funds Traveller Education Services in over one hundred and twenty Local Education Authorities in England, supporting three thousand four hundred schools which have Traveller children. Over seventeen thousand Traveller children are benefiting from this program, and we believe the results are showing educational improvements.

The Bradford Service

The Service works to ensure that all Traveller children have access to a full curriculum within mainstream schools and that education is a positive experience (Bradford Education Service for Traveller Children, 2002). The Service aims to do this by:

- encouraging Travellers to take full advantage of the educational opportunities which are theirs by right;
- working with parents/carers to ensure they are aware of their responsibilities towards the education of their children;
- working with schools to ensure Traveller children are welcomed and accepted and their educational needs are understood and met. (See also Leeds LEA Traveller Education Service, 2000).

The work of the Service can be described as follows:

Access

If requested the Service assists parents to obtain school places. Parents choose the school they wish their child to attend and the Service approaches the school to obtain a place. Unless the classes are full, a place is provided. If the classes are full and the parents wish, an appeal is made to an independent local authority panel under the Education Act 1996 (UK DfEE, 1996).

Attendance

The Service works to ensure regular attendance at school. It has a specialist Education Social Worker whose role is to work with Traveller families and the mainstream Education Social Work Service to ensure that children attend school as regularly as possible. Help and advice is also given on a range of issues affecting children's education.

Achievement

The Service has teachers who provide direct teaching support to children who have interrupted education. The support can be individual or group or class, depending on the situation. The main focus of the support is teaching Traveller children to read as quickly as possible. If, for example, a child starts school at the age of nine, learning to read is the important way in which they can start to access many other curricula areas. Some children make excellent progress, quickly learning to read and write.

In the initial stages of a family's contact with a school and if they wish, Service staff liase with school and sort out problems. This advocacy role is gradually reduced to ensure direct contact between home and school.

The Service employs Travellers as trainee classroom assistants both to enable Travellers to work in education and for them to give schools in which they work greater insight into Traveller culture.

INSET and Traveller Awareness Programs

Information is supplied to schools on Traveller culture and lifestyle. The service lends and sell to schools learning materials that reflect Traveller culture. This enables children to see their culture reflected in school, and helps to make it a friendly place. The Service provides Traveller Awareness training to staff in schools, to trainee teachers, trainee nursery nurses, and a range of professionals in jobs related to education.

Challenges for the Service

The Service has been successful in securing the attendance of primary school age Traveller children (age four to eleven), but less successful in ensuring secondary school (age eleven to sixteen) attendance. We seek strategies to increase the number of Traveller children enrolled at and successful in secondary school.

There should be greater direct community involvement in the Service and also in the education system in general.

Gypsy Travellers have been in England for about five hundred years and are still not accepted by the majority communities. There are high levels of discrimination and racism against them. The Service has a direct role in contributing to rectifying this situation, and should further develop this aspect of its work.

References

Bradford Education Service for Traveller Children (2002). Children of Romany Asylum Seeker Families Views of English Schooling (Video). Bradford: Bradford Education Authority.

Leeds LEA Traveller Education Service (2000). Gypsies and Travellers in their Own Words. Education Leeds: Leeds, UK

UK DoE Dept. of Education (1967). Children and Their Primary Schools. The Plowden Report. London: HMSO.

UK DfEE Dept. for Education and Employment (1993). Education Act. London: HMSO Her Majesty's Stationery Office. (http://www.legislation.hmso.gov.uk/acts/acts1993/Ukpga_19930035_en_3.htm)

UK DfEE Dept. for Education and Employment (1996). Education Act. London: TSO The Stationery Office. (http://www.legislation.hmso.gov.uk/acts/acts1996/1996056.htm)

UK OfSTED, UK Office for Standards in Education (1996). Education of Travelling Children. HMR 12/96/NS. London: OfSTED Publications. (http://www.ofsted.gov.uk/public)

14. INTERCULTURAL EDUCATION: DELIVERING THE CURRICULUM FROM FAMILIES' STORIES

Maggie Power and Eileen Sparks,
Bradford Community College, UK

Introduction
An inclusive education cannot be achieved by treating all pupils in the same way.

To be effective, schooling has to take account of the often very varied life experiences, assumptions and interests of different pupils and different groups, including sometimes their differing responses to schooling itself. (UK Teacher Training Agency, 2000).

The above quote originates from a publication by the British Teacher Training Agency that seeks to support students training to be teachers, in their endeavours to encourage and enhance achievement of pupils belonging to minority ethnic groups.

We are all aware that the first place in which a child learns and grows is within the family, the home and the extended community that s/he has been born into. Schools are often strange and challenging places for both children and members of their families. If there is a significant difference between the culture of the school and that of the family members it can be difficult to see where they can fit in, and it can be even harder for children and family to contribute to the learning their children are engaged in once they have crossed the school threshold.

Getting to know the individuality of families is one of the most difficult tasks for any teacher because there are so few opportunities for them to get to know parents as people. (Corbett & Slee, 2000).

However the importance of valuing and working with family members has been acknowledged as crucial to the development of learning for the young child. Parents, family members and others from the wider community must feel they have something to contribute. They should feel they can work in partnership, alongside those within the school and classroom, in helping and supporting their children.

Lubeck, cited in Blatchford–Siraj and Clark (2000), urges educators to understand how early childhood practices help to maintain social inequality by creating status differentials between and among people and by reinforcing ideologies most likely to have been acquired by those of the dominant classes. Too often institutions and those working in them make assumptions about parents and their potential contributions that are, in reality, false. For many mothers in our inner cities who are of minority ethnic backgrounds, there is a sense of helplessness, a feeling that they are outside the school gates with little to offer. Many of these women have had little access to formal education, some are not able to read or write in English and feel unable to help their children in the context of our education system, which often appears to value achievement through academic ability. However, this does not mean that they are any the less interested or concerned about the education and progress of their children: they need access and appropriate support.

This paper looks at ways in which a group of women in Bradford have been helped to grow in confidence. The strategies developed by the school have enabled this to happen. These women came to realise that they had talents and skills that were useful to the school and much appreciated by the teachers of their children. All concerned have been helped to discover that so much more can be achieved by working in collaboration to support, develop and extend opportunities available to the children, the school and the wider community.

Experiential learning: children collect families' stories
Mel Ainscow (in Corbett & Slee, 2000) argues that inclusive education is a process which involves people enquiring into their own context and seeing how it can be developed: he sees inclusion as a process of growth. This supports the approach that was undertaken by Maggie Power in a Bradford inner city school that involved collecting stories from within the local community. In small groups the children were encouraged to interview teachers and other adults who worked in the school. Then, accompanied by a teacher, they went out into the community. Their initial question was 'How did you come to live in Bradford?' The children collected accounts of how individuals and families had come to be settled in this industrial city in the north of Britain.

The children and their teachers unfolded a rich tapestry of stories, which lead to a shared understanding that all of us have a story to tell. Whether our routes to it were local, national or international everyone had something to relate that the school could value and use.

Researching and using grandmothers' stories

Following on from this, research was carried out by the children into stories their grandmothers knew and cherished. In class the children considered which of the stories were a part of a shared heritage and what could be learnt from them. A video was made of grandmothers telling stories, usually in mother tongue. As discussed earlier, many of the women had no formal education but shared a richness of knowledge and experience that was inspiring, informative and thoroughly absorbing. The stories they offered were written up in both the home language and English. These and other stories about grandmothers were used and shared in class and small group work throughout the year. Like the original stories, these class and group discussions based around the stories were in home languages, facilitated by classroom assistants or by bilingual teachers, as well as in English. Some of the children's grandmothers did not live in England. These children were encouraged to write to them wherever they were in the world. The responses were significant for the individual children and for everyone involved in the project. The children felt that their languages, cultures and families were being valued. They all had a voice, even if the contribution was not part of an immediate, local network. They grew in confidence as result. They were able to see the relevance of being able to write letters and to gather information using both English and their home language. The school staff recognised that it was not difficult to give such opportunities to children. All that was needed was a willingness to think and plan together and to consider the importance of creating schools which include rather than exclude the wider community.

Building bridges with communities

Within all we want to do and make possible for children there is a need to build bridges, to forge links within and between communities, and the work with grandmothers made it possible to involve the children in writing to family members wherever they were in the world. The messages, poems and stories that came back were of value. The children felt they and their languages, cultures and families were of use to the school. The indication was that those who came from a culture or society that was different from the norm could succeed. Schools need to be inclusive not exclusive wherever they are.

The importance of using stories, both fiction and non–fiction, that children can identify with is an essential element in building inclusivity within the curriculum. Inge Cramer (1997) emphasised this:

Children should be asked which stories they might like to tell; which they get told at home and so on. A teacher is thereby more likely to give every child a chance of bringing all their cultures into the classroom rather than simply replicating the almost inescapable dominant cultural messages offered by the choice of texts from publishers.

To involve children meaningfully in the education process, teachers must build the bridges that forge the links with pupil's extended families and the local community. Opportunities for both young and old have often been limited by their race, sex, cultural or religious background. Such barriers and limitations must be deplored and challenged. Wherever we are, we all need to have an ongoing commitment to ensure that all the children in our schools can grow up within a Europe where there is opportunity for all.

The Teacher Training Agency (TTA: UK Teacher Training Agency, 2000) gives a strong lead to teacher trainers in England on these issues. It outlines key priorities to be addressed by all those involved in training future teachers and those practitioners already working in classrooms. It offers detailed guidance on the areas of competence and the knowledge needed for those who care about the minority groups within our schools.

The TTA document states that:

- inequality can operate at institutional, structural, cultural and individual levels;
- prejudice and discrimination can affect the emotional, social and intellectual development of all pupils;
- inclusive schools respect the identities of their pupils, when taking account of a wide range of allegiances, and help pupils and teachers hold them in balance.

It goes on to identify particular priorities such as:

- because of mobility, some pupils, especially refugee pupils, asylum seekers, some Gypsy–Traveller pupils and some pupils with English as an additional language may need to become more familiar with school language, customs and rules or to experience what other pupils take for granted;
- policies within schools must recognise and respect the cultural experiences of all pupils, recognise the contribution to knowledge of a wide diversity of human groups, promote an understanding of cultural, religious and linguistic diversity.

These are fine ideas. They are achievable if the practice of educational inclusion does not depend solely upon the efforts of teachers. It requires commitment from policy makers across a range of institutions and contexts beyond the school gate. However as educators, wherever we are working, be it in Brno or Bradford, we do have a special responsibility to ensure that in our classroom practice, in the way schools are organised and in the way the curriculum is delivered, all children know that they are valued and respected.

One of our lasting memories was a young Roma woman's story. When asked by a researcher what her hopes for the future were, she said that she would like to be a waitress, adding that this would not be possible for 'Who would like to be served by a Roma? No one would employ me'. This starkly emphasised the perspectives under discussion at the conference and in this book. As educators our priority must be to celebrate and value the richness and diversity within humankind and to make a difference to the opportunities available for every individual in our care.

References

Blatchford–Siraj, I. & Clark, P. (2000). Supporting Identity, Diversity and Language in the Early Years. Oxford: Oxford University Press.

Corbett, J. & Slee, R. (2000). Inclusive Education Policy Contexts and Comparative Perspectives. London: David Fulton.

Cramer, I. (1997). Why you don't eat bananas: an exploration of a child's possible worlds in story. In E Gregory (ed.), One Child, Many Worlds. London: David Fulton.

UK Teacher Training Agency (2000). Raising the Attainment of Minority Ethnic Pupils. Publication number 114/5. London: Teacher Training Agency.

SECTION V

MULTICULTURALISM AND MULTICULTURAL EDUCATION

15. THE PROBLEM OF MULTICULTURAL SOCIETIES IN WESTERN AND EASTERN EUROPE

John Rex, University of Warwick, UK

Western Europe

Subnational Autonomy and Devolution

In western European societies there have been two problems of social integration. One is that of the coexistence of several geographically concentrated national units politically dominated by one of them. In Britain this is the problem of the existence within what is often called 'the United Kingdom' of Wales, Scotland and Northern Ireland. In Spain there are the Catalonian and Basque territories. The British and Spanish cases are the clearest of this kind but there are claims to separate nationhood by the occupants of distinguishable territories in most west European nation states. If the central national government is unable to impose its rule directly in these territories there is likely to be a political struggle in which the subordinate groups claim some degree of autonomy and the central government responds by proposing a degree of devolution. Obviously this problem has been dealt with most successfully and peacefully in the case of Wales, Scotland and Catalonia, whereas in the case of Ireland and the Basque country there has been armed conflict.[23]

Economic Migrants

Quite different from the problem of these territorially concentrated units seeking autonomy is the problem of integration posed by immigrant

---

[23] It is not possible in a short paper to deal with the detailed complexity of these problems. Two may be important. One is that the subordinate national minority might seek affiliation to a neighbouring territory as do the Republican Irish and the Basques. The other is that the central government is dominated by a national group which does not see its own existence as problematic until devolution to the subordinate nations raises the question of its own national rights. This seems to be the position of the English in Britain after devolution to Wales and Scotland.

minorities who are likely to be dispersed across the territory of the host nation and who have no interest in seeking autonomy. Western European governments have dealt with such groups in principle in four ways:

- they may seek to exclude them or expel them;
- they may demand their total assimilation organisationally and culturally to the host nation and their disappearance as separate units;
- they may be treated as denizens who live within the host society's territory but are denied the rights of citizens;
- they may be recognised as separate units within some kind of multicultural society.

Extreme host society nationalists advocate the first of these alternatives; the second is most widely accepted in France, the third in the German speaking countries. The multicultural alternative is thought of as having been pursued in various ways in the Netherlands, Sweden and the United Kingdom.

Types of Multiculturalism

Multiculturalism however may have several different forms divided broadly between those which involve unequal treatment for recognised minorities and those which combine the recognition of these minorities with a demand for equality for their members. It was this second type of multiculturalism which the British Home secretary, Roy Jenkins, referred to when he defined integration as involving 'cultural diversity, coupled with equal opportunity in an atmosphere of mutual tolerance' (Rex & Tomlinson, 1979). In supporting this type of multiculturalism I have suggested that it involves the recognition of two cultural domains or sets of values. On the one hand there is the set of values in the public domain based upon the idea of equal citizenship, on the other there is that of the values expressed in the cultures of separate ethnic communities.

So far as the first of these is concerned there is a limited conservative view which calls only for equal opportunity and a more radical view which calls for some degree of equality of outcome. The latter alternative is the one suggested by T. H. Marshall who suggests that the various institutions of the welfare state should guarantee a minimum standard for all citizens even if there is still inequality above this minimum (Marshall, 1951). So far as the second set of values is concerned the suggestion is that the private communal cultures of separate groups should be preserved through the continued use of mother tongues in private, through the continued practice of separate religions and through the preservation of domestic customs and family practices.

There are in fact many difficulties involved in sustaining this view of two sets of values or cultural domains within multiculturalism. Some will maintain that the public political culture should involve the universal assertion of human rights and that these apply within the separate ethnic minority cultures. Taking this further, some may insist upon the supremacy of the host society's language and religion. On the other hand some of the proponents of minority cultures may claim that their values should hold and their culture should be expressed in the public as well as in a private domestic and communal sphere. Moreover the educational system is concerned with both primary socialisation where it competes with minority cultures and with preparation for the more public world of the economy where it encourages individual rights and a concept of shared citizenship.

It should be clear from the last paragraph that there is no simple blueprint for a democratic and egalitarian multicultural society. The most which one might expect is some commitment both to the notion of the recognition of cultural diversity and to the creation of conditions of equal opportunity and to some extent equality of outcome. There may be some variety in the detailed ways in which these commitments are fulfilled and it is possible that within the detail the ideal commitments will be subverted.

Political Migrants

So far, however, we have dealt only with migrants whose primary reasons for migration are economic. Today, however, immigration by economic migrants has been halted except for family completion and the principle group of migrants are those seeking asylum or more generally escaping from political conditions in their homelands. These political migrants are subject to different constraints from those migrating for economic reasons. They may look forward to changed political conditions in their homelands which will permit their return in the near or more distant future; but they may have no hope of return and seek acceptance in their country of refuge. The receiving society will have policies which balance the obligation to provide immediate protection against the perceived undesirability of allowing political migrants to become economic migrants in disguise. In these circumstances refugees and other political migrants may be given only temporary status while being required to return to their homelands after a defined period or being given only what is called 'exceptional leave to remain' after such a period. On the other hand those who succeed in their claims to asylum may, after a further period, seek naturalisation, and with this, the normal rights of citizens in a democratic and egalitarian multicultural society.[24]

Jews and Roma

Two other problems might have to be faced in western European societies. The first is that there may be certain occupations which must be filled and

[24] There are extended discussions of these topics in my book Ethnic Minorities in the Modern Nations State (Rex, 1996).

certain tasks which must be performed which are at odds with the society's values. This leads to the existence of 'pariah' groups. On a macro scale Jews who engaged in money lending and some other commercial operations in the middle ages have represented such a group, but there are many other groups who fulfil pariah roles, such as those of landlords, even in modern societies. The second problem arises where and to the extent that there is a conflict between the cultural values of a group and those of modern industrial and democratic societies. Roma and Sami are often given as examples. There is very little empirical evidence about Roma values and how much they have changed and are changing, but what there is suggests that they are family based and may well have origins in India. Conflict with modern society would be consistent with a longterm history of exclusion and subsequent disadvantage. Clearly a full account of multicultural societies must deal with policies towards both pariah groups and these other groups. In the absence of such policies it is likely that there will be demands for their elimination. It has to be noted here that historically both Jews and Roma suffered a holocaust at the hands of the nazis.

Muslims in Western Europe

A final set of considerations applies to the position of Muslims in societies which are primarily Christian or secular. One extreme view which has been advanced by Huntington is that Muslims belong to a different civilizational period to that of western Europe, and that in this civilizational period the distinctions which we have made here between the two value domains do not apply. Again some are inclined to see all Muslims as 'fundamentalist' and incapable of moving flexibly between different roles in a modern society. On the other hand, there are clearly other trends amongst Muslim immigrants and other policies towards them advocated by some members of the host society. Many Muslims do in fact accept the idea of two coexisting value systems and the idea of equal citizenship in the welfare state, and there are those in the host society who accept the policy of making a place for Muslims within a multicultural society. While this is true, it is, however, the case that the integration of Muslims within predominantly Christian and secular society does pose special problems which have to be attended to.

Eastern Europe

There are two particular types of problem which arise in eastern European societies which make difficult the development of the notion of a fair egalitarian and democratic multicultural society. The first is that a number of these societies were previously part of the communist and Soviet Empire and when communist rule was overthrown had large Russian and Soviet settler populations. The new independent national governments therefore had to deal with a numerous minority population which had enjoyed numerous social and economic privileges and who certainly had not had to adapt to the rule of the indigenous people. This was the case in Ukraine, and particularly in the Baltic Republics and in Kazakhstan. Here these Russian minorities might have claimed a degree of territorial autonomy and devolution, or they might have claimed the right to recognition of their language and customs on an equal basis with those of the ruling indigenous minority. This, however, has not happened. Rather the new independent governments have insisted on the territorial unity of their states, have given the Russian language at best a subordinate role and have exercised centralised control of the schools. The result is that the Russian speaking minority feels itself culturally attached to Russia and the other former Soviet territories and, like Irish Republicans in Northern Ireland, feel themselves attached to neighbouring territories even though they have no prospect of returning there. Clearly this situation is not one that can be understood in terms of the theory of subnationalisms or immigration. Rather it has to be understood in terms of a theory of empire and postimperial situations (Rex, 2001).

The other problem which looms large in eastern Europe is that of the position of the Roma[25] within the separate nations and internationally across eastern and western Europe. There are no totally agreed statistics on the numbers of Roma, but a recent estimate in a British newspaper gives the following: Romania two and a half million; Spain eight hundred thousand; Hungary six hundred thousand; Bulgaria five hundred thousand; the Czech Republic, Slovakia and Yugoslavia each half a million, France and Russia, each one third of a million and the United Kingdom one hundred and fifty thousand.

Some Roma, as we suggested earlier, see themselves as having distinct values from those of modern industrial societies, whether of the capitalist or communist sort. Some of them are also Travellers. In the wake of communist rule, however, this kind of detachment from mainstream society no longer appears possible for many, and they may seek to gain equal rights to employment, housing and education. Roma politics therefore have an inherent ambiguity. They are based both upon a claim for Roma to be allowed to stay outside mainstream society if they so wish but to receive equal treatment if they wish to enter it.

Some Roma are Travellers, others are sedentary. There are also many groups of Travellers including some new ones, the New Age Travellers, who are not Roma. The different national and local governments also may have different policies to Roma and to Travellers. The result of this is that Roma in some countries see themselves as subject to racist

---

[25] The term Roma is used here as the one least likely to give offence to the groups involved. They are also commonly called 'Gypsies' or 'Tsigaan' but these terms are more likely to have a derogatory connotation.

attack, to oppression and to discrimination. They may well wish to move to countries where they are more favourably treated and may claim political asylum because of their well founded fear of persecution in their homelands. Governments in their chosen lands of refuge have almost universally refused to accept their claim to asylum while also lacking a clear policy towards Roma and Travellers in their own countries.

The problem of the position of Roma clearly has to be tackled on a European basis and the various European bodies, such as the European Union and the Council of Europe, have in theory addressed themselves to it. However it remains largely unsolved in practice and the Roma find themselves with few political friends. In the Czech Republic where Roma constitute one in thirty of the population this is one of the most important problems involved in any attempt to create a fair, egalitarian, multicultural society. At the same time the paradox of policy in the western countries is that, while they see themselves as having fairer policies towards Roma than do the Czechs and Slovaks, they are not prepared to accept them as asylum seekers.

References

Marshall, T. H. (1951). Citizenship and Social Class. Cambridge: Cambridge University Press.

Rex, J. (1996). Ethnic Minorities in the Modern Nation State. Basingstoke: MacMillan and NY: St Martin's Press.

Rex, J. (2001). The basic elements of a systematic theory of ethnic relations. Sociological Research Online, 6, 1, u36–u61.

Rex, J. & Tomlinson, S. (1979). Colonial Immigrants in a British City – a class analysis. London: Routledge and Kegan Paul.

16. HOW STUDENTS COMPREHEND HUMAN RIGHTS

Elena Ivanova
Kharkov State University, Ukraine[26]

Human rights is one of the key problems in the building of a democratic society, implying certain specific measures and steps on the part of the state, and of the citizens of the given society. The observance of human rights presupposes the people's common awareness of this problem, their knowledge of the mechanisms for its implementation, and the energy they invest in the issues in this arena. In this connection the development of the problem of perception of human rights in the post–Soviet Ukraine is up to date, urgent, and important, as for all the countries that are building a democratic society.

One of the tasks of contemporary Ukrainian society is the democratic education of young people, developing their consciousness of law. It means giving them knowledge of human rights and freedoms, and skills to observe them. In this perspective a special subject *Introduction to the Science of Law* has been introduced to the school curriculum. It is taught for one or two years in the tenth and eleventh grades of high schools, when students are about sixteen and seventeen years old. Of course our schools have no experience of this new subject, and they have had very little guidance about delivering it, and also we are without feedback on this teaching. Thus it is important to monitor the schools' success and failures in their task of developing consciousness of the rule of law. Similarly, there is no psychological literature regarding human rights, and we refer only to western publications (eg Diaz–Veizades et al., 1995; Helwig, 1995).

This empirical study focused mainly on school students' understanding and knowledge about human rights, their evaluations of the observation of

[26] Professor Ivanova's research was supported by the John D. and Catherine T. MacArthur Foundation.

human rights in Ukraine, their attitudes to it and sources of information about it, and prioritisation of rights.

Research design and sample

There is very little research into attitudes to human rights in Ukraine (Ivanova, 1996), and none that investigates urban and rural differences, even though the Ukrainian population is largely rural: an urban – rural comparison was therefore built into this investigation. The research was carried out in three regions of Ukraine: the central, the eastern and the western, which differ in their population structures, their economic development, political preferences, historical and cultural traditions and native language. The eastern part was most influenced by Russia. The native language of most people is Russian, and the political orientation is pro–Russian. The western part was absorbed into Soviet Ukraine and the USSR only in 1939, and has always seen a strong desire for a Ukrainian sovereign state, and strong recalcitrance against both Soviet and Russian influence. The language here is Ukrainian and a strong national and even nationalist movement continues. The central part is more moderate and less radical. It is also more rural with fewer opportunities for employment. It was included in the Soviet Union very soon after the 1917 Revolution, but in contrast to the eastern part of Ukraine, the central region has remained traditionally more Ukrainian regarding language, customs and cultural stereotypes.

The sample

The sample consisted of three hundred and fifty tenth and eleventh grade students (age about sixteen and seventeen) from urban and rural schools from these three regions of Ukraine. Half were from urban schools and half from rural ones, with equal proportion of males and females in each subsample.

Methods and procedure

We used three techniques, all specially developed for this research:

- **Incomplete sentences:** there were ten incomplete sentences to tap the students' abstract understanding of human rights and freedoms, and their understanding as shown in practical examples of individual people's rights, their attitudes to human rights, and understanding of conditions for their observance and infringement.
- **Questionnaires:** One questionnaire consists of multiple choice questions on observance of human rights in Ukraine, the possibility of defence in case of infringement, the respondents' estimation of their own knowledge of human rights, their the sources of information on human rights and their views about ways of improving human rights protection. The second questionnaire deals with the individual

students' experiences of human rights violations in their own lives and in public life, and the responsibility for these violations.

- **Ranking Rights:** Respondents ranked twenty human rights and freedoms, including civil, political, economic, social and cultural rights and freedoms, according to the degree of importance he or she attached to them.

The young people completed the sentences, questionnaires and ranking in their classes. There were four order variants to maintain the integrity of individuals' views. All the received data were subjected to statistical processing with the help of the software package SPSS, the significance of differences was considered by F–criterion.

Analysis of data

Satisfaction with human rights in Ukraine

One third of the whole sample consider the situation with human rights in Ukraine to be unsatisfactory and only six per cent satisfactory. Although they were required to make this evaluation, less than a half of the students could give a definite answer about whether they were satisfied or dissatisfied, see Table 1. Students in the eastern and central rural schools were most satisfied, in comparison to city schools and western village schools.

Table 1: Students' satisfaction, human rights in Ukraine: (% sample for each place)

	East		Centre		West	
	Kharkov city	Eastern village	Poltava city	Central village	Lvov city	Western village
Satisfied	1,7	11,7	6,6	7,8	5,0	5,0
Partly satisfied	40,0	51,7	39,3	54,9	30,0	36,7
Dissatisfied	40.0	23.3	39,3	27,5	46,7	30,0
Cannot answer	18,3	13,3	14,8	9,8	18,3	28,3

Effective means of redress

These adolescent students in our sample were very uncertain that there would be an effective means of defending their rights if they were violated (Table 2). More than a half of the sample either answer that they cannot be defended, or are unsure ('Don't know'). The relative contrast between the rural areas and the east on the one hand, where there is more satisfaction, and the cities and the west on the other is again clear in Table 2:

Table 2: Possibility of defending rights if violated
(% of sample for each place)

	Eastern		Central		Western	
	Kharkov	Village	Poltava	Village	Lvov	Village
Yes	28,3	50,0	23,0	27,5	25,0	26,7
No	40,0	15,0	29,5	47,1	23,3	18,3
Don't know	31,7	35,0	47,5	25,5	51,7	55,0

Methods of improving human rights

We asked the students to choose between the following six methods of improving the human rights situation in the Ukraine: improvement of laws; prosecution of guilty officials; accessibility of legal help; more effective human rights legal protection; promotion of the development of non–governmental human rights protection organizations; active assertion of one's own rights. Responses showed high proportions in the west and in the central village trusting prosecution of guilty officials as the best means of bringing about improvement, while students in the eastern city and the western village felt that individuals had to fight for their own rights. Universally, there is little faith in improving legal defence, and there is open scepticism about the value of promoting human rights NGOs. Students in villages more than those in cities believe that improving the laws will be effective.

Table 3: Trust in measures to improve human rights protection
(% each place)

	Eastern		Central		Western	
	Kharkov	Village	Poltava	Village	Lvov	Village
Better laws	18,3	38,3	16,4	31,4	20,0	23,3
Prosecute suspect officials	18,3	21,7	29,5	45,1	36,7	28,3
Defence by lawyers	18,3	6,7	9,8	9,8	20,0	21,7
Effective protection	8,3	6,7	13,1	15,7	15,0	5,0
Rights NGOs	6,7	6,7	8,2	0	8,3	8,3
Actively assert own rights	30,0	21,7	24,6	17,6	21,7	33,3

Knowledge and sources of information about human rights

Regarding human rights violated and observed, more than one third of the school students answered that they do not know which rights are violated.

They answer: 'All the rights' or 'Almost all'. Even more students could not answer which rights are observed. They answer that they cannot reply because they do not know what kinds of human rights exist. However, they are inconsistent in that at the same time only 14.7% students evaluate their knowledge of human rights as 'bad'.

Thus, another group of data are connected with the students' evaluation of their knowledge about human rights, sources of information available to them, and their opinion about their own rights have been ever broken. Since this is a new topic in our country, the large number of students (52.5% of the total sample – Table 4, "Not well") who evaluate their knowledge of human rights as poor may be reassuringly realistic: it seems to show that the new generation are open to change. However, the many students who believe that they have good knowledge of human rights are shown to be naïve by their answers to many other questions, which demonstrate poor understanding of the issues. This naïvité is also reflected in the fact that only half of students believe their human rights were ever broken, which seems unlikely in a state with a very recent totalitarian history.

Table 4: Students' evaluation of their own knowledge of rights
(% each place)

	Eastern		Central		Western	
	Kharkov city	Village	Poltava city	Village	Lvov city	Village
Well	35,0	45,0	55,7	17,6	23,3	15,0
Not well	55,0	41,7	41,0	72,5	50,0	55,0
Badly	10,0	13,4	3,3	9,8	26,7	30,0

Mass media is a very big source of information in the villages (with families providing information as well), and in the central city, Poltava, while students in the eastern and central city say they use legal literature, presumably referring to material they are given in school (see Table 5). An interestingly high proportion of students in the west (city and village) believe they receive no information at all, in spite of the new courses I referred to above. Again this suggests their openness to more and better teaching.

Table 5: Sources of information on rights protection
(% of respondents)

	East		Center		Western	
	Kharkov city	Village	Poltava city	Village	Lvov city	Village
Legal literature	38,3	13,3	44,3	19,6	20,0	16,7
Mass media	21,7	38,3	39,3	39,2	26,7	38,3
Family	21,7	26,7	1,6	43,1	25,0	28,3
Lawyers	1,7	10,0	3,3	3,9	5,0	0
H Rights NGOs.	0	1,7	1,6	3,9	0	3,3
Others	15,0	10,0	14,8	9,8	13,3	11,7
No information	5,0	1,7	1,6	2,0	13,3	16,7

Ranking human rights (data not included)

When ranking the twenty civil, economic, political and social rights and freedoms, most students value most highly the rights for freedom and for privacy. The least important are the right to participate in the activities of any political party, the right of absence of ethnic discrimination and the right to practice any religion. There is a tendency for students in the central region to value the rights to work, for education and for health insurance more highly, probably because of more unemployment in this more rural part of Ukraine, but on the other hand, these priorities of rights are similar in urban and rural students.

Semantic analysis of 'uncompleted sentences' technique showed that the emotional attitude of these students to human rights can be defined as uninterested. They consider the rights to be concepts existing only on paper, having nothing to do with real life. This, together with their low prioritising of religion and of the rights of ethnic minorities, leads us to agree with Ruck et al. (1998) who argue that what adolescents and children think about rights appears to be influenced by how they view rights in their own lives – these students tended not to have experience of ethnic minorities, and had little experience of religion. On the other hand, the majority of students do understand human rights as separate freedoms (of actions, decisions, speech, thoughts, and so on). This can be considered as one of the first steps in development of their consciousness of the rule of law.

Summary:
Critical of human rights standards

My evidence is that throughout Ukraine, students in tenth and eleventh grade (UK Further Education) are critical of the human rights situation in our country, especially students in the western region and students in urban areas (Table 1).

Defence of own human rights

Approximately one third of students say that they do not know how to defend their human rights. Eastern students and rural students are most optimistic about this (Table 2). This greater confidence may arise from lack of awareness and lack of experience of the situation, as is also suggested by the fact that students in the west tend, probably realistically, to evaluate their knowledge as poor. Lack of the students' awareness and experience is also reflected in the sentence completion tasks.

Improving human rights

Students of the different regions have different views about most important measures for improving human rights protection. Rural students and especially eastern students trust improvement of legislation. Rural students and those in the western city also believe in prosecution of officials. Rural students from the western region believe more in asserting their own rights than their peers from the central and eastern regions. But students in all regions, rural and city, distrust NGOs and many distrust lawyers (Table 3).

Information on human rights

Regarding sources of information, mass media are the main source in all regions, followed by the family in the west and legal literature in the east the Centre. Legal literature is also used more by urban students: by this we believe they mean literature they receive through the new school courses. Only western students say they get no information on rights protection. Again human rights NGOs are universally distrusted: they are ranked lowest as sources of information (Table 5).

Prioritisation of human rights

Students from all parts of Ukraine value most highly rights for freedom and for privacy, and have no wish for political or religious activity, or to defend ethnic minorities. Students in the more rural centre of the country where unemployment is higher tend to prioritise economic and health rights.

Significance of regional differences

So students' prioritisation of human rights reflects their own situations, with employment related rights important in the more rural centre where unemployment is high, and with no students aware of issues connected with ethnic minorities or with religion.

The various regional differences described above are significant. Consistently students in the west of Ukraine are more sceptical about human rights in the country: they seem to be more aware of inadequacies in our human rights situation and are also more realistic about their own lack of understanding and experience. On the other hand, the majority of Ukrainian students do understand human rights as separate freedoms (of actions, decisions, speech, thoughts, and so on). This can be considered as one of the first steps in development of their consciousness of the rule of law.

New subject: Introduction to the science of law

Thus the new subject: *Introduction to the Science of Law* is a first step. But we have a grave need for better teaching methods, textbooks and other materials, both to support the awareness of students who recognise the needs for improvements in national human rights practice and in their own knowledge of human rights, and to develop conciousness in the students who are, understandably, less sophisticated.

References

Diaz–Veizades, J., Widaman, K., Little, T. & Gibbs, K. (1995). The measurement and structure of human rights attitudes. The Journal of Social Psychology, 135, 3, 313–328.

Helwig C. (1995). Adolescents' and young adults' conceptions of civil liberties: freedom of speech and religion. Child Development, 66, 1, 152–166.

Ivanova, E. (1996). Attitudes to Human Rights in Ukraine. Paper presented at the European Congress of Psychology, Dublin, Republic of Ireland.

Ruck, M., Keating, P., Abramovitch, R. & Koegl, C. (1998). Adolescents' and children's knowledge about rights: some evidence for how young people view rights in their own lives. Journal of Adolescence, 21, 275–289.

17. A TEACHERS' TRAINING COLLEGE AS A JOINT FRAMEWORK FOR DRUZE AND JEWS

Zipora Oshrat and Judith Lapidot–Berman,
Gordon College of Education, Haifa, Israel

Background and previous research

The Israeli education system maintains separate programs for Jews (the majority) Arabs, and Druze (minorities). Thus, youth of different ethnic groups meet only during their last stages of adolescence, at a stage when their views and attitudes are already formed. Relationships between young Jews, Arabs and Druze are rare, so that the intercultural knowledge they have of each other is based mainly on information from the media. The images they have are mostly composed of stereotypes, and are influenced by prejudices about the other group from indirect sources, rather than as a result of personal acquaintance.

In some respects Druze are treated as an integral part of the Arab minority, but in other respects, as a separate group. This may be due to the fact that Druze, unlike Arabs, serve in the Israeli army. Unlike Druze students who have some knowledge about Jewish life style, Jewish students have only a vague idea about Druze culture.

Previous studies conducted in Israel have investigated perceptions Jews have of Arabs and vice versa, but no similar studies were carried out regarding the Druze minority.

The present research was conducted at a Teachers' Training College. Jews and Druze who major in fields such as literature and grammar study in separate study programs, referred to as homogeneous study groups. Those who major in subjects such as science and mathematics study in integrated programs, referred to as heterogeneous study groups. The students remain in these frameworks for four successive years, and interact at various intergroup and interpersonal levels. Therefore the college serves as an appropriate setting to monitor and examine change and resistance processes in relation to attitudes and relationships between the two ethnic groups.

Several issues were investigated in this study:
1. Are there differences between the students in the homogeneous and in the heterogeneous programs with regard to:

- the nature of the characteristics which each ethnic group attributes to the other?
- the willingness to form social relationships with the other ethnic group?
- the extent of intercultural knowledge, that is knowledge which each ethnic group has about the heritage of the other?

2. To what extent do the Druze attribute characteristics to the Jews in symmetrical ways, and vice versa?
Symmetrical consideration (Schwartzwald & Yinon, 1978) is defined as a situation in which members of a certain group perceive themselves exactly as they perceive the members of the other group.

3. What is the contribution of a preplanned intervention?
What effect has intervention such as a meeting in a Druze village between the two homogeneous groups, on the views and knowledge about each other?

Sample
Four hundred and seven student teachers at a Teachers' Training College took part in the investigation. All were women. Two hundred and forty five were Jews and one hundred and sixty two were Druze. Two hundred and nine of the sample were in heterogeneous and one hundred and ninety eight in homogeneous study programs.

A three part questionnaire was developed for the purpose of this study. The questions dealt with: (a) attribution of characteristics; (b) willingness to establish friendly relationships and (c) knowledge about the heritage of the other ethnic group. The questionnaire was completed anonymously by each student, once in relation to her own ethnic group and once in relation to the other ethnic group. Students participating in the Druze village meeting completed the questionnaire prior to and after the meeting.

Results and Discussion
1. Differences between the students in the homogeneous and in the heterogeneous programs
(i) Findings indicate that Druze students of the heterogeneous groups attributed more positive traits to Jewish students than do Druze students of the homogeneous groups. Among the Jewish students such differences were not found. It appears that the intensive interaction between Druze and Jews in the heterogeneous groups explains the above findings. The daily contact

in the same study setting enables Druze students to know Jewish students on a more individual basis, and to form their views and attitudes not only on the basis of stereotypes and prejudice.

(ii) No differences were found between the homogeneous and heterogeneous groups in regard to the willingness to establish friendly relationships with members of the other ethnic group. It appears that this sort of interaction in not enough to motivate willingness for social relationships. Perhaps a heterogeneous study setting in an earlier age could lead to different results. In addition, initiating more intensive interaction, such as demanding more cooperation between students from the two ethnic groups in project work, may lead to more friendly approaches.

(iii) Findings indicate that the knowledge about Jewish heritage by Druze students who studied in the heterogeneous group is significantly greater than that of Druze students from the homogeneous group. This knowledge was not due to a preplanned intervention, but probably was a result of the ongoing contact between students from both ethnic groups.

2. Symmetry in attribution of characteristics

The results also indicate considerable difference in the knowledge students of each ethnic group have, on subjects related to the heritage of the other ethnic group. The Druze gave on average seventy percent correct answers to questions dealing with the Jewish heritage, while the Jews gave only forty percent correct answers to questions dealing with the Druze heritage.

In analyzing the extent of the symmetry in trait attribution, a clear interaction was observed: an overwhelming majority of the Druze, ninety five percent, attributed more positive traits to themselves than to the Jews, while most of the Jews (sixtyfive per cent) attributed more positive traits to the Druze. Only a minority (four per cent of the Jews and one per cent of the Druze) has expressed a symmetrical evaluation. Tajfel (1981) notes that people tend to present an extremely exaggerated positive social identity especially when they experience a threat to their group identity (usually the identity of the minority group) by the other group (usually the identity of the majority group). Regarding these findings, it is possible to understand the clear asymmetry, which is expressed by the traits that the Druze attribute to the Jews and to themselves. As members of a minority group, whose language and appearance differ from that of the majority, it is reasonable that they feel uncomfortable and this spurs them to present themselves in an extremely positive light. This may result from a defence mechanism that serves the minority group. On the other hand, the fact that most of the Jews attribute to the Druze more positive traits is surprising and possibly expresses the Jews' social desirability, presenting themselves as having no prejudice and racist perceptions.

3. Contribution of preplanned intervention

Attempts to encourage friendly relationships between the two different ethnic groups were made by arranging a meeting. Jews and Druze from homogeneous study frame works met in a Druze village and attended lectures given by key figures in the Druze community. The only variable indicating a change following the meeting was Jewish students' knowledge about the heritage of the Druze.

The lack of change in attributing traits to members of the other ethnic group and also in the willingness to establish friendly relationships with them (above 1 (ii)) can be explained on the basis of reports made by other researchers. Amir and Ben–Ari (1987) as well as Cook (1978) note the knowledge factor about the other's heritage as a significant factor in establishing interethnic relationships, but not sufficient in order to establish close and deep relationships between ethnic groups.

Conclusions

It seems that processes that influence the mutual perception of students from different ethnic groups who study together are very slow. They take place mainly at the declarative level, act to a very small extent at the knowledge level and are hardly expressed at the behavioural level. It may be that in order to create a change in the willingness to establish friendly relationships between the groups, more meaningful interventions should be made, preferably at an early age, at earlier stages of personal development when personal perceptions are not yet fully shaped.

References

Amir, I. & Ben–Ari, R. (1987). Meetings between Jewish and Arab youth in Israel – reality and potential. Megamot, 30, 3, 305–315. (Hebrew).

Cook, S.W. (1978). The systematic analysis of socially significant events: a strategy of social research. Journal of Social Issues, 18, 66–84.

Schwartzwald, I. & Yinon, I. (1978). Symmetry and asymmetry in inter–ethnic perceptions. Megamot, 24, 45–52. (In Hebrew).

Tajfel, H. (1981). Human Groups and Social Categories: studies in social psychology. Cambridge: Cambridge University Press.

18. COMMUNITY ORGANISATION: A HUMAN RIGHTS APPROACH FROM THE 'BOTTOM UP'

Clare Beckett and Maggie Pearse
University of Bradford and Bradford Community College, UK

Introduction

One argument in the British House of Lords[27] refusal of asylum to the Horvath family, who claimed to have fled racist persecution in Slovakia, was that no state can ensure freedom from persecution for all communities within it. If state action alone cannot mend division within society, then other avenues must be recognised and strengthened. Our argument is that community organisation and education are fundamental processes in supporting human rights and countering community division. Structural inequality continues, and unequal resource allocation perpetuates social division, but there is a vital place for support and education programs that enable community actions to counter negative stereotypes. Our experience is from working within British communities, and from sociology and social policy. We advocate resource allocation by the state with funding to, and respect for, individual communities.

In this paper, we use case studies to examine how a 'bottom up' organisation confronts intercommunity labelling and encourages community cohesiveness and active social participation. We advocate a new role for community workers, with the focus of human rights within the community group, encouraged by flexible but peripheral support from professionals. The common factor in our studies is that members of the community act as agents of change, with professional community organisers and formal education remaining on the sidelines, members of a different social group, to be used when and how community members request. In practice, this watching brief is difficult to pursue and to resource.

---

[27] BBC News discussion, 6 July 2000. Case decision 13 July 2000.

Community organisation in practice.

Case Study 1:[28] Bradford's Bangladeshi community

Less than one per cent[29] of the large Asian population of Bradford are of Bangladeshi origin, thus numerically and politically at a disadvantage while sharing a common religion with the larger Pakistani community. They live close to the city centre, in an area known as the 'Cornwalls'. The men are now predominantly employed in local restaurants, but older people entered England before 1975, to work in the textile industry.

The Bangladeshi Youth Organisation (BYO) was set up in the nineteen seventies by UK born, English speaking young people, to provide social and welfare support for their older people who often had no English. Depending on immigration status, many elderly had no access to welfare benefits when nineteen eighties recession and unemployment hit the textile industry. Young people used formal welfare provision for their extended family. In learning to manoeuvre around that system, they developed skills of presentation and articulation that could be supported through formal education: some are now professionally qualified themselves. Our role was to facilitate contact between members of the community, and to provide the practical resources needed to understand and use the benefit system.

The BYO identified three major community needs, and solutions:

1. Obtaining food that was familiar to Bangladeshi elders, but which British shops saw as part of a stigmatised culture. The group established allotments, where elders and women, who often came from a rural background, could grow and sell traditional vegetables.

2. Access to computers and homework space for children, to break down perceptions of different ability in the classroom. The organisation established a homework scheme in the local community centre.

3. Specialist housing, Apart from health and safety issues, the multi-occupation and disrepair of many houses in the 'Cornwalls' added to local perception of a deprived community. The City Council opted not to provide grants after 1985. Bangladeshi families wanted to stay near to their community in larger inner city houses, with culturally appropriate bathroom and kitchen facilities: council houses on estates did not appeal. The BYO helped to establish Manningham Housing Association, using government funds with community control to build and renovate homes. Once houses were available, the group worked to create an area with an ethnic and cultural mix, vetting potential tenants for both housing need, and suitability for a racially and culturally diverse setting.

---

[28] We would like to thank the current organisers of the BYO for their permission to write up this experience

[29] 1991 Census figures

The stereotype of the Bangladeshi community as small and insular, reliant on central government welfare, has been reversed. The area has a vibrant community, looking to support its own needs and to provide housing and support to others.

Case study 2: Five women's lives

A group of two Scottish and three Irish women lived on an all white council estate. They were friends, two married, one widowed, and two divorced. Four of the five had large families. They were marginalised on the estate because, according to a common English stereotype of Irish and Scots, they were perceived as 'loud' (drinking, singing, swearing and argumentative). The criminal behaviour of some of their children, including adult children, added to community perceptions.

The women were individually invited to join a literacy class run by adult education on the estate. Over time, the role of the class and the community tutor became one of facilitation. The group stayed together for approximately ten years, examining their lives individually and as a marginalised minority. They used oral exchange (taped interviews of reminiscence, childhood songs) and photography. This exploration of their common culture and heritage, particularly through photography, was a new skill. They developed the work into a travelling exhibition, *Five Women's Lives*, that toured Britain and was well received by local and national media.

On a personal level, the women found new interests which moved them from seeing every day incidents as isolated an individual, and new skills such as public speaking and dealing with media. They developed a sense of value in their own community and culture, and became more involved in other initiatives. The youngest woman qualified as a youth and community worker. They helped raise funds, plan and manage a purpose built community centre, and were pivotal in activities like forming a local credit union.

On a cross community[30] level, their own development challenged the stereotypes held by other families on the estate. They were seen to move from dependency and marginalisation, to a point where their actions and opinions were sought and respected. This personal challenge to others' stereotypes was supported by increased knowledge of the differences and similarities between their experiences as an ethnic and cultural minority, and those of women from the majority community. The process both strengthened awareness of the value of actual differences, and blurred awareness of perceived differences in both local and national arenas.

---

[30] While Cockburn (1998), among others, uses this term to describe specific work across the Irish 'peace line', we use it more generally to describe any work across community borders.

Discussion

In Case Study 1, professionals from college were peripheral to the community organisation, but their support and resource role was central. With the Five Women, a community education tutor at Bradford College was a catalyst through the literacy class, after which the professional role became resource based. Common to these disparate groups is a determination to change their own situation: both organised collectively and cooperatively around a set of principles determined by themselves. In both, ownership and achievement are at the heart of a 'bottom up' approach to community organising, and hold the key to destabilising stereotypes and disadvantage (Batten & Batten, 1967). The professionals were supportive and available with their flexible, resource based service. The salutary part of our role was that any attempt to lead or to force the pace was counter-productive! This involves personal as well as academic acceptance of human rights as including the right to selfdetermination.

Ownership of their projects gave both groups the confidence to move into the mainstream of community work. As well as the Manningham Housing Association, the BYO went on to help manage the Bradford Law Centre. The 'Five Women' helped change both the experience, and the public perceptions of living on housing estates. Both groups reacted to their own needs, and in doing so extended to change the community in general.

Context and Theory

Access to employment is crucial to people's ability to participate in many of the economic and social opportunities of society. Inequality in access to jobs contributes substantially to poverty and social exclusion, with debilitating effects on the morale, health, family status, and even social networks of individuals and communities (Gordon & Pantazis, 2000 p. 59).

We dispute the assumption that the welfare system and equal opportunities legislation reduce social divisions: action from government needs to be understood in a context of community and group pressure for resources. For example, in Britain, government resources make up the major source of housing, education, social services, and health care, but they are not received equally by all communities or individuals: there are differences in access within as well as between race, class, gender and geographic groups. Further, over time and generations, structural and perceived inequalities change disproportionately. Currently, different communities and geographic areas, including both in our case studies, lose out differentially far more than in most of Britain, thus a stereotype of disadvantage has been generated for the areas.

Institutions and individuals help form and destabilise stereotypes and therefore oppression. We use Paolo Freire's (1970) model of education – coming from and being for the people. We believe 'bottom up' organisation, as in the network of community groups which make up informal education, is a prerequisite of intercommunity tolerance, and support for human rights.

To label (Becker, 1963) a group is to identify it in the positioning process which is part of the struggle for resources. Thus to label is to control, through state action and personal interaction. In our examples, the terms 'Bangladeshi' or 'Irish' were used to allocate formal services like housing, and to create informal divisions in popular perception. Further, any identified group can be perceived as a threat, as in Cohen's (1985) model of moral panic, and social division becomes inevitable: thus our Irish families were perceived as a threat to public order. Axiomatic to this process is that disproportionate value is given to perceived community behaviours, while actual community behaviours are unvalued: a group may be perceived as dangerous while performing activities that are not only unthreatening but are culturally valid and reasonable when seen more rationally. For example, Irish women found digging for potatoes among the estate rubbish were seen as threatening rather than hungry, and Bangladeshi community members choosing to live in run down housing as 'difficult' rather than as trying to maintain community links.

Formal and informal education must challenge such perceptions by helping stigmatised groups, who cannot alone alter the competitive barriers for resources that arise where action is only from a central state. However, awareness of difference, and the value of identity, can and must be strengthened at the community level to ensure a just society. Every individual and every institution shares the responsibility of raising awareness of and valuing actual difference, while countering stereotypes and assumptions about other communities.

Conclusion

On the basis of our experience, we suggest four ways to stop the erosion of human rights.

- Community organisers should use their resource base and skills to help specific groups to help themselves in the unequal battle for resources.
- Only community members understand community priorities regarding needs and activities: outsiders cannot recognise the value of the cultural experience of a stigmatised group. Communities themselves must value their own culture as well as it be valued by others.
- We must also work with the prejudiced to counter prejudice and oppression. All actions and interactions reflect a hierarchy of power and government equal opportunities policy is only meaningful if carried through at a community level.
- Inequality in education will continue until all service personel question stereotypes and counter assumptions on a daily basis.

We finish on a note of hope. The community itself, supported by strong state direction and finance, is a powerful force for social justice and human rights. Community action has and will continue to achieve tolerance and peace between communities.

References

Batten, T. R. & Batten, M. (1967). The Non–Directive Approach in Group and Community Work. London: Oxford University Press.

Becker, H. S. (1963). Outsiders: studies in the sociology of deviance. New York: Free Press of Glencoe London: Collier–Macmillan.

Cockburn, C. (1998). The Space between Us: negotiating gender and national identities in conflict. London and New York: Zed Books.

Cohen, A. (1985). The Symbolic Construction of Community. Chichester: Ellis Horwood

Freire, P. (1970). The Pedagogy of the Oppressed. Harmondsworth: Penguin Books

Gordon, D. & Pantazis, C. (2000). Tackling Inequalities. London: The Polity Press.

19. CULTURAL SYMBOLISM AND THE INTEGRATION AND EDUCATION OF DIFFERENT COMMUNITIES

Krystyna Węgłowska–Rzepa and Jolanta Kowal,
University of Wrocław, Poland

Introduction

In Poland, our largest minorities are Belorussians, Roma, Lithuanians, German, Ukrainians and Jews. The System of Education Act 1991 and the Ministry of Education Decree 1992 regulate the education of minorities and preserve minority pupils' sense of national, ethnic, and language identity. Minority languages can be taught, at parental request, at kindergartens, Basic[31] and secondary schools. The following arrangements are allowed: schools with a minority language as language of instruction; bilingual schools; additional study of the mother tongue at Polish schools, or at classes for groups of schools. The schools which teach pupils in their mother tongue also supplement standard lessons in history and geography with material about the pupils' country of origin. The decision whether to introduce such changes is devolved onto the individual schools, which also issue bilingual certificates. Some schools even teach ethnic languages and local dialects (Janowski, 1995).

The lifestyle of Roma children can challenge conventional educational methods, for example, by frequent journeys and older daughters caring for their young siblings. Also, as in many countries, Roma probably suffer most social ostracism, which the Polish pupils bring into school. Two educational programs for Roma children interestingly compare approaches to minority education. In the first program to prepare pupils for school, which gained full certification from the Ministry (Nowicka, 1998), the syllabus covered such basic topics as hygiene, personal property rules, respect for green areas, pets, plants and classroom equipment, reading, Polish history etc. This knowledge based program simply introduced children to Polish basic education. It failed to win acceptance from Roma people. However, the Roma class in Olsztyn (Bułatek, 1996) to which the Ministry allowed only

---

[31] See Glossary, p.195, this volume for description of school structure which had similarities in various east central European countries.

temporary, qualified certification, was more successful. To accommodate late bedtimes, classes started with school lunch at noon and lasted four hours. The two women teachers, one Pole and one Roma, both accepted unorthodox behaviour: walking around during the lesson, humming, going out for a smoke, and frequent absence. They countered their Polish students' disdain for the weak academic skills of many Roma children and encouraged them to see the unique Roma culture and language. Soon this class gained full Ministry certification: attendance was good, loss of books and conflicts were few. Roma and Polish pupils played together, Roma pupils started to request homework, and they prepared their own artistic programs.

Thus we must embrace culturally unique elements and promote their positive content and values. One way to do this is through cultural symbolism (Dyczewski, 1993; Moven, 1995; Sobol, 1993).

Cultural symbolism

Fromm classifies symbols three ways: conventional, accidental, and universal. Words are the best example of conventional symbols:

the only reason why this word symbolises that object is the convention by which we give particular objects their unique names (Fromm, 1994 p.18).

Symbols of the second kind, accidental symbols, also have no inner relationship with the objects they symbolise. This kind of symbol relies on personal experience, which makes it the symbol of a particular mood. The third kind of symbol, the universal symbol, exhibits an inner relationship with the object it symbolises: we have the feeling of near integration of emotions and reasoning on the one hand, and sensual experiences on the other. These symbols can involve all people; basically, they are the only universal language developed by the human race.

Cultures, including elitist, popular and youth culture (Filipiak, 1996), have different visions of the world in which the same material and immaterial products carry different significance (Kryszewski, 1993). Such products are typically transferred to members of respective societies by means of symbols (Levy, 1981; Mowen, 1995). Thus communities have rich forms and meanings laid down sometimes over millenia, in the arts, mythology, rituals, as well as in national holidays, dress code, food, everyday forms of addressing people, and even in dreams. Symbols can help cope with dark sides of the human psyche and can give purpose to our lives (Brun, Pederson & Runberg, 1995; Jacobi, 1993; Levy, 1981; Prieur, 1982; Samuels, Shorter & Plaut, 1995).

Education workshops employing cultural symbolism: Who are we?

Using cultural symbolism in workshops with young children and adolescents can decrease stereotyping through knowledge about other communities, and can create the category 'We', in addition to that of 'I – You'.

Our cycle of fortnightly meetings are devoted to the role of symbols in culture and in everyday life, from getting to know one another to throwing the final party. They last one school semester, about one hour per meeting, and are as follows:

- *Let's meet:* the leader introduces him or herself, some relevant problems are aired, and the children introduce themselves verbally or through drawings.
- *Participation in the group:* these activities help children experience happier contacts with the children from the other minority group, and learn what the mixed group means for themselves and for the school, also what friendship means in terms of normal expectations between friends, and in what ways the common rules and norms help in the mutual contacts.
- *Cooperation:* the objective here is to provide experiences which would bring about the feeling of one's own value which stems from the affiliation to the group and the feeling of satisfaction with working together and helping friends.
- *Symbols in culture and in everyday life:* the aim is to explain to the students what a symbol means, its role in human life and the forms in which it appears.

Students now:

- learn about **similarities and differences between people, nations and cultures** and they try to express them by means of symbols;
- **tell their stories and the stories of their families**, bring in family souvenirs and symbols;
- **prepare legends, fairy tales and stories** with regard to a particular nation;
- **search for symbols** specific to a given minority group and symbols which are shared by more than one minority, or with the majority;
- **refer to religious symbols** and decode their meanings;
- **invite guests** – people they know and parents who are the representatives of the minorities;
- **build the history of their own group** and elaborate the symbolic drawing, for example the emblem of the group.

5. Final activities – recapitulation and plans; an artistic evening and a meal together
The above cycle took place several times in the 1990s in the area of Wrocław, southwest Poland. We witnessed the following effects:

- Full imaginative play between pupils of different ethnicities, including Roma pupils. This play extended the young students' awareness and understanding of the symbols of the other cultures.

- Open discussion of inter–ethnic problems, including by pupils as young as first grades of Basic school.
- The development of friendships out of school, including visits to each others' homes, between majority and minority pupils. Several Roma children were included in such friendships with majority children.
- Cooperation between majority and minority parents, particularly in contributing to our final parties.

Effects such as these, after only a year of working with the students, were obviously very interesting and worth continuing (see Weigl & Maliszkiewicz, 1998 for report of longer program). The contents of the courses should be adjusted according to the specific conditions existing in a given environment; also, personnel should be properly trained and support from the local authorities granted.

Conclusion

The issues discussed in this paper have educational value for a very broad band of children and adolescents, if we bear in mind that modern technology is instrumental in replacing individual consciousness (reasoning, feeling, imagination, decision making) with the modern collective consciousness provided by the virtual worlds of mass media. On the other hand, helping children and young people both to understand how symbolism works, and to recognise the symbols of their own culture and the cultures with which they co–habit, is an important service which can increase just, peaceful settlement in whole nations. If we turn towards symbols present in traditional as well as contemporary cultures and decipher their meanings, we will be better prepared consciously to take decisions in our lives and to help others with their lives.

References

Brun, B., Pedersen, E. W., & Runberg, M. (1995). Symbole duszy. Warszawa: Jacek Santorski.

Bułatek, M. (1996). Cygańska klasa. Problemy opiekuńczo–wychowawcze, 2, 14–16.

Dyczewski, L. (1993). Wartości w kulturze polskiej. Lublin: Wydawnictwo Fundacji Szkołom Polskim na Wschodzie im. T. Goniewicza.

Filipiak, M. (1996). Socjologia kultury: zarys zagadnień. Lublin, Wydawnictwo Uniwerystetu Marii Curie–Skłodowskiej.

Fromm, E. (1994). Zapomniany język. wstęp do rozumienia snów. baśni i mitów. Warszawa: PWN.

Jacobi, J. (1993). Psychologia C. G. Junga. Warszawa: Wydawnictwo Wodnika.

Janowski, A. (1995). Szkolnictwo dla mniejszości: skromny fragment systemu. Społeczeństwo otwarte, 2, 25–33.

Kryszewski, W. (1993). Encyklopedia powszechna. Warszawa: PWN.

Levy, S. J. (1981). Interpreting consumer mythology: a structural approach to consumer behaviour, Journal of Marketing, 45, 3, 49–61.

Minister of National Education Decree 24 03 (1992). Concerning organization of education which would preserve the national, ethnic and language identity of pupils belonging to national minorities, Journal of Law, 34, item 150.

Moven, C. J. (1995). Consumer Behavior. New Jersey: Prentice Hall.

Nowicka, E. (1998). O naprawie systemu oświatowego w Polsce. Dzieci romskie w szkole. Społeczeństwo otwarte, 5, 28–31.

Prieur, J. (1982). Les Symboles Universeles. Paris: Editions Fernand Lanore.

Samuels, A., Shorter, B. & Plaut, F. (1995). Krytyczny słownik analizy Jungowskiej. Wrocław: Oficyna Wydawnicza UNUS.

Sobol, E. (1993). Mały słownik języka polskiego. Warszawa: PWN.

Weigl, B. & Maliszkiewicz, B. (1998). Inni to także MY. Sopot: Gdańskie Wydawnictwo Psychologiczne.

20. MULTICULTURALISM AND MULTICULTURAL EDUCATION: CHALLENGES IN TEACHER TRAINING

Susana Gonçalves,

Escola Superior de Educação de Coimbra, Coimbra, Portugal

Multiculturalism in Portuguese society: a challenge to schools

Labour migrations, decolonisation, the fall of communism, political instability and poverty in undeveloped countries have all contributed to the emergence of new sociocultural and ethnic communities in Portugal, (Fassman & Munz, 1994; Gonçalves & Coelho, 2000; Perotti, 1997) which can only continue given current migratory pressures from south to north and east to west (Castles, 1993). Linguistic, ethnic, cultural and religious heterogeneity is highlighted by historic events, as well as by political, economic and demographic factors (Rocha–Trindade, 1995) which extend their effects to the school population. For example, over eighty per cent of the pupils in some schools around Lisbon are African Portuguese from former colonies, we have over one hundred thousand immigrants from east European countries, and some isolated communities of west European origin still maintain mother tongue. All these groups suffer limited knowledge of Portuguese language and traditions, and feel in 'no man's land' in society and at school. The clearest link between ethnicity and material deprivation is the decline of street trade and many other circumstances which force the Roma community to find new subsistence methods and to abandon nomadism or travelling. School attendance is legally required, so the poorest families may be supported by subsidies to the children.

As all over the western world, poor achievement and exclusions from Portuguese schools (Cardoso, 1996; Souta, 1998) show minorities and the poor as among the most vulnerable, suggesting that Portuguese schools respond inappropriately to diversity (Carvalho, 1999). Particularly regarding Roma children, schools have negative stereotypes, and schools' and families' principles and values conflict (Borreicho, 1996; Liégeois, 1994; Medeiros, 1996). Low expectations and attribution of lack of success to external factors exacerbate the effects of poverty and lead to exclusion of minorities

(Ferreira, 1994; Geremek, 1996). This phenomenon is revived whenever social and economic difficulties are intensified.

Legislators, teachers and communities must debate relevant multicultural curricula, and schools must develop their role beyond providing information, to promoting social understanding and tolerance (Albert & Triandis, 1994). We maintain that, rather than considering all these problems as obstacles, facing them will stimulate analysis and reexamination of the role of the school. Educating teachers in relevant management skills is a crucial element in this transformation. This paper reports our courses which have run over several years with highly experienced teachers, whose mastery of multicultural education was often rather slight.

Principles of our courses
Training involves psychological and moral development of teachers' qualities as individuals and citizens
Thus training should include reflection on current dominant and normative social values, and facilitate responsible, and balanced personalities (D'Orey da Cunha, 1996; Gonçalves, 2001a, 2001b, 2001c; UNESCO, 1983, 1998). Our frame is the critical questioning model (Zeichner, 1983), that is, stimulating reflection and interpretation of social reality, the school and the teacher's own role as an educational agent, able to lead in determining needs, resources and pedagogical aims.

Emotional knowledge and control are fundamental to intercultural competence
We must know the origin of our own emotions, and why they are experienced as good or bad. Their control is the first step to tolerance. Opportunities for such learning pervade the curriculum (Elias et al., 1997), and to offer them to his or her pupils a teacher must deal both with his own emotions and those of the pupils and their families. This includes understanding cultural filters on children's emotional behaviour, for instance inhibition of male weeping. (Puig–Rovira & Martin García, 1998)

Teacher training should be experiential
First it should provide rewarding activities (Csikszentmihalyi, 1990, 1993), later setting out the theory. Games, projects, debate, problem solving exercises, teamwork, case studies, and analysis of films, images and texts all encourage active analysis of social reality and stimulate reasoning.

Multicultural education is for all children
It is not only those in heterogeneous classes. It is a contribution to whole societies' management of diversity.

Themes and procedures adopted

The cultural and professional background of the group was used for:

- analysis and comprehension of teaching and its problems;
- identifying and avoiding stereotypes, prejudices and misinformation;
- critically analysing school practices, encouraging active participation in the building of knowledge;
- encompassing various topics relevant to minorities in European schools as follows:

Minorities in Europe: their history and current situation

Historical, sociological and economic information on migration led to critical exercises on media material referring to minority groups' problems. Through organising files, portfolios or posters we analysed themes such as relations between poverty, minorities and social exclusion; human rights and minorities; minority children's problems in our schools.

Relationships between culture, socialisation and education

Assuming formal education tries to make children compliant with society's accepted cultural models, we analysed the impact of school upon both majority and minority children's identity. Through exercises, debates and case studies we explored the multiple identity concept (Banks, 1981) of three hierarchical levels: ethnic identity shaped before school through family socialisation, national identity united by cultural elements, and global identity as members of the world wide human society where unifying realities *can* be broader and deeper than divisive ones.

Relationships between social identity, social image and intergroup conflict

We explored social identity theory (Tajfel, 1983) and social image formation, including intergroup conflict, in particular the notions of in-group, out-group and intra-group favouritism, and the mechanisms of stereotypes, prejudice and discrimination towards outgroup members. Portuguese examples were Roma, Black Africans and minority religious groups such as Jehovah's witnesses. Texts, films and trainees' self reports made the analysis of all kinds of prejudice more subtle.

Curricula, pedagogical relationships and multicultural education

Awareness that the curricula represent conscious or unconscious choices of whom to educate is a step towards cultural diversity in the classroom (Powel & Anderson, 1994). Consistent with the principle that multicultural education is for all pupils (Taylor, 1995; Tomlinson, 1990) not only those in heterogeneous classrooms, trainees reflected on the meaning of multicultural and antiracist curricula and deduced that they must actively:

- promote positive cultural pluralism that recognises explicitly that all persons belong to cultural groups;
- facilitate awareness of and pride in ethnic roots, including educational activities about ethnic and cultural belonging;
- promote children's self esteem and curiosity for artefacts from foreign cultures, fighting racial prejudice and discrimination against people and groups;
- use the principles of equal opportunities and human rights as organisers and criteria for evaluation of practice;
- promote mutual intercultural respect as a way to fight ignorance, fear and indifference;
- help remove barriers to the success, well being and equality of opportunities of groups vulnerable to social exclusion.

Multicultural education: how to fight discrimination and intolerance in the classroom

Finally in the training process, we imagined ourselves in actual classrooms and, following our principles above, tried to devise criteria for resources, methods, activities and practical strategies for teachers' working routines with children, families and communities. The projects actively developed by the trainees have focused on very varied practical subjects. They include the use of juvenile literature, music or movies in a multicultural perspective; strategies to promote cooperation between school, parents and minority communities; school educational projects; multicultural principles; activities for the development of moral values; developing strategies and resources for human rights teaching and learning.

Assessing the results

Many of our participating teachers have reviewed their practices, methodologies and patterns of pedagogical interaction. Above all, they understood that multicultural education is not limited to the actual presence of minorities in the classroom, but that it constitutes an educational procedure which can be adapted to all classrooms. Even teachers who had little contact with ethnic minorities showed progressively more interest during the training, including trying to obtain information about the minorities in Portugal. Also teachers concluded that curricula and practices in common use are ethnocentric and devalue minorities' ethnic identity: they made several suggestions for reform.

We believe our course helps schools to become true democratic laboratories of a society where pluralism, tolerance and the respect for difference will be a reality. The teachers' own voices express their high degree of satisfaction in quotes from their evaluations of the course.

Evaluation of the 'Multicultural Education' In service Course for Teachers: some comments

- I became a lot more watchful, in order to put these notions into practice in the classroom...
- This module influences our 'conscience', it makes self seeking people feel the need to reexamine some ideas, thus creating a positive uneasiness that induces reflection and self criticism. It makes us think...
- It is very important to think of these themes related to globalisation in a humanist perspective, and of respect towards difference...
- The contents were important, the resources were rather diversified and motivating, and the group participated actively. We are all different, but there is a special magic in each one of us. Sometimes, it is asleep and help is necessary to find it again. It was worth the time...
- This should become a compulsory theme in teacher training...

References

Albert, R. D. & Triandis, H. C. (1994). Intercultural education for multicultural societies: critical issues. In L. A. Samovar & R. E. Porter (eds.), Intercultural Communication: a reader. (Edn 7, 425–434). Belmont California: Wadsworth Publishing.

Banks, J. (1981). Multiethnic Education: theory and practice. Boston: Allyn and Bacon.

Borreicho, A. M. (1996). Absentismo e aproveitamento das crianças ciganas numa escola do 1º Ciclo. Multicultural, IV, 6. Escola Superior de Educação de Setúbal / C.I.O.E. (Absenteeism and achievement among Gypsy children in primary school)

Cardoso, C. M. (1996). Educação multicultural. Percursos para práticas reflexivas. Lisboa: Texto Editora. (Multicultural education. Pathway to reflexive practices)

Carvalho, I. (1999). Da violência da homogeneização à heterogeneização da escola. Perspectivar Educação, 5, 23–31. (From the violence of homogeneity to diversity in schools).

Castles, S. (1993). Migrations and minorities in Europe. Perspectives for the 1990s: eleven hypotheses. In J. Wrench & J. Solomos (eds.), Racism and Migration in Western Europe, pp.17–34. Oxford: Berg Publishers.

Csikszentmihalyi, M. (1990). Flow: the psychology of optimal experience. New York: Harper Perennial.

Csikszentmihalyi, M. (1993). Novas atitudes mentais. Lisboa: Círculo de Leitores. (Portuguese translation of the original: The Evolving Self)

D'Orey da Cunha, P. (1996). Ética e educação. Lisboa: Universidade Católica Editora. (Ethics and Education).

Elias, M. J., Zins, J. E., Weissberg, R. P., Frey, K. S., Greenberg, M. T., Haynes, N. M., Kessler, R., Schwab–Stone, M. E. & Shriver, T. P. (1997). Promoting Social and Emotional Learning. Alexandria, Virginia: Association for Supervision and Curriculum Development.

Fassmann, H. & Munz, R. (1994). Patterns and trends of international migration in western Europe. In H. Fassmann & R. Munz (eds.), European Migration in the Late Twentieth Century: historical patterns, actual trends, and social implications, pp.3–34. Luxemburg, Austria: IIASA.

Ferreira, C. C. (1994). Pobreza, cidadania e desqualificação social– uma abordagem sociológica da exclusão social em Portugal. Coimbra: Faculdade de Economia da Universidade de Coimbra (ed. policopiada). (Poverty, citizenship and social disqualification – a sociological approach of social exclusion in Portugal).

Geremek, B. (1996). Coesão, solidariedade e exclusão. In Delors, J. Educação, um tesouro a descobrir, pp.201–204. Lisboa: Edições ASA. (Cohesion, solidarity and exclusion. (In Delors (ed.). Learning: the treasure within).

Gonçalves, S. (2001a). A componente ética da formação de professores: interdisciplinaridade e transversalidade, Colectânea de Artigos Científicos. Coimbra: Instituto Politécnico de Coimbra. (Ethics in Teacher Training: interdisciplinar and transversal domain).

Gonçalves, S. (2001b). Reflexões sobre a educação moral no ensino superior. Actas do Encontro Internacional Educação para os Direitos Humanos. Lisboa: Instituto de Inovação Educacional e Comissão Nacional para as Comemorações do 50º Aniversário da Declaração Universal dos Direitos do Homem e da Década das Nações Unidas para a Educação em Matéria de Direitos Humanos. (Thoughts about moral education in higher education).

Gonçalves, S. (2001c) (Coord.). Educação Multicultural e Para os Direitos Humanos: materiais de apoio às escolas e aos educadores/ professores. Coimbra: ESEC (in press). (Multicultural Education and Human Rights Education: materials for schools and teachers).

Gonçalves, S. & Coelho, A. (2000). Minorities: past and present. In T. Van Praag (coord.), Multicultural Education in European Perspective. Rotterdam: Hogeschool Rotterdam.

Liégeois, J. P. (1994). A escolarização das crianças ciganas e viajantes'. Relatório síntese da Comissão da Comunidade Europeia. Lisboa: ME – Departamento de Programação e Gestão Financeira, Série 'Documento'. (Schooling Gypsy and Traveller children. European Community Report).

Medeiros, R. (1996). Escola, uma instituição distanciada da criança cigana. Multicultural. IV, 7; ESES / C.I.O.E. (School, an institution distanced from Gypsy children).

Perotti, A. (1997). Apologia do Intercultural. Lisboa: Secretariado Coordenador dos Programas de Educação Multicultural, Ministério da Educação. (The apology of intercultural).

Powel, R. G. & Anderson, J. (1994). Intercultural education for multicultural societies: critical issues. In L. A. Samovar & R. E. Porter (eds.), Intercultural Communication: a reader, Edn. 7, 322–330. Belmont, California: Wadsworth Publishing Company.

Puig–Rovira, J. M. & Martín García, X. (1998). La educación moral en la escuela: teoría y práctica. Barcelona: Edebé. (Moral Education in Schools: theory and practice).

Rocha–Trindade, M. B. (1995). Sociologia das migrações. Lisboa: Universidade Aberta. (Sociology of Migrations).

Souta, L. (1998). Escola de excluídos: reflexões críticas sobre multiculturalidades, Pensar Educação, 1, 25–32. (A school of excluded: critical reflections about multiculturalism).

Tajfel, H. (1983). Grupos humanos e categorias sociais (vol. I e II). Lisboa, Livros Horizonte. (from the original <u>Human Groups and Social Categories: studies in social psychology</u>, London: Cambridge University Press, (1981).

Taylor, W.H. (1995). Ethnic Relations in all–white schools. In S. Tomlinson & M. Craft (eds.), <u>Ethnic Relations and Schooling: policy and practice in the 1990's.</u> London: Athlone.

Tomlinson, S. (1990). <u>Multicultural Education in White Schools</u>. London: Batsford.

UNESCO (1983). <u>A Sense of Belonging: guidelines of values for the humanistic and international dimension of education</u>. CIDREE/ UNESCO.

UNESCO (1998). <u>World Declaration on Higher Education for the Twenty– First Century: vision and action</u>. http://www.unesco.org/education/educprog/wche/declaration.htm

Zeichner, K. (1983). Alternative paradigms of teacher education. <u>Journal of Teacher Education. 4</u>, 3, 3–9.

21. FROM ASSIMILATION TO THE CELEBRATION OF DIVERSITY?

Marie Macey, University of Bradford, UK

Multiculturalism is a fact in most advanced industrial societies in Europe, North America and Australasia. The potential for enduring conflict is real. A new vision must be one that celebrates our common humanity and seeks to reconcile differences. (McLellan & Richmond, 1994, p.680).

In an increasingly postmodern, globalised world, multicultural societies are the norm, and here to stay. Yet this diversity is often associated with conflict: cultural differences are viewed as a problem rather than a resource, a cause for concern rather than celebration. Here I explore Britain's experience of multiculturalism in education and wider society, analysing some of the mistakes made and the thinking that has developed from this. I conclude that it is imperative for multicultural societies to work towards genuine pluralism, not only in the interests of social justice, but to avoid conflict and fragmentation in society itself.

The making of multicultural Britain

Britain's long history of ethnic diversity can be traced back to the Celts, Romans, Saxons and Vikings. Contemporary Britain includes Irish, English, Welsh and Scottish nationalities, as well as populations of Indians (eight hundred and thirty thousand), Caribbean and Pakistani (both half a million), Black African (two hundred thousand), one hundred and fifty thousand Bangladeshi, Chinese, Arab, Cypriot, Guyanese, and east European descent. There are also an estimated one hundred and fifty thousand Roma in Britain (OSCE, 2000). Despite this diversity, in Britain today *visible* minorities are defined as a problem.

There have been Black people in Britain for over five hundred years (Fryer, 1984), but significant immigration from outside Europe began only after the second world war with recruitment from colonies and former colonies for reconstruction and expansion. Despite these workers holding British citizenship, their eventual return home was assumed. By the early nineteen sixties however, families had settled and it was realised that they were 'here to stay' (Gilroy, 1987), and that 'something had to be done', at least about children without English in British schools. So began a series of interventions, defined by Mullard (1982) as assimilationist, integrationist and pluralist.

Education and Diversity
Assimilation (nineteen fifties and early nineteen sixties)
During the assimilationist phase, the concern was to absorb immigrant children into the British way of life as quickly as possible. It was felt that a harmonious nation depended on minimising difference, best accomplished by instilling English language and culture into Black and Asian children. Thus children were sent to reception centres, language units or, in the nineteen sixties and nineteen seventies, dispersed via 'bussing'. Wider society saw growing antagonism to immigration, fuelled by politicians' overt use of 'the race card', which lead to the introduction of restrictive immigration laws.

Integration: late nineteen sixties and early nineteen seventies
The integrationist phase saw the government demanding a shift from the ideology of assimilation to one of 'equal opportunities within a framework of cultural diversity' (Rattansi, 1992), thus acknowledging that 'the problem' was not entirely with minorities, but with white racism. In schools, however, the approach was to teach indigenous children to be tolerant of other cultures. In 1971, Bernard Coard published a damning indictment of racism in education in his book *How the West Indian Child is Made Educationally Subnormal in the British School System.* The government simultaneously promoted integration, but also restricted Black and Asian immigration: in 1971, primary immigration virtually ended, with entry restricted to family reunification.

Cultural Pluralism: nineteen seventies and nineteen eighties
Cultural pluralism represented a significant shift from the assumption of a culturally and politically united society to acceptance of distinct cultural/ ethnic groups in Britain. The government took a strong stance against racial discrimination: the school curriculum was to take account of the multiracial society, and in 1979, it also launched an official investigation into the educational underachievement of minority ethnic children. *The Swann Report* (UK DES, 1985) provided semi–official legitimation for tackling prejudice in schools and promoting cultural pluralism in education *and* society.

Meanwhile, the state continued to fuel public antagonism to visible minorities, for example with the 1977 distinction between British citizens and British *overseas* citizens. Racialised relations deteriorated and in 1980–81 there were a number of urban uprisings, resulting in an official enquiry, which called for an urgent response from the education system (Scarman Report, 1982).

From multiculturalism to antiracism

From the nineteen sixties to the nineteen eighties education engaged in a form of multiculturalism

> *...based on the premise that the key issue facing schools is how to create tolerance for black minorities and their cultures in a white nation now characterised by cultural diversity or cultural pluralism. (Rattansi, 1992, p.25).*

This was despite such evidence as that of the UK Commission for Racial Equality (1988) which endorses Rattansi's comments.

> *The sheer prevalence, intensity and normality of abuse, harassment and violence directed by white students against British Asian and Afro–Caribbean students as part of the informal, popular culture of schools is horrifying. Accounts abound of the distress, trauma and injury involved. The acts range from verbal abuse – continual taunts of 'Paki', 'Nigger', 'Blacky', 'Chocolate face', 'Black bastard' – to vicious physical attacks by both boys and girls in corridors, on playing fields and at bus stops; hospitalization for broken bones, stitches and broken noses is not uncommon. (Rattansi, 1992, p.21).*

Multiculturalism's failure to eliminate racism led to the development by the 1980s of an antiracist movement. This viewed racism as embedded in social structures and institutions and proposed that institutional ideologies and practices must be challenged, along with oppression based on class and gender. *Murder in the Playground* (Macdonald et al., 1989) reported an inquiry into a thirteen year old boy's murder on school premises by a white boy. The report castigated the antiracist policies of the school and local education authority as *doctrinaire, divisive, ineffectual and counterproductive* (Rattansi, 1992). This highlights that an antiracist approach was no more exempt from mistakes than a multicultural one. These mistakes have had negative consequences for individuals, institutions and society itself.

Mistakes in the British approach to cultural diversity

Analysis of the British approach to cultural diversity reveals wide ranging mistakes at all levels: macro, mezzo and micro; political, academic and activist. There are conceptual, analytical and theoretical errors in academic analyses and empirical research *and* in the practical application of multiculturalism and antiracism. Here are a few examples.

Educational Underachievement: the Cycle versus the Culture of Poverty Theses
The relationship between socioeconomic status and educational attainment
is persistent and highly resistant to change: middle class children usually
succeed whilst working class children fail. Thus both Britain and the USA
conducted a series of educational interventions during the nineteen fifties
and nineteen seventies aimed at improving the attainment of children from
materially deprived homes. These programs rested on two theories about
the *causes* of poverty, one blaming the culture of poor people (Lewis, 1966),
the other blaming social structures (Pahl, 1971).

The Culture of Poverty

The culture of poverty is a psychological thesis proposing that financial
hardship, squalid environment and inadequate family support produce
a pathological pattern in which apathy, alienation, fatalism and pessimism
are internalised by the age of seven, rendering children from poor families
unable to take advantage of educational and other opportunities. The
culture of poverty transcends geographical, social and racial boundaries: the
poor habituate to, and perpetuate, their own poverty.

The Cycle of Poverty

The cycle of poverty is a sociological model which views poverty as
a *consequence* of low income, poor housing and inadequate education and
employment opportunities. It is cyclical: unskilled work/unemployment
leads to low income/poverty resulting in poor living conditions and access to
poor educational opportunities. Poor educational qualifications trap people
in a cycle of unskilled work/unemployment and low income. Responsibility
for poverty is located within social structures, not individuals, families
or communities: the belief is that the cycle can be broken by effective
intervention at any of its points.

Although, logically, interventions to enhance educational achievements
of *children* should be based on a *cycle* of poverty model, in fact compensatory
programs were implemented by educationists who subscribed to a *culture* of
poverty thesis. Thus children were defined as culturally and linguistically
deprived and treated to large doses of white, middle class language and
culture to correct these deficits. Educational programs can have far reaching
social consequences, and the failure of these intervention programs
contributed to a genetic 'explanation' of educational underachievement
which proposed that Black innate intelligence is of a different, inferior, type
to white intelligence (Eysenk, 1971; Jensen, 1969; for critiques see Kamin,
1974; Richardson & Spears, 1972). Few noticed that the programs were
fundamentally flawed: being designed to correct deficits, they ignored the
roots of the problem – poverty.

Minority Ethnic Underachievement: Cultures versus Structures

Black and Asian people's cultures were blamed for their problems in British society and culture provided an easy answer to their children's educational underachievement. This is bad enough, but a more basic criticism of the literature of the time, including official inquiries, is that educational failure was both exaggerated and generalised and the influences of social class and gender ignored. In fact, some minority ethnic children, mainly from materially comfortable homes, and particularly girls, have always achieved in British schools. The correlation between socioeconomic background and educational attainment cuts across ethnic boundaries: middle class children succeed in school whether they are black, brown or white. Thus racism in education received scant attention with the exception, at times, of an over emphasis on it at the expense of such other variables as class and gender. This resulted in both antiracists and multiculturalists disseminating the same inaccurate information, the only difference being in the explanations they offered: multiculturalists blamed minority cultures, antiracists blamed institutionalised racism, both ignored *successful* Black and Asian children.

Multiculturalism versus Antiracism

Troyna (1987) scathingly criticised the psychological paradigm underpinning early educational approaches as *3 Ss – Saris, Samosas and Steel Bands*. The suggestion is that multicultural education was largely restricted to cosmetic, token referrals to esoteric aspects of minority cultures. Later, the pendulum swung to a crudely Marxist sociological approach which focused on racism as institutionalised and embedded in social structures. Few attempted to develop a more balanced approach which acknowledged the ignorance, prejudice *and* racism, and tried to develop strategies to tackle them all (Macey, 1995). Schools had become ideological battlegrounds and minority ethnic children were casualties of war.

Education for cultural diversity

From one perspective education is simply a reflection of society (Durkheim, 1926), from another there is a dialectical relationship between the two (Reid, 1987), from yet another, schools can transform society (Freire & Shor, 1987). Despite some changes, including the implementation of a national curriculum, and increased access to higher education, education in Britain still largely reflects the stratification in wider society where racial discrimination and disadvantage operate in employment, health, housing, the judicial system and social services (Modood et al., 1997), profoundly affecting the lives of Black and Asian people. The cycle of poverty begun with the early immigrants continues to blight the lives of their children, exacerbated by the unemployment caused by globalisation and the revolution in communications technology (Allen & Macey, 1995). Together, these factors put children from many minority ethnic groups into situations of poverty which risk school failure.

Neither schools nor individual teachers can change wider social structures in the short term. Good pedagogical practice, however, demands that they facilitate positive change for individual children and thereby contribute to societal change in the longer term. See for example the issue of racism in all white schools (Gaine, 1987, 1995) and the Children's Legal Centre advice for these schools (Hamilton et al., 1999). Such education for cultural pluralism demands professional awareness of such additional factors as:

- *Institutional racism:* taken–for–granted processes and procedures can have racist consequences, even though no individual in the school intends this.
- *Material deprivation vs. cultural/linguistic deficit:* poverty does not constitute cultural deprivation, nor do differences in the surface forms of language constitute linguistic deprivation.
- *Stereotypes and expectations:* living in a racist society is a racialising experience so that we are all likely to have internalised some negative racist stereotypes. These can lower teachers' expectations, lead to differential teaching, and depress attainment.
- *Essentialism:* there is a danger of assuming unjustified similarities between people from the same ethnic group. Black and Asian people, like white ones, are gendered and class located; they are also individuals (see Cagler, 1997 on plural identities).
- *Cultural differences:* possible differences between the various categories defined as ethnic groups should not be assumed. Cultures are dynamic, not static, and change in relation to, and in interaction with, other cultures (Gilroy, 1990). Teachers should be aware of cultural differences that do exist, and deal sensitively with them.
- *Prejudice:* schools reflect society and there will be prejudiced individuals among any staff and students. Expressing such prejudice, however subtly, can erode the confidence and lower the self esteem of minority ethnic children, thus adversely effecting achievement.
- *Racial harassment and bullying:* schools should adopt a 'zero tolerance' policy in this sphere and teachers need to be alert for signs (Katz et al., 2001; Smith, 2000).
- *Psychological tests:* all contain a degree of cultural bias so they should either be avoided in multicultural classrooms or their results interpreted with great caution.
- *Sanctions:* when any sanction is found to impact disproportionately on students from a particular ethnic group, its use needs to be assessed for institutional racism. This currently applies to the exclusion from school of African Caribbean boys.

These suggestions represent a commonsense that has to be interrogated in order to overcome the taken–for–granted racism of most white people. This is hard work but essential for achieving a stable multicultural society.

Conclusion: from ethnic conflict to the celebration of diversity

The world that is irretrievably multiracial, multicultural and multifaith is often marred by conflict, which has reached grave proportions and includes physical violence, rape, murder, war and ethnic cleansing. Physical and cultural differences are used to mobilise antagonism against a variety of groups defined as 'other' in terms of their racial or ethnic origin, nationality, immigration status, religion or any combination of these (Ford, 1992; OSCE, 2000; Virdee, 1995). Racism, ethnocentrism and scapegoating are widespread, and at times of rapid change, insecurity and uncertainty, they can increase (Macey, 1996; Macey & Moxon, 1996). Every society has at least one group which it scapegoats, whether Asian, Black, Jewish, Polish or Roma, and their members are variously marginalised or excluded from mainstream society. However, this has negative economic, political and social consequences, not least the tendency for marginalised people to retreat into older, more rigid variants of ethnicity, thereby possibly exaggerating the very cultural differences to which the dominant group objects. Thus ethnic segregation is dysfunctional for both majority and minority groups; it leads to tension, conflict and even violence in mainstream society.

No European society has developed pluralism to the point where there is genuine equality and sharing of power between diverse groups. However, a number including Britain have moved some way from rampant monoculturalism. From a starting point of assimilation, the road to pluralism has gone through various forms of integration and numerous struggles to reach its current stage of approaching not the mere tolerance of cultural difference, but its celebration. The various methods of change have included government initiatives and the development of policy and practice in fields such as education and social work (overview in Macey, 1995), and not least through the minority pressure groups themselves.

Arguably, schools are in a key position to influence society, both structurally and ideologically. In the case of the former, the conventional social divisions of class, gender and race are mediated through educational qualifications which determine roles in the labour market. Schools may not be able to change social hierarchies, but they could change the membership of them through ensuring genuine equality of opportunity, irrespective of social class or ethnicity. In terms of the latter, Althusser's (1972) definition of education as a key ideological state apparatus has optimistic implications for the transformation of individual, group and societal thinking. Neither social structures nor ideologies are any more immutable than are cultures:

they are man made, not God given, and are therefore amenable to change, if only we have the will:

As society creates social differences so it can affect, change and abolish them. There seems little incapable of change or avoidance in the social manifestations of social class, sex, ethnicity and age. What appears crucial is that people should be freed from those inequalities, injustices, constraints or lack of choice imposed upon them by the structure of the society in which they live. (Reid, 1987).

References

Allen, S. & Macey, M., (1995). Some issues of race, ethnicity and nationalism in the 'New' Europe: rethinking sociological paradigms In P. Brown & R. Crompton (eds.), The New Europe: economic restructuring and social exclusion. London: UCL Press Ltd.

Althusser, L. (1972). Ideology and ideological state apparatuses. In B. R. Cosin (ed.), Education, Structure and Society. Harmondsworth: Penguin.

Cagler, A. S. (1997). Hyphenated identities and the limits of 'culture'. In T. Modood & P. Werbner (eds.), The Politics of Multiculturalism in the New Europe. London: Zed Books Ltd.

Coard, B. (1971). How the West Indian Child is Made Educationally Subnormal in the British School System. London: New Beacon Books.

Durkheim, E. (1926). Sociology and Philosophy. London: Cohen and West.

Eysenck, H. J. (1971). Race, Intelligence ad Education. New York: Temple Smith.

Ford, G. (1992). Fascist Europe: the rise of racism and xenophobia. London: Pluto Press.

Freire, P. & Shor, I. (1987). A Pedagogy for Liberation. London: MacMillan.

Fryer, P. (1984). Staying Power: the history of black people in Britain. London: Pluto Press.

Gaine, C. (1987). No Problem Here. Stoke on Trent: Trentham Books.

Gaine, C. (1995). Still No Problem Here. Stoke on Trent: Trentham Books.

Gilroy P. (1987). There Ain't No Black in the Union Jack. London: Hutchinson.

Gilroy P. (1990). The end of antiracism. In W. Ball and J. Solomos (eds.), Race and Local Politics. London: Macmillan.

Hamilton, C., Rejtman–Bennett, R. & Roberts, M. (1999). Racism and Race Relations in Predominantly White Schools: preparing pupils for life in a multicultural society. Colchester, Essex: Children's Legal Centre.

Jensen, A. R. (1969). How much can we boost IQ and scholastic achievement? Harvard Educational Review, 39, 1, 1–123.

Kamin, L. (1974). The Science and Politics of I.Q. Harmondsworth: Penguin

Katz, A., Buchanan, A. & Bream, V. (2001). Bullying in Britain. East Molesey, Surrey: Young Voices.

Lewis, O. (1966). La Vida. New York: Random House.

Macdonald, I., Bhavnani, R., Khan, L. & John, G. (1989). Murder in the Playground. London: Longsight Press.

Macey, M. (1995). Towards racial justice? a re–evaluation of anti–racism. Critical Social Policy, 15, 2/3, 126–146.

Macey, M. (1996). Alienation and racial discrimination in the European Union, in F. Geyer (ed.), Alienation, Ethnicity and Postmodernism. Westport CT: Greenwood Publication Group.

Macey, M. & Moxon, E. (1996). An examination of anti–racist and anti–oppressive theory and practice in social work education, British Journal of Social Work, 26, 297–314.

McLellan, J. & Richmond A. H. (1994). Multiculturalism in crisis: a postmodern perspective on Canada. Ethnic and Racial Studies, 17, 4, 662–683

Modood, T., Berthoud, R., Lakey, J., Nazroo, J., Smith, P., Virdee, S. & Beishon, S. (1997). Ethnic Minorities in Britain: diversity and disadvantage. (fourth national survey of ethnic minorities), London: Policy Studies Institute.

Mullard, C. (1982). Multiracial education in Britain: from assimilation to cultural pluralism. In J. Tierney (ed), Race, Migration and Schooling. New York: Holt, Rinehart & Winston.

Organisation for Security and Co–operation in Europe (2000). Gypsies in the European Union, reported in The Guardian, 8 April.

Pahl, R. E. (1971). Poverty and the urban system. In M. Chisholm & G. Manners (eds.), Spatial Policy Problems of the British Economy. Cambridge: Cambridge University Press.

Rattansi, A. (1992). Changing the subject? Racism, Culture and Education. In J. Donald & A. Rattansi (eds.), 'Race', Culture and Difference. London: Sage Publications.

Reid, I. (1987). Social Class Differences in Britain: life chances and life styles (3rd edn). London: Fontana Press.

Richardson, K. & Spears, D. (1972). Race, Culture and Intelligence. Harmondsworth: Penguin.

Scarman, The Rt. Hon. Lord (1982). The Scarman Report. Harmondsworth: Penguin.

Smith, P. (2000). Bullying in Schools. Association of Educational Psychology Highlight 174.

Troyna, B. (1987). Swann's Song: the origins, ideology and implications of Education for All. In T. Chivers (ed.), Race and Culture in Education. Windsor: NFER–Nelson.

UK CRE Commission for Racial Equality (1988). Learning in Terror. London: CRE.

UK DES Department of Education and Science (1985). Education for All. London: HMSO (The Swann Report).

Virdee, S. (1995) Racial Violence and Harassment. London: Policy Studies Institute.

CONCLUSIONS AND LOOKING AHEAD

Hilary Gray, University of Nottingham, UK, Christopher Alan Lewis, University of Ulster, UK, and Vladimír Smékal, Masaryk University, Brno, Czech Republic

This book about the educational predicament of ethnic minority children contains general material about inclusive schooling for multiethnic communities. It also includes some material relevant to the education of children from marginalised[32] and underachieving groups – Roma in central Europe about half of whom are in segregated schooling, many ethnic groups including Roma in Portugal, Travellers, Bangladeshi Muslims and also underachieving Pakistani and African Caribbean pupils in Britain. Substantial proportions of all of these groups have gained relatively little from their national education provision (eg Gillborn & Gipps, 1996; Gillborn & Mirza, 2000). For members of such groups, social exclusion tends to go hand in hand with exclusion from the economic life of the society and material disadvantage.

Our Introduction (p.18)[33] raised five questions. Here we also note the adjunct to each which follows from our papers.

I. What principles, hypotheses and needs underlie the aim for inclusive education? But also which type of equal opportunities are we content with: Marxist formal equality, equality of outcome, or equality of opportunity? How far are we prepared to allow equality to members of ethnic minority groups, especially those who tend to be severely disadvantaged?

II. What are the minority and majority processes that prevent ethnic minority children, especially those from marginalised groups, using the education systems offered by host societies? But also, can we dispel cultures

[32] See Footnote, p.14 regarding the terms 'marginalised', 'severely marginalised' and 'underachieving'.

[33] In this concluding chapter, page numbers given alone or with Author's names refer to papers in this collection.

of hopelessness more quickly than Britain's slow but steady rate up to now? Can we reverse cycles of disadvantage other than via welfare payments?

III. What is assessment's role in fostering inclusion? Assessments can be *honest* and must be responsible in the use of any instruments. But child development is context dependent, and its various routes are not parallel. How therefore can assessments be *neutral* with respect to major issues such as inclusion of disadvantaged groups?

IV. What is the hope that ethnic minority children can progress as or more successfully than children from majority groups. In particular, what is the hope that children from marginalised communities can make progress when their education is provided on an inclusive basis in local mainstream schools. What can central and local *governments* do? What can *schools* do?

V. How can we foster minority and majority will to reverse cultures of hopelessness and successfully facilitate celebration of diversity by majority children and their families? In particular, teaching programs or even living together with other communities may increase *knowledge*, but how can we engage with the emotional and largely unconscious processes involved?

Our papers have considered some aspects of these intergenerational, interethnic processes. Some generation of inclusion occurs through local authority and government activities and depends on standardised testing of children and / or on ethnic monitoring, about which former totalitarian states are right to be cautious. In any case, with or without monitoring, our Conclusions lead to four broad methods for *schools* to conduct intercultural work. These are largely independent of governmental procedures.

First we will summarise the five Sections, which offer some answers to the above five questions.

I. Principles of Inclusive Education

Inclusive education is based on various principles: the right to education according to potential (UNICEF, 1989) confirmed by the Dakar declaration to include severely marginalised children (UNESCO, 2000). It is also based on the social justice (UNESCO, 1994) and political and economic wisdom (European Commission, 1993) of this education taking place in a child's local school. These are statements of human rights, and this makes it clear that inclusive education is a value. This implies that, although one can show that a band of pupils can make equally good progress in mainstream as in special school (eg Smékal et al., p.54, Study 2), cultural changes within schools and their support systems are necessary for the policy to be effective for all pupils.

Tomlinson's quotation of the Australian State of Victoria's principles (p.27) asserts this right for all children, then elaborates with four further principles which are open to empirical investigation. For example, that all children can learn and that inclusive education for pupils with special educational needs can be offered efficiently are also testable: our papers by Smékal et al., Mehmet, and by Minhas and Trickett include some evidence. Tomlinson's conditions show that successful inclusive education depends on more than resources. Whole school approaches in the form of good school management, evaluated planning for changing curriculum delivery and school organisation, and good interprofessional and parent – professional collaboration are all essential.

Verma introduces dynamic change through educationists' traditional ideal of preparing citizens who know and respect their culture. In modern times this must include many cultures: education must meet *the broader issue of preparing all pupils for life in a multi–racial society* (UK DES, 1985). Verma, based on Saunders (1989), refers to wide systemic change at the level of national legal systems, to redress the inequalities experienced by different groups of people. More satisfactory education of minorities helps the majority by improving social harmony and by reduction of welfare payments (European Commission, 1993; Koucký et al., 1999). However, the latter processes alone are not sufficient: legislation is essential, and the legislation must target each of the various areas of public life including education. We noted in the Introduction that Britain only recently achieved this with the UK Race Relations Amendment Act (2000).

II. Development of attitudes

These papers from Czech psychologists looked at some origins of the problem at the level of individual children and families, and their relationships with the wider society through schools. Matějček identified the emotional, barely conscious intergenerational forces: individual children learn from their parents to fear difference or to tolerate it (p.47). He also identified the school's role as society's crucible: experiences in school induce fear or facilitate tolerance. Smékal et al. showed (above, p.55, Study 2) that Roma parents are already materially and educationally severely disadvantaged and the skills of some of the children seem to be weak at an early age. Roma mothers' closeness to their children, probably rooted in the cultural tradition of maternal responsibility for children's welfare (Hübšmannová, 1996; Zlnayova et al., 1996) can encourage them to help with their children's education (Smékal et al., p.54). However, Samková–Bučková et al.'s work suggests that the problems have continued for so long that many Roma mothers are without hope about reversing the situation. It seems that few mothers believe their children can be both successful and happy in school and educational success seems to be subsidiary to peaceful relationships with the teachers to whom they must entrust the children (Samková–Bučková et al., pp.62–66). But encouragingly, Smékal et al. found that a broad band of pupils with initially similar academic profiles made equally good progress in mainstream as in special school.

III. Fair educational assessment

Section III's discussion of better educational assessments begins the consideration of changing cultures as opposed to individual children and families. In this case we refer to the culture within one entire profession, educational psychology. There is unanimity in this book that 'neutral' educational assessment is not a useful concept (eg Tomlinson p.28; Verma, p.37). Childhood is developmental, and many individual children substantially change their positions relative to their peers (Smékal, p.55; Hindley & Owen, 1980; Sameroff et al., 1993). This high rate of individual difference means that conventional IQ tests are so fraught with risk that their use can often maintain exclusion by supporting categorisation and contributing to a low self image in children.

The *Learning Potential Test for Ethnic Minorities* (LEM: Hamers et al., 1991) is the most complete example, at least for early school age, of a new form of 'Dynamic' test. The test session includes standardised teaching, mainly non–verbal, and the assessment relies in part on the learning that the child achieves from that teaching. In Hamer's development sample in Rotterdam, LEM appeared to predict the ability to make progress in mainstream school for a substantially higher proportion of ethnic minority pupils than did a conventional Dutch intelligence test (p.85 and Hamers et al., 1996). Pilot use of LEM with Bulgarian Roma and minority Turkish children pointed in the same direction (above p.86).

LEM incorporates teaching into a set of tasks for use in a relatively conventional single session test situation. In contrast, Pokorná explains (pp.95-97) how Feuerstein's Instrumental Enrichment programs (Feuerstein, 1990; Feuerstein et al., 1980) have been used for longterm assessment and facilitation of socioculturally disadvantaged children. The program changed the intellectual functioning of a significant proportion of this Czech sample (Pokorná, p.97). Cline also opposes single session samples of a child's abilities for assessing his or her educational needs, both when that session is based on comparisons with so called 'normally functioning' children as in conventional, norm based tests, and also when that one–off session is 'Dynamic'. Cline relates how some multicultural cities in the UK first developed principles for fair assessment of ethnic minority pupils' educational needs (ILEA, 1986; Joyce, 1988; Manchester SPCGS, 1983). British law slowly but increasingly recognised these principles. For example, the 1994 Education Act strengthened the legal duty to consider parental opinion, and also required assessments to take into account the learning context which the school offers to the child (UK DfES, 2001: Code of Practice). For Cline (p.74) the good teaching which should provide that context for assessment includes mother tongue support teaching and the elimination of racial harrassment and isolation. Assessments that attempt to categorise children and / or take into account mainly skills which fit the requirements of intelligence tests and / or identify weaknesses rather than strengths are excluding children who could make progress in their local schools if only the schools were managed and staffed appropriately.

IV. Government strategies and schools' methods for inclusive education

Part IV's array of good practice in inclusive education takes forward the process of changing cultures in education. For convenience we divide local or central *government strategies* on the one hand from *school based methods* on the other, although on the ground the distinction is not so clear cut.

Cycles of mistrust and disadvantage are intergenerational (Matějček, p.46; Smékal et al., pp.54–56; Samková–Bučková et al., pp.59–66) so one strategy is to begin early in one cycle with young children. This approach is often validated by Schweinhart and Weikart's (1993) longitudinal monitoring of 'graduates' of American Black preschool education. They showed that good preschool education represents an efficient use of resources with economic, social and emotional benefits that last into young adulthood for the individuals concerned. The wider society also benefited, through reduced welfare costs and reduced criminality. An earlier analysis by this team found three components of 'Good' preschool education: a good curriculum, delivered through experiential learning styles, and with involvement of the parents. (Berrueta–Clement et al., 1984; see also Smékal et al., Study 1 p.54).

The local education authority of Britain's second largest multicultural city, Birmingham, seeks to meet *every* child's needs in *mainstream* preschool. Birmingham then systematically monitor the education the children receive by a series of Standards. As well as good curricula, leadership etc, Birmingham includes relationships with parents as an essential Standard (Ford, p.104). That is, preschools are encouraged to work in *'multilevel'* fashion, with families as well as with individual children (Green, 2000[34]). The concept of 'multilevel work' echoes Tomlinson's call for good parent – teacher relationships, (p.30) but also includes work with other members of families, (grandparents or siblings), and with leaders of minority communities. Below we show multilevel work as one broad method which can help solve several dilemmas in the education of ethnic minority pupils, especially those from marginalised groups.

In papers 10 and 11 above, Mehmet from the London Borough of Camden LEA (p.107) and Minhas and Trickett from Education Leeds (pp.119–120) describe how many education authorities monitor their strategies for inclusion. We referred (p.15) to British weakness in teaching literacy and mathematics. These two chapters should be read within the context of recent

---

[34] Diecec is a cross–European network of teachers and local authority education officers from 18 cities committed to advancing the education of marginalised ethnic minority groups. See: www.bradford.gov.uk./educate/diecec

national campaigns (Minnis & Higgs, 2001; the UK National Literacy and Numeracy Strategies, UK DfES, 1999) to improve this teaching, and to assess each child's progress by regular, nationally standardised testing[35]. Especially at age eleven, average reading and mathematics scores are improving irrespective of ethnic group, socioeconomic status or gender, due to the National Literacy and Numeracy campaigns (eg Mehmet, Figure 5, p.111, All Groups; Minhas & Trickett, Table 1, p.120, All Leeds averages). London / Camden and Leeds monitor this pupil achievement data for each of the UK's main ethnic groups, to ensure that children from all groups benefit from this national campaign.

In our Roma context, the signs are interesting that the methods used by mainstream schools in London / Camden, Leeds and elsewhere are beginning to succeed even with children from some of Britain's most marginalised ethnic groups. For example, in London / Camden the 'gap' narrowed from 1996 –2000 between the percentage of eleven year olds from the marginalised Bangladeshi community who achieve the criterion 'Level 4' in the national tests for English, and all Camden's eleven year olds (Figure 6, p.112). Similarly in Leeds the gap narrowed from 1998 to 2000 between African Caribbean, and to a lesser extent Pakistani, eleven year olds and all Leeds' eleven year olds (Table 1, p.120). Although the gap becomes more stubborn as it gets smaller, it does seem that these pupils from underachieving groups are receiving more appropriate help and are catching up. Improvement is patchy. For example, marginalised Bangladeshi in Camden maintain their improvement at age sixteen (Mehmet, Figure 4, p.110), but African Caribbeans' acceleration is not yet sustained at age sixteen in either Camden or Leeds (Mehmet, Figure 4, p.110; Minhas & Trickett, p.120). This patchy improvement in pupils' achievement reflects similar patchiness across the UK, and includes disadvantaged white groups. However, encouraging analysis of such disaggregated pupil achievement data for over half of UK education authorities shows that, for each ethnic group monitored including the marginalised Bangladeshi pupils, there is at least one local education authority where that group is performing better than any other group in the nationally standardised examinations (GCSE) at age sixteen (Gillborn & Mirza, 2000, p. 9).

Our reason for drawing attention to this data is because it suggests that with good help, pupils from marginalised ethnic groups *can* succeed in *mainstream* schools. There is wise caution in former totalitarian countries about monitoring citizens[36]. In any case, many varieties of help such as

[35]See Footnote, pp.107–108 about monitoring techniques for pupils achievements and disaggregation of this data for different ethnic, socioeconomic and gender groups.

[36] See for example the judgement of the Czech Council for National Minorities (1997), that ethnic monitoring contravened human rights (ČR Council for National Minorities, 1997, p.9). This was relaxed in the recent Act on the Rights of Members of National Minorities (ČR, 2001).

teacher training, provision of preschool classes, and affirmative action in provision of same ethnicity teachers and classroom assistants do not depend on ethnic monitoring.

Also, there are other powerful educational methods which have contributed to this success, and which *schools* can use. These include multilevel work with families and communities, discipline procedures to ban racism, and work in the minority languages. All these methods help ethnic minority children, and they also reduce majority pupils' fear of difference. Thus the team who support Bradford's highly marginalised Traveller children work in multilevel fashion with the parents, so that they play their part in the children's attendance at school (Johnson, p.130; UK OfSTED, 1999).

Classroom assistants can significantly contribute to a culture of inclusion in any multiethnic school (Meluzínová, p.125), but their modelling role is probably even more important among marginalised groups where educational success can be hard to find. Meluzínová's tasks for Roma classroom assistants include the multilevel work of building trust with the parents whom Samková–Bučková et al. (p.65) found to be without hope of success and happiness at school. Understanding mother tongue is one of her criteria for good assistants. Agreeing with her, we should note that children's general cognitive skills and skills in *second* language can be promoted by *encouraging* their *first* language (Baker, 1996; Cummins & Corson, 1997; Trickett, 2000). Further, Hakuta proposes that an 'oasis' of bilingual teaching or mother tongue support is especially useful in the late preschool and early school years (Bialystok & Hakuta, 1994).

In Part IV's final chapter, Power and Sparks (p.132) helped children conducting simple ethnographic work with their mothers and their grandmothers. This work uses several of the broad methods we suggest for successful intercultural education:

- the teaching is clearly *multilevel,* involving elders from the children's own families;
- the work is clearly *experiential:* the children collect the stories, often in mother tongue, then they work with the stories, developing their crucial skills in investigation, language, and other curriculum areas;
- the work *reduces the excluding effect of 'received' knowledge,* that is knowledge that is judged by the establishment to be correct. This is because the families themselves are the source of knowledge. Thus for example language development can take place in small groups with classroom assistants working in mother tongue or in English.
- Majority and minority children also *work with information about each others' cultures.*

This ethnographic, multilevel method clearly asserts that the teacher values all pupils. However, like the modelling role of same ethnicity classroom assistants (p.125) such work seems especially valuable for children from marginalised groups because:

- the simple ethnography is oral, therefore highly appropriate within oral traditions such as Roma (Introduction, p.17);
- such multilevel activities are especially appropriate for work within the many ethnic traditions which still strongly value their elderly.

V. Multiculturalism and intercultural education

Part V continued to look at generating inclusion by discussing multiculturalism and intercultural education. Multiculturalism has occurred for many reasons, and modern industrial societies show various forms of it (Rex, p.139). In particular host societies have tended to use their ethnic minority groups for particular roles, such as the humble service roles of Roma in east Slovakia (Smékal et al., p.52; Samková–Bučková et al., p.59). Such positions of dependency may themselves perpetuate different attitudes to time and to planning (Rex, p.142), and are probably linked to Roma mothers' feelings of hopelessness regarding their children's success. But sound relationships do not develop only by majority and minority members living or being educated together, nor only by rational means (Matějček, p.45; Lapidot – Berman, p.155). How can education systems deepen majority children's understanding? How can teacher training, curricula, and school management best deliver inclusive education's second theme: *the broader issue of preparing all pupils for life in a multi–racial society* (UK DES, 1985; quoted Verma, p.39).

Firstly Ivanova monitored new human rights education in Ukraine. Her work emphasises the deep twofold challenge facing such states (above, Introduction p.13). The situation is especially complex where, as in Ukraine, the largest minority group is the former colonial power. Oshrat and Lapidot–Berman (Results (ii) p.154) illustrate how little is gained by the majority in conditions of living or working together (see also eg Amir & Ben–Ari,1987 for adults; Cairns, 1995 for children). But encouragingly Pearce and Beckett's multilevel facilitation of the younger members of Bradford's marginalised Bangladeshi community contributed to the well being and independence of this entire community. Kowal and Węgłowska–Rzepa engage at both cognitive and emotional level by helping children understand minorities' symbols, and further at the emotional level through interactive play and shared festivities with Polish and Roma children and their families.

Gonçalvez bases her training of teachers at the emotional level. If sensitively presented, tasks such as analysing text and media for stereotypes can facilitate teachers' reflection on prejudice, including their self reflection (Goncalvez, p.168). At the same time, Gonçalvez makes the very important statement that if only teachers have the will to discover them, the curriculum as found in many European states offers rich opportunities to improve majority pupils' knowledge and tolerance of other groups, and also to reduce minority pupils' defensiveness. All curriculum subjects have something to offer (Kenrick, 1994; Pumfrey & Verma, 1992, 1993; Sharon–jeet & Bailey 1991; Verma & Pumfrey, 1993, 1994). Taking science as an example, many ethnic traditions have simple health practices which can help to teach concepts in biology. In some ways, the Roma practice of mánuš or bodily separateness is such an example (Frazer, 1995; Johnson, p.129; Rao, 1975).

Finally, Marie Macey traces British education's cultural shift from the 1960s' aim of assimilating the newly arrived immigrants, to some recognition at the turn of the Millennium that diversity is desirable. But better inclusive provision as described in Part IV cannot succeed where there is teasing, bullying or ostracism: responsible schools must guarantee protection of all pupils through systems of zero tolerance of racism (See also Macey, p.179; Mehmet, p.115; Minhas & Trickett, p.122).

Final conclusions: four broad methods for successful Education for All
Majority children's understanding of peers from other cultures *can* increase. Also gaps can diminish between the achievements of pupils who gain most and pupils who gain least from education systems. Various strategies that depend on government finance are helpful, including teacher training, the appointment of same ethnicity classroom assistants and reaching disadvantaged children through preschool provision.

Ethnic monitoring of achievements of different groups, based on nationally standardised examinations, may help to target resources. But *schools* do not need ethnic monitoring to use the four broad methods for successful intercultural education which we find in this book. They are:

1. **Multilevel work:** Successful work with ethnic minority pupils is multilevel: it offers support and works actively to develop strong positive relationships with families, and it involves families and leaders of minority communities as sources of information and as partners in creating and implementing policy.
2. **Experiential Learning:** Children need an experiential learning mode, especially when they are young. But experiential learning is especially useful for children in danger of marginalisation, because the excluding effect of 'received' knowledge (footnote, p.15) is reduced, sometimes substantially. The concept of 'received' knowledge can be extended to include language skills: especially young children can be helped by bilingual education or mother tongue support.
3. **The Whole Curriculum:** Clearly subjects such as Citizenship education

can include material which helps majority pupils understand other cultures, and which helps minority pupils engage better in school. However, many elements of *most* curriculum subjects can be delivered with cultural sensitivity to extend pupils' intercultural understanding.

4. **Antiracist procedures:** No child should have to cope with, or can be expected to progress, where there is racist bullying, teasing or ostracism. The methods described above cannot work satisfactorily unless schools establish discipline and counselling systems which demonstrate to all that racism is not acceptable, and which deal appropriately with individual incidents of racism. (UK CRE, 2000, pp.41–45 for practical advice).

If the above broad methods are followed together, intercultural education will move beyond 'tokenism' and also the increase in majority pupils' understanding of minority cultures will help ensure that antiracist protection has a wider, less dogmatic base.

The Dakar declaration (UNESCO, 2000) bids us attend to the educational needs of children from severely marginalised groups. Concerted efforts by governments and also by their agents such as teachers are needed to reverse centuries of slavery and colonialism in the west, and stigmatism, holocaust, and forced assimilation in central and eastern Europe. Cultures of inclusion that will accelerate this reversal depend on training and targeting, and work by schools according to broad methods including the four above.

Finally, we are delighted that the Government of the Czech Republic has recently announced two new educational reform projects, one to prepare all pupils for life in a multicultural society and the second to help accelerate skills of Roma pupils *(EUROPEAID/112286/D/SV/CZ and 112287/D/SV/CZ)*. We congratulate the Government that the first project also specifies use of skills based rather than knowledge based learning. It will be clear to our readers that the authors and editors of this book sincerely wish the very best to these and of course to all similar projects as they arise across east and central Europe.

References
Amir, I. & Ben–Ari, R. (1987). Meetings between Jewish and Arab youth in Israel – reality and potential. Megamot, 30, 3, 305–315 (in Hebrew).
Baker, C. (1996). Foundations of Bilingual Education and Bilingualism. Clevedon, UK: Multilingual Maters Ltd.
Berrueta–Clement, J. R., Schweinhart, L., Barnett, W., Epstein, A., & Weikart D. (1984). Changed Lives: the effects of the Perry pre–school program on youths through age 19. Ypsilanti, Michigan: The High/Scope Press.
Bialystok, E. & Hakuta, K. (1994). In Other Words: the science and psychology of second language acquisition. New York: Basic Books
Cairns, E. (1995). Children and Political Violence. London: Blackwell Publishers.

Cummins, J. & Corson, D. (1997). Bilingual Education. Boston, MA: Kluwer.

ČR Council for National Minorities (686/1997). Report on the situation of the Roma Community in the Czech Republic and Government Measures assisting its Integration in Society. Prague: Government Council for National Minorities.

ČR Act (273/2001). Act on the Rights of Members of National Minorities. (http://www.vlada.cz/1250/eng/vrk/vybory/vybory.htm)

European Commission (1993). The European Discussion of Education. (Green paper). COM(93) 457. Brussels: European Commission.

Feuerstein, R. (1990). Theory of Structural Cognitive Modifiability, in B Presseisen (eds), Learning and Thinking Skills: classroom interaction, pp. 68–134. Washington DC: National Education Association Research for Better Schools.

Feuerstein, R., Hoffman, M. B. & Miller, R. (1980). Instrumental Enrichment: an intervention program for cognitive modifiability. Baltimore: University Park Press.

Frazer, A. (1995). The Gypsies of Europe. Oxford: Blackwell.

Gillborn, D. & Gipps, C. (1996). Recent Research on the Achievements of Ethnic Minority Pupils. UK OFSTED (Office for Standards in Education). London: HMSO

Gillborn, D. & Mirza, H. S. (2000). Educational Inequality: mapping race, gender and class. UK Government Office for Standards in Education. MHI/232. (http://www.ofsted.gov.uk/public/docs00/inequality.pdf)

Green, P. (2000). Raise the Standard. Stoke on Trent: Trentham Books.

Hamers, J. H. M., Hessels, M. G. P. & van Luit, J.E.H. (1991). Leertest voor Etnische Minderheden: test en handleiding (Learning Potential Test for Ethnic Minorities: test and manual). Lisse: Swets & Zeitlinger.

Hamers. J. H. M., Hessels, M. G. P., & Pennings, A. H. (1996). Learning potential in ethnic minority children. European Journal of Psychological Assessment, 12, 3, 183–192.

Hindley, C. B. & Owen, C. F. (1980). The extent of individual change in IQ for ages between six months and 17 years, in a British longitudinal sample. Journal of Child Psychology and Psychiatry, 19, 329–350.

Hübšmannová, M. (1996). Postavení a role některých členů tradiční romské rodiny (Role and status of some members of the traditional Roma family). Romano džaniben 3, 1–2 (Special issue on the traditional Roma family in Slovakia in early and mid twentieth century).

ILEA (1986). Anti–racist Developments in the Work of the Schools Psychological Service. Report to Subcommittees. London: Inner London Education Authority.

Joyce, J. (1988). The development of an anti–racist policy in Leeds. Educational and Child Psychology, 5, 2, 44–50.

Kenrick, D. (1994). Histoire Locale & Minorite. (Helping pupils conduct ethnographic work on the Roma holocaust). Seminar CoE DECS/SE/BE/Sem(19)17. Strasbourg: Council of Europe. (http://www.coe.int/publishing)

Koucký, J. et al. (1999). Czech Education and Europe: pre–accession strategy. Phare project CZ 9405 01 03 01 UIV Tauris.

Manchester SPCGS (1983). Promoting Racial Equality: a statement of service policy. Manchester: City of Manchester Education Department School Psychological and Child Guidance Service.

Minnis, M. & Higgs, S. (2001). Evaluation of the National Literacy and Numeracy Strategies. Windsor: National Foundation for Educational Research. (http://www.qca.org.uk/ca/5-14/eval_nlns.asp)

Pumfrey, P. D. & Verma, G. K. (1992), (eds.). Cultural Diversity and the National

Curriculum (Vol. 1): the foundation subjects and RE in secondary schools. London: Falmer Press.

Pumfrey, P. D. & Verma, G. K. (1993), (eds.). Cultural Diversity and the National Curriculum (Vol. 3): the foundation subjects and RE in secondary schools. London: Falmer Press.

Rao, A. (1975). Some mánuš conceptions and attitudes. In F. Rehfisch (ed.), Gypsies, Tinkers and Other Travellers. London: Academic Press.

Sameroff, A. J., Seifer, R., Baldwin, A. & Baldwin, C. (1993). Stability of intelligence from preschool to adolescence: the influence of social and family risk factors. Child Development, 64, 80–97.

Saunders, P. (1989). The question of equality. Social Studies Review, 5, 2, 77–82.

Schweinhart, L. & Weikart, D. (1993). A Summary of Significant Benefits from the Perry Preschool Project Through Age 27. Ipsilanti, MI; High Scope UK.

Sharon–jeet, S. & Bailey, P. (1991). Multiple Factors: classroom maths for equality and justice. Stoke–on–Trent: Trentham Books.

Trickett, D. (2000). Bilingualism in Education: a critical evaluation of the role of bilingual support assistants. Leeds: Leeds Metropolitan University Centre for Race, Culture and Education.

UK CRE Commission for Racial Equality (2000). Learning for All (Equality Standard for Schools). (http://www.cre.gov.uk/gdpract/ed_lfa.html)

UK DES Department for Education and Science (1985). Education for All: Report of the Committee of Inquiry into the Education of Children (The Swann Committee). London: Her Majesty's Stationary Office.

UK DfES Department for Education and Skills (1999). National Literary Strategy: review of research and other related evidence. London: Her Majesty's Stationary Office.

UK DfES Department for Education and Skills (2001). Revised Code of Practice for the Identification of Special Needs. (http://www.dfes.gov.uk/sen/documents/SENCodeOfPractice.pdf)

UK OfSTED (Office for Standards in Education) (1999). Raising the Attainment of ethnic minority pupils. HMI/170. (http://www.ofsted.gov.uk/public/docs/raising)

UK Race Relations Amendment Act (2000). London: The Stationery Office. http://www.hmso.gov.uk/acts/acts2000/20000034.htm

UNESCO (1994). The Salamanca Statement and Framework for Action on Special Needs Education. UNESCO Special Education Program, 7 Place de Fontenoy, 75352 Paris 07 – SP.

UNESCO (2000) World Education Forum, (Dakar, Senegal) – Final Report UNESCO Special Education Program, 7 Place de Fontenoy, 75352 Paris 07 – SP.

UNICEF (1989). Convention on the Rights of the Child (http://www.unicef.org/crc/crc.htm)

Verma, G. K. & Pumfrey P. (1993), (eds.). Cultural Diversity and the Curriculum (Vol. 2): cross–curricular contexts, themes and dimensions in secondary schools. London: Falmer Press.

Verma, G. K. & Pumfrey P.(1994), (eds.). Cultural Diversity and the Curriculum (Vol. 2): cross–curricular contexts, themes and dimensions in primary schools. London: Falmer Press.

Zlnayova, E. a kol./et al. (1996). Postavenie a uloha ženy–matky a muža–otca v romskej rodine (Position and role of mother and father in the Roma family). Romano džaniben 3, 1–2.

GLOSSARY OF TERMS

Table 1: **Approximate equivalence of types of school in Czech and UK education systems.**

For more information see:
http://www.eurydice.org/Eurybase/Application/frameset.asp?country=CZ&language=EN
And http://www.eurydice.org/Eurybase/Application/frameset.asp?country=UK&language=VO
Also the website of the Czech Ministry of Education Office for Education Statistics:
http://www.uiv.cz/

Czech Republic	United Kingdom
Nursery school ('jesle').	**Day nursery** (Social Services responsibility).
Kindergarten ('Mateřská škola') since 1994 subject to fees.	**Nursery school or class.** (Local authority or private).
Possibility of **Zero grade class** ('nultý ročník') depending on decisions of headteachers and local educational department; these are free classes in mainstream or special schools to accelerate progress of pupils who are not ready for Grade 1 (almost entirely Roma).	
Basic or Uniform school. ('Základní škola') offering grades ('ročník') 1 – 9. Základní škola were the only schools in the communist regime. There have been some curriculum changes, supported by inservice retraining of teachers. They still serve most Czech children.	**Primary school** – statutory schooling age 5 – 11. It is very rare for pupils to be away from their chronological peers.
	Secondary school – UK – age 11 – 16+ (or 18).
Stage ('stupeň') 1 – **Grades** ('ročníky') 1–5; Stage 2 – Grades 6–9; usually two departments of the same school.	In UK education, school years are rarely different from pupils' chronological ages. The four Key Stages therefore end at ages 7, 11, 14 and 16. (see Footnote p. 107 = Mehmet).
Middle or secondary school ('Střední škola') offering general education; also specialized schools for industrial and commercial skills and lower rank professions. All from Grade 10, that is, follow Basic schooling as UK further education, but smaller, more specialised establishments.	**Further education** – age 16 onwards, as E European Secondary education from age 15.
Four – eight year Gymnasium – selective high school, grades 10 – 13 or 6 – 13 (now 25% of pupils).	**Selective grammar schools.**

Higher education – Universities, Institutes of Science & Technology etc.	**As ČR.**
Remedial or special school ('Zvláštní škola').	Schools for pupils with **Moderate learning difficulties / Area special schools**. Formerly ESN(M) – (educationally subnormal) schools until 1981 Act introduced concept of continua of needs.
Helping school ('Pomocná škola').	Schools for pupils with **Severe learning difficulties**; until 1981 Act, ESN(S) – educationally subnormal, (severe) schools.
Základní školy – not separated, could be body of all day institutions ('výchovné ústavy').	Schools for pupils with **behavioural and emotional difficulties**.
Maturitas – is awarded on passing special exams ('maturitní zkouška') and satisfactory completion 'of all statutory subjects required at Grade 13 – qualification for higher education.	**GCSE General Certificate of Secondary Education, advanced level** (see: GCSE below).
National curricula. In communist system statutory curricula for Basic schools for each of thirteen subjects, specifying hours per subject per week and detailed attainment targets. Minimum attainments in each subject for satisfactory Grade completion are also specified. At all levels including Maturitas, this judgement is the school's, but nationally standardised school leaving baccalaureates are now being developed for pupils around Grade 13. Similar separate curricula for the various special schools, Střední (Middle) schools, Gymnasia and specialist (eg sports) schools have specified options. Reforming legislation, of which the first alternative curriculum was the 1994 Obecná škola curriculum, includes subject specific curricula for each legal form of education, with flexible hours in the case of Národní škola (see below).	**National Curriculum** From 1988. Centralised curriculum in ten Levels of work in three 'core' subjects, seven foundation subjects and five cross curricular elements. Supported by some Programs of Study in all subjects, particularly by the National Literacy and Numeracy Strategies. The levels of work divide into four Key Stages, at the end of which each pupil's progress is evaluated by nationally standardised tests in core subjects, and at the end of Key Stage 4 also in as many option subjects as the pupils can manage. Schools' effectiveness is monitored by these test results. (http://www.ofsted.gov.uk > inspection reports). The Foundation Stage curriculum refers to pre–school. Pupils with Statements of special educational needs can be excused from the National Curriculum in one or more subjects.

Active learning – see Experiential learning.

Affirmative action – policies which seek to reverse cycles of exclusion and disadvantage. Used particularly about employment, but can apply to any actions of the local authority, eg purchasing. Less radical than positive discrimination.

Antiracist – activities and policies to reverse racial discrimination.

Assimilation – where minorities are expected to become identical with the majority; Integration referred to equal opportunities within a framework of cultural diversity; cultural pluralism recognises diversity more strongly than does integration; celebration of diversity is the fourth self explanatory phase.

Bohemia – Former Czech kingdom. Prague was capital of the Holy Roman Empire under Emperor Charles IV in the second half of the 14th century, and a very important centre of European culture, with the first university north of the alps. From 1526 – 1918, Bohemia was part of the Austrian Empire, along with Moravia and Slovakia to the east, as well as to the North.

For 1918 to 1993 see below, **Czechoslovakia**. Today Bohemia is the eastern half of the present day Czech Republic, with Prague both regional and national centre.

More information see:
http://www.czech.cz/index.php?section=3&menu=0&action=text&id=11
http://www.czech.cz/index.php?section=3&menu=0&action=text&id=12
http://www.czech.cz/index.php?section=3&menu=0&action=text&id=13

Bilingualism – education conducted in two languages

Charter of Fundamental Rights and Freedoms – Czech equivalent to the European Convention on Human Rights.

ČR MŠMT – Czech Republic Ministry of Schools, Youth and Sport, otherwise known as MoEYS (Ministry of Education, Youth and Sport).

Czech legislation:
About Roma:
Edict 74/1958, enforcing settlement of Travellers.

Edict 502/1965, enforced quotas for each ethnic group, which led to resettlement in industrial cities in western Czechoslovakia.

About special schooling:

ČSSR School Law 29/1984: Education Act which defined mental handicap as needs that cannot be met in mainstream school.

Czech Ministry of Education Regulation 10 433/99–24: Allows parents to request reassessment of their child's educational needs.

Czech Ministry of Education Regulation 19/2000: Allows entry to mainstream 'secondary', (UK Further) education without matriculation from Basic school.

Major restructuring legislation is moving through the Czech parliament, in part connected with EU accession. This is overviewed (in Czech) at: www.vlada.cz/1250/vrk/eu. Thus, www.vlada.cz/1250/vrk/eu, April 2002, 393/2002 sets out the longterm direction of education in the Czech Republic. Other reforming legislation relevant to ethnic minorities is the **Rights of National Minorities Act 273/2001**: http: // www.vlada.cz/1250/eng/vrk/vybory/vybory.htm.

Czechoslovakia – formed as a democracy at the end of World War I, under the great President T. G. Masaryk. Following the Munich agreement between Britain and Germany, Bohemia and Moravia were occupied in 1938 as the nazi Protectorate, Slovakia keeping nominal independence. Czechoslovakia was unified and again democratic in 1945. It became the Czechoslovak Socialist Republic in 1948 until 1989 and the Czechoslovak Federal Republic until 1992 when Slovakia and the present day Czech Republic parted. Now Bohemia and Moravia form the western and eastern halves of the Czech Republic.

Dynamic Assessment – assessment of educational needs based on child's learning, often in specially devised tests. In the latter case, give rise to a Learning Potential score.

ECHR – **European Convention of Human Rights**, administered by the Council of Europe and overseen by the European Court of Human Rights at Strasbourg. All seven EU access east central European countries are signatories, with no Reservation relevant to ethnic minorities. The European Union is a signatory, the UK became so in 1974. With the UK Human Rights Act, 2000, integration of the ECHR into UK domestic law was very significantly accelerated.

ECML - European Charter on Minority Languages. Framework agreement. Various reservations were registered since the Charter came into force in 1998. (http://conventions.coe.int/treaty/en/Summaries/html/148.htm)

Equal Opportunity – provides a level initial playing field. Equality of Outcome – seeks equal endowment for all; Formal Equality refers to assumptions that equal treatment guarantees equal outcome.

Experiential learning – learning by experiencing and problem solving – close to active learning, but the latter is sometimes interpreted as physical activity.

Formal Equality – see Equal Opportunity.

Gadžo, UK gaugo, Romani term for members of non–Roma ethnic groups.

GCSE – General Certificate of Education. National examination in separate subjects usually at age 16 or thereafter. Moderated by four Councils which in turn are regulated by the UK Department for Education.

Instrumental Enrichment – Reuven Feuerstein's extensive methods for active facilitation of thinking and intelligence in children.

Key Stages 1–4 – four phases of delivery of the UK National Curriculum education, with SATs (Standard Assessment Test) at the end of each.

LEA, Local Education Authority. Local government body with responsibility for administration of education in towns, cities, etc. Traditional discretion reduced since the 1988 Education Reform Act which set up the National Curriculum, national monitoring of schools' effectiveness etc.

Learning Potential – see Dynamic Assessment.

Mánuš – Romani term for bodily separateness which regulates food and sexual behaviour and also relationships with Gadžo.

Marginalised / severely marginalised / underachieving ethnic groups: For purposes of discussion, we refer to Roma as 'severely marginalised' echoing the opinion of the European Commission (1999, p.4), to some ethnic groups in Britain, eg Bangladeshi Muslims as 'marginalised', and to larger British African Caribbean and Pakistani groups, whose children's needs have also been poorly met by the education system, as 'underachieving'. This does *not* imply a genetic theory of difference, or that the 'underachievement' is the fault of the pupils, their families or their communities. See also Gilborn & Mirza (2000 p.7).

Moderate (and Severe) Learning Difficulties – see Table 1 above.

Moravia – of which the capital is Brno, is the eastern half of the present day Czech Republic, and was the central third of Czechoslovakia. Towards the end of the first Millennium, the Great Moravian Empire extended west beyond Bohemia and east beyond Slovakia. The Empire was the site of the earliest Christianity in the region, and had alliances across east and west Europe. From the eleventh century Moravia was ruled by Bohemia. In 1526, with Bohemia, it became part of the Habsburg Austrian Empire. Later, in the first half of the seventeenth century, Moravia was a very important centre of progressive, child centred educational theory and practice lead by the great protestant, Comenius. The protestant Moravian Brethren were targets in the Austrian—led Counter Reformation, and very many thousands left for north west Europe as religious and political refugees.

Národní (National) škola – reformed (1996) schooling grades 1–9. Experiential and values based curriculum. Favours core curriculum and elective tasks to respond to special interests and to needs for different rates of progressing through the work of the grade, with weekly individual pupil – teacher consultation on components of the electives. See http://www.mtu-net.ru/sgerisee/papers/gray.doc

Nursery school – preschool provision – mateřská škola.

Občanská škola – Citizen school – alternative curriculum for grades 6–9 from 1996 reformed schooling, favouring education based in skills, experience and values with individual programs, later rather then earlier career choices; and offering emotional support to pupils.

Obecná škola – reformed schooling from 1994, grades 1–5 – alternative curriculum as Občanská škola greater emphasis on experiential learning. See http://www.mtu-net.ru/sgerisee/papers/gray.doc

Olach Roma – the ethnic sub–group which most maintains cultural traditions. Other subgroups represented in the Czech Republic are those from the various regions – east and west Slovakia and Hungary. There are also descendants of the 1,000 holocaust survivors in the Protectorate of Bohemia and Moravia. For information about Roma in the Czech Republic see:
http://www.romove.cz/
http://www.czech.cz/index.php?section=3&menu=0&action=text&id=30

Positive discrimination – policies which actively seek to reverse minority discrimination (more radical than affirmative action).

SEN – special educational needs. Denotes a *continuum* of *changeable* needs rather than categories. The term is slowly replacing "mental handicap" internationally.

SENCO – Special Educational Needs Coordinator. All UK schools are required by law to appoint one teacher who coordinates the SEN work of his or her colleagues.

Statement of SEN – multidisciplinary description of needs, opinions of key involved persons, effects of help to date, recommended provision which legally guarantees additional help and its mainstream or segregated setting.

Slovakia – was part of the Great Moravian Empire, (see Moravia) and part of Hungary from the fall of the Empire. It escaped the Turkish occupation of Hungary from 1526, then with Bohemia and Moravia became part of the Austrian Empire. Its capital was for some years the seat of Austrian government during the Turkish campaigns against Vienna. Slovakia remained part of Hungarian Austria until 1918. It became the eastern third of the country when Czechoslovakia was formed in 1918. It was nominally independent during the second world war and the nazi occupation of Bohemia and Moravia, and in 1944 was a major centre of rising against the nazi regime (the Slovak National Rising). Slovakia was part of the newly democratic Czechoslovak Federal Republic from 1989 until it separated from the Czech Republic at the end of 1992. See http://www.slovak.sk

Technicalist education program – similar to knowledge based program

Tokenism – activity by institutions and governments that gives the impression of inclusion, rather than actually responding to the needs of the minority group. In Troyna's images from colonial Britain, (Indian) saris, (Muslim) samosas and (African Caribbean) steel bands.

UK Department for Education and Science / Employment / Skills – the many names for the UK Ministry of Education, reflecting priorities of the Government of the day.

UK legislation:
About Race:
Race Relations Act 1976: Exempted the police and security services from the general prohibition on racial discrimination.

Race Relations Amendment Act 2000: Included the police and security services and strengthened the requirement for all statutory bodies to actively promote racial harmony.

About Education:

1981 Education Act (Special Educational Needs): Introduced the concept of a continuum of changeable needs, multiprofessional assessment of needs with various levels of help including a statement of special needs with legally binding additional help, the requirement to take parental opinion into consideration and to report openly to them, and the desirability of placement with local peers.

1988 Education Reform Act: established the National Curriculum and nationally standardised testing (SATs) with published aggregated results to monitor each school's effectiveness. Since 1988 various Acts have refined the process, eg effectiveness now takes into consideration the test results of pupils entering the school and the socioeconomic profile of the catchment area according to number of pupils eligible for free school meals.

1994 Education Act: Established requirement for assessment of needs to take into consideration the learning environment provided for the child by his or her school, with a Code of Practice on the Identification and Assessment of Special Educational Needs to regulate responsibilities for help. Revised again 2001: http://www.dfes.gov.uk/sen/documents/SENCodeOfPractice.pdf

1996 Education Act: Established tribunals to oversee rights of pupils to join their school of choice, including pupils such as Travellers who may not be longterm resident in the area.

UNICEF 1989: Universal Declaration of Rights of the Child.

UNESCO 1994: Salamanca *Statement and Framework for Action on Special Needs Education:* 92 governments and 25 international organisations. The statement supported inclusive schools: Inclusion and participation are essential to human dignity and the exercise of human rights. (p 11)

UNESCO 2000: Dakar Declaration: Called for attention to the educational needs of the most disadvantaged, including working children, remote rural dwellers and nomads, and ethnic and linguistic minorities, children, young people and adults affected by conflict, HIV/AIDS, hunger and poor health, and those with special learning needs... (UNESCO 2000).

INDEX

The high frequency words: *education, minority, parents, school, teacher* are not indexed as such, only for their subcategories. *g* refers to a glossary entry.

Vladimír Smékal, Hilary Gray
and Christopher Alan Lewis (eds.)

TOGETHER WE WILL LEARN:
ethnic minorities and education

Sazba a obálka Čestmír Kučera
Tisk Reprocentrum Blansko s.r.o.
Vydalo nakladatelství Barrister & Principal
Martinkova 7, 602 00 Brno
www.barrister.cz
e-mail:barrister@barrister.cz
Tel.: +420 545211015, Fax: +420 545210607
Vydání první
Brno 2003

ISBN 80-86598-40-3